Filosofia aziendale secondo Enzo Ferrari

Dall'automobilismo alle imprese

di PATRICK HENZ

Prima edizione italiana, ottobre 2017 – maggio 2018
Secondaa edizione italiana, luglio 2019

Copyright © 2014, 2019 Patrick Henz. Materiale fotografico di Patrick Henz, alcune eccezioni sono segnate. Design della copertina di Patrick Henz.

Tutti i diritti riservati.

ISBN: 9781077253179

DEDIZIONE

Dedico questo libro alla mia famiglia, i miei genitori Falko e Ursula, che mi hanno preparato a crescere, mia moglie Claudia e mia figlia Valeria, che mi hanno dato il loro tempo e sostegno per lavorare in questo libro.

CONTENUTO

	Prologo	i
1	Uomo e Mito	6
2	Leadership basata sull'Integrità	41
3	Gestione Rapporto Clienti	120
4	Sostenibilità	171
5	Aziende	270
6	La Bandiera a Scacci	328
7	Bibliografia	356
8	Chi 'Autore	370

PROLOGO

Fin dalla sua nascita nel 1898, sia la vita di Enzo Ferrari che la sua filosofia basata sull'integrità, il rispetto e l'umiltà rimangono rilevanti, come anche i valori, che sono i pilastri sostenibili per il successo e la protezione contro frode e corruzione. Molte delle sue decisioni hanno permesso di mostrare risultati tangibili, quest'ultimo può essere direttamente correlato ai campionati e allo sviluppo di automobili uniche.

È stato affascinante scoprire il mondo di Enzo Ferrari, non solo per il suo viaggio in passato, se non perché spiega la cultura aziendale che rimane ancora fino ad oggi. Questo libro è più di una biografia, mostra i miei 10 anni di esperienza nel mondo degli affari in Messico e in alcuni paesi dell'America Latina. Essa espone i paesi latini non come un fattore di rischio, ma come una cultura aziendale, che ci ispira ad attuare le idee di Enzo, che sono simili a quelle di Steve Jobs, Bill Gates o Richard Branson. La cosa interessante di queste persone menzionate è che hanno vissuto quasi mezzo secolo dopo Enzo, ma non solo, ma anche che le loro attività commerciali sono state sviluppate in diverse regioni culturali e tipi di attività.

Grazie alla sua intelligenza emotiva e all'apprendimento autodidatta, Enzo Ferrari potrebbe gestire situazioni complesse e diversi tipi di personaggi, che si confrontano oggi con la generazione Millennium. Abbiamo teorie e vocabolario moderni, ma se analizziamo la persona, le competenze e i metodi di Enzo, oggi sarebbe ancora un leader di successo.

L'integrità basata sulla leadership non è l'unica cosa necessaria per i lavoratori, ma è un importante fattore di successo per l'azienda. Secondo la consulenza globale "Brand Finance", che elenca le marche più potenti del mondo, Ferrari è qualificato in tutto il mondo con la gamma totale AAA+, perché sono stati analizzati categorie come la lealtà, la percezione, il sentimento dei consumatori, la presenza online, identificazione visiva e soddisfazione dei dipendenti; che per Enzo è una "élite di lavoro". Essere il leader di queste categorie permette alla società di vendere le loro auto con un margine attraente e utilizzare il loro cavallo rampante per la fabbricazione di altre merci, come i vestiti, orologi e anche passeggini. La Ferrari Corporation, non fa eccezione, che l'integrità regola e conduce il business redditizio e sostenibile.

Scrivere un libro è come viaggiare, si prepara il suo bagaglio, li mette nel bagagliaio della macchina e inizia il suo corso. Ma anche la pianificazione del viaggio, alla fine non si sa in dettaglio quello che si sta per vedere e chi sta per sapere. È successa la stessa cosa a me. Grazie alla prima edizione, sono stato in grado di rimanere in contatto con persone nuove e viaggiare in luoghi diversi. Per quanto precede, le nuove edizioni del libro erano inevitabili. Ringrazio le seguenti persone che sono pronte in ordine alfabetico: Eduardo Aguilar (Electronic Arts), Alain Bellehumeur (Musée Gilles Villeneuve situato in Canada nella provincia del Quebec), Verónica Bellinazzi (Enzo Ferrari Museum), Jim Glickenhaus (Scuderia Cameron Glickenhaus), Richard Hilleman (Amazon Games), Jack Koobs di Hartog (autore ed esperto di Bizzarrini), David Lee (Hing Wa Lee Group), Gene Leeds (Scuderia Cameron Glickenhaus), Joe Leigh (Ferrari World Abu Dhabi), Eric Hutchison (Electric GT), Rick Koenig (MPerpeto), Daniele Martin (ATS Automobili Turismo Sport), Paolo Martin, Gianluca Perdicca (Autodelta Italia), Mathias Pfaffel (Audi Tradition Unternehmsarchiv) e Raffaella Quaquaro (Museo Storico Alfa Romeo).

San Gimignano, Italy

Oggi più che mai spero che il mio libro "Filosofia Aziendale secondo Enzo Ferrari" oltre ad essere un libro con basi scientifiche diventi un libro di gestione dell'intrattenimento. Forse si può godere meglio con un bicchiere di buon vino bianco italiano, perché no? Un vino di San Gimignano, questo bellissimo borgo medioevale della Toscana che si trova a 84 km dalla pista del Mugello, qualcosa da vedere, in quanto questa pista è la rinascita del famoso Rally stradale disputato ventiquattro volte in Italia nel Tre 1927 e 1957 chiamato "Mille Miglia"

Anche se la storia di Enzo Ferrari inizia molto prima, quest'anno è il 70 anniversario della Ferrari Company, che è il motivo per cui mi ci vuole per aggiornare alcuni dettagli del mio libro. Facendo quanto sopra, è importante per me includere un capitolo aggiuntivo, spiegando come lo spirito di Enzo rimane ancora vivo nei valori e nel codice di condotta di questa società, in quanto sia i dipendenti che gli azionisti possono continuare a Apricandolo come il comandante "Il Commendatore "della società. Quanto precede dà un vantaggio al datore di lavoro, in quanto i valori non rimangono astratti perché hanno un volto e voce, così come il gran numero di video e materiali che ancora esistono all'interno della società.

Prendendo uno dei suoi appuntamenti "devo mettere qualcosa di nuovo nella mia auto ogni mattina", così ho rilevato in me che io sono un cambiamento costante ed è per questo che ho aggiunto parti al mio libro, è per questo che questa sesta edizione (primo spagnolo) comprende molte cose diverse per la Prima edizione.

Ovunque e quando è possibile leggere queste linee e scoprire che le competenze di sostenibilità e di leadership non sono nuovi modelli di business come questo date in modo simile nel secolo scorso e prima; Le aziende di Enzo Ferrari sono ora un modello di ispirazione rilevante come sono stati dalla metà del XX secolo e ancora di più, grazie alla recente tecnologia all'avanguardia, come l'industria 4,0 che fa celebrare e rinascere per Enzo.

Patrick Henz, Atlanta 2017

BUSINESS PHILOSOPHY ACCORDING TO ENZO FERRARI

1 MAN & MYTH

1.1) *Il Commendatore*
1.2) *Il Cavallino Rampante*
1.3) Creating a Myth
1.4) *"I want to build a car that's faster than all of them."*
1.5) *"I am an agitator of men."*
1.6) *"Divide et Impera"*
1.7) *"I am a cop, not a racing driver"*

BUSINESS PHILOSOPHY ACCORDING TO ENZO FERRARI

1.1 *Il Commendatore*

Enzo Ferrari was born on August 18, 1898. Even if he did not had a strong formal school education, me made his way up to the top of the world's most famous sports car company; self-founded and named. As second son of a rural metal worker[1], he got used to wake up with the hammering noise from the foundry. Typical for a family company, his father not just worked many hours inside the garage, but also was the manager, designer, salesman and filled any other needed position. An early experience what should characterize Enzo for his whole life, as he always underlined the need of hard work to reach high goals.

Destiny hit his family in 1916, as his father and older brother died because of a widespread flu outbreak. Two years later also Enzo should suffer of the illness, but survived it and as result got discharged from the Italian military, where he served in World War I. As the family business went into bankruptcy due to loss of the family members and the negative effects of the war, Enzo went to Milan and got his first job in a small company, who refurbished trucks and create smaller passenger cars out of them.

Even if his formal education finished with high school, he received the opportunity to join the Alfa Romeo racing team in the 1920s to become one of their drivers in local events.[2] Due to his early success doing so, he competed later in more prestigious races.

In 1929 he founded the "Scuderia Ferrari". Originally the racing team was born out of financial needs. Due to the legend, the idea came up November, the 19th in 1932, where Enzo met with the potential financial investors Augusto and Alfredo Caniato plus the wealthy gentleman-driver Mario Tadini. As they accepted, the idea became reality. The team started with several Alfa Romeo 8C cars.

---

[1] Formica, Piero (fetched July 29, 2014) : Enzo Ferrari – The Making of the Motor Racing and Sport Cars Knowledge Cluster

[2] Levin, Doron (1988, in The New York Times): "Enzo Ferrari, Builder of Racing Cars, Is Dead at 90"

1932 became a turning point, as in that year the team used for a first time the famous prancing horse logo at the 24 Hours of Spa, Belgium, and furthermore Enzo retired as active racing driver to concentrate on his role as team manager. This because of the birth of his son Alfredo (Dino) and his wife, who pressured him to give up his driving passion, so that the son would not lose his father in one of the numerous accidents at that time. Further the Scuderia went growing to more than 50 drivers, which needed Enzo's full attention.[3] With this the Scuderia Ferrari became the racing department with the most numerous drivers ever. This could be reached as Enzo organized them similar to sales executives, meaning they not gained a fixed salary, but got paid according their success. Furthermore, a part of them had been so-called "Gentlemen Drivers", wealthy men of the upper classes, which not only had been drivers, but also bought the race cars themselves. Independent from this, their level of talent varied. Some of them could even compete with the hired professional drivers, one of these examples had been Clemente Biondetti. Originally born 1898 into a working-class family, based on his talent he achieved a seat at the Maserati factory team, before he switched to Alfa Romeo.[4] His early success enabled him to invest into race cars, so that he won the Mille Miglia 1938 with a private Alfa Romeo 8C 2900B Spider MM Touring and 1947 with an Alfa Romeo 8C 2900B Berlinetta Touring.

1948: Ferrari 166 S Allemano, 2.0L V12, 110hp @ 6000rpm, 170km/h, 800kg, design by Carrozzeria Allemano

---

[3] Sidepodcast (fetched 28.08.2014) : « F1 People – Enzo Ferrari »

[4] Grandprix.com (2019): "Clemente Biondetti"

In 1948, the Scuderia Ferrari entered two 166 Allemano Mille Miglia. The stronger SC was driven by the legendary Tazio Nuvolari, the S by the gentlemen driver Clemente Biondetti. Due to technical problems Nuvolari couldn't finish the race, what opened the way for Biondetti's third triumph at this traditional event. Due to respect for Nuvolari, Biondetti started this speech at the latter awards dinner with the words *"excuse me for having won."*

Enzo Ferrari once justified motor sports: *"What has instructed all of the world's builders of safe, efficient cars? Auto racing. Any theory, any laboratory experiment needs practical support, and only the race can offer it because during the race the driver submits the car and its parts to intense, unpredictable, unthinkable testing."* For him the gentlemen drivers had been important for two reasons, they helped to finance the professional racing team, but also they volunteered to test his products. Not only in average use, but right at the limit. This showed already in beginning of his managing career his practical and non-romantic approach. At the same time, we find this practice still today, but in a complete different industry.

Software companies hand-out so-called beta versions to the most technical involved clients, which volunteer and register for this perceived privilege. In opposite to the gentlemen drivers, these users do not risk their lives, but at least the functionality of their private computer system, as such early software versions still include bugs and other incompatibilities. Due to their knowledge, the beta-testers can give precious feedback to the manufacturer and support the internal development team to create the final product.

Clemente survived his racing career, and with four victories became the uncrowned *"King of the Mille Miglia"*, including a monument at the Raticosa Pass.

Enzo was a pure racer, but well aware that he needed to sell cars to finance and justify his racing department. This included that the racing team had to produce success to create selling arguments for the street cars and had to be as effective as possible organized. His employer Alfa Romeo, as also other car manufactures, appreciated the idea that companies, which are active in motor sports seek a tangible output as sales numbers. For example Alfa Romeo announced in the 1950's its 1900 as the *"family car that wins races."* This was not just a marketing slogan, but the car proved it in the famous

"Targa Florio".

Alfa Romeo 1900, 1.9L, Straight 4, 90hp, 171km/h, 1100kg, design by Orazio Satta

In 1937 Enzo's position got reduced to sports director, with less authority for decision making. As autonomy was one of his key motivators, he decided to leave the company in '39.

Of course, it was not only this one reason, but a combination of different factors. Alfa Romeo was in financial difficulties, and besides, lost its luck in motorsports. The '36 12C and the '38 Tipo 308 are both very elegant cars, but on the track not competitive. Based on the missing positive results, Enzo's friend Vittorio Jano had to leave the company at the end of 1937. Enzo himself blamed the Spanish engineer Wilfredo Picart and that his creation, the racing car, was *"outdated, good only for scrap or a museum."* Wilfredo had an opposite biography than Enzo, he had first his own company, where he already developed two prototypes, and then joined Alfa Romeo in 1936. Due to his background, he wasn't shy and both characters collided.[5] Later after World War II, Wilfredo left Alfa in '45 (earlier he designed in '40 the Alfa Romeo 512. A monoposto racer, which at the end never raced due to the war) and founded in 1951 Pegaso. Its focus was on trucks, but nevertheless the company produced with the Z-102 also a sports car. Thanks to its V8 engine, the car reached a maximum speed of nearly 250km/h. On the other hand, its handling was very difficult and it had not any relevant success in motorsports. For Wilfredo no problem, as the Z-102 was nevertheless a success for Pegaso's reputation. As for Enzo the manufacturing of race and sports cars was a precious craftsmanship, he

---

[5] Dymock, Eric (1981): "Postwar Sports Cars"

could not respect the combination of trucks with such exclusive vehicles. A fact what became relevant again later for his relation with Ferruccio Lamborghini.

Already one year after Enzo left Alfa, he manufactured two race cars for the famous open-road endurance race "Mille Miglia", still under the brand "Auto Avio Construzioni", as due to a release clause, he was not allowed to work under his own name for 4 years. Then after the end of the Second World War, he could finally establish "Ferrari S.p.A."

This book wants to go back in time with you and to figure out what an old-school entrepreneur, sportsman and business leader said to the topic "business philosophy". Still something to learn and understand or are ethics and leadership really complete new issues? Therefor the book is not a direct biography, but will present and interpret some of Enzo's famous quotes and business decisions. Luckily he was a man of open words, so we have a real treasure, even if we have to see and understand that he lived before the time of political correctness. Meaning, if we read some of the quotes now, honestly in today's times it would be not possible anymore to say it that way; even if you analyze it, he was not on a wrong way.

People often referred to him as "Il Commendatore", what is the Italian name of "Knight Commander", a high medal of honor, which Enzo received in 1927. The name came half for the medal, but also half due to his success and direct leadership style.

Enzo's career was enrooted in Italy and the local region, as he nearly never left the country and the Italian Grand Prix of Monza were the only Formula 1 races he attended personally. Even more, he never took holidays, *"The best holiday for me is spent in my workshops when nearly everybody else is on vacation."* For this, let's take a short look on the country.

Italy's development after World War II was somehow similar to Germany. The country was included in the Marshall Plan, what gave it the opportunity to build up its major cities, including Turin, Milan and Rome. For this the period from 1950-63 should be remembered later as "il miracolo economico". Source of "the economic miracle" had been the high demand after the war, the money from the Marshall Plan and relatively cheap human labor. As the country developed unevenly, many immigrants came from the poorer agricultural structured south to the industrial north of the country, especially to the "economic triangle", the area between Turin, Milan and Genoa. In this period Italy as country could reach economic growth rates of over 6% and the triangle should become one of Europe's most important industry regions.

Even if Modena was not based inside the triangle, the city was still near enough to profit from its economic structures, as in general all parts of the Italian society benefited from the strong economic growth. The legendary Fiat 500 mobilized the masses and based on its concept and design, the company decided to develop more than 50 years later a 500 for the next millennium. This new car hit the markets in 2007 and became a huge success, regarding sales, but also critics, as the car was even exhibited in the Museum of Modern Art in New York. For Ferraristi, Fiat presented 2011 the Abarth 695 "Tributo Ferrari".

1957: Fiat 500, 0.5L, Straight 2, 13hp, 499kg, design by Dante Giacosa

BUSINESS PHILOSOPHY ACCORDING TO ENZO FERRARI

2011: Abarth 659 "Tributo Ferrari", 1.4L, Straight 4, 180hp @ 5500rpm, 225km/h, design by Roberto Giolito

Besides a better life for all citizens, the 50s should boost the Italian economy, likewise it produced a new generation of business men and company founders, with fresh ideas and determined to reach their goals, one of them Enzo Ferrari. As the financial situation of most of its citizens became better, also the cultural life should develop new quality standards. Italy became famous for its movies, created by the movie city in the outskirts of Rome, "Cinecittà". One of its most famous ones, 1957's "La Dolce Vita" (The sweet life) analyzed the new Italian upper class, which tended to life in decadence, similar to the Old Romans, who lived over thousand years ago. Even if Ferrari cars fitted perfectly to the new super rich, Enzo Ferrari with his nearly ascetic lifestyle was the complete opposite. This led to the situation that we was not always happy about the client groups, which could afford his cars, as they bought them as status symbols, but in fact were not really appreciating the quality and racing quality of the sports cars. *"The real Gran Turismo Ferrari is an offshoot of my racing cars."* defined his original business idea to sell street cars, which could be used also for a racing weekend. Nevertheless he understood the business opportunity and the 50s saw now also luxury sports cars, which still could offer an extreme driving experience, but also had been capable to be used as a luxury vehicle. As before, Ferrari offered handcrafted automobiles. Originally this had its focus on driving specifications, but now included also luxury features and went up to individual designs.

Apart from Federico Fellini and Aldo Fabrizi, Roberto Rossellini was one of Italy's most famous and critical acclaimed directors. On the screen he preferred the neorealism and showing also the less glamour's sights of life, in private he enjoyed his success and became a loyal client of the still young Ferrari company. As he had once a front-end accident with his 375 MM, he went in '54 to coachbuilder Sergio Scaglietti to include some visual changes to his car. The result was presented one year later and was an impressive unique creation with an aluminum body.[6]

1954: Ferrari 375 MM Scaglietti, 4.5L, V12, 330hp @ 6500rpm, 280km/h, design by Silvio Scaglietti

---

[6] Owen, Richard (fetched 17.11.2015) : «1954 Ferrari 375 MM Coupe Scaglietti »

1954: Ferrari 375 MM Berlinetta Speciale Ingrid Bergman, 4.5L, V12, 335h, 1200kg, design by Pininfarina[7]

Roberto Rossellini not just treated himself with individual luxury, but the same year he commissioned Pininfarina to create a special version of the 375 MM to have a gift for his wife Ingrid Bergman. Unique was not only the design of the car, also the grey color was at that time not available for other Ferrari clients. Because of its timeless elegance and its famous owner, the car became famous, so that Ferrari started offering the color as "Grigio Ingrid", which stayed until today in the company's catalogue.

---

[7] Automobile catalog (fetched 22.11.2015): "1954 Ferrari 375 MM Berlinetta Speciale Pininfarina Ingrid Bergman"

"Somewhere in Tuscany"

Italy as country has the image of being a highly corrupt place. To analyze, if this had an influence on Enzo's business, we review two anti-corruption indices, published by the non-governmental organization "Transparency International":

- "Corruption Perception Index": The CPI "ranks countries and territories based on how corrupt their public sector is perceived to be." In 2016 Italy can be found on position 60 (with a score of 40) in a total of 176 countries. This due to the relative high perception of corruption in this country, at least in relation to other European countries.[8] 2001 Italy ranked on position 29 in a total of 91 positions. The score was 5.5, what would be today 55. Keeping in mind a given statistic uncertainty; it is not sure to say that the situation in 2016 became worse than in 2001, but Italy is a country with a medium to higher perceived corruption level.

---

[8] Transparency International Corruption Perception Index 2016 (2017)

- Bribe Payers Index: The BPI "ranks 28 of the world's largest economies according to the perceived likelihood of companies from these countries to pay bribes abroad."[9] The BPI is less known than Transparency International's other index, the CPI; nevertheless it is very interesting, as beside its primer results, to show how likely it is for a company to bribe outside its home-country, you can assume that companies normally start growing inside a country, before they expand into other ones. So if they use bribes outside their home territory, likely they have learnt this "strategy" as a successful business behavior before inside of it. The 2011 results present Italy on position 15 of a total of 28 countries, quite in the middle of the list.

Even if Italy has the image of corruption, on a global view, the country is on a good midfield position, what means that there is a higher risk that sometime in your business life you may face such requests and temptations, but on the other hand this can be clearly no excuses that clean business would not be possible. Ferrari cars played a role as bribery objects, but Enzo Ferrari and his company never had been involved in a corruption case.

Starting after the Second World War counting to 2014, the country had 64 governments. This makes it quite understandable that Italians have not the highest opinion of politicians. Even though governments changed often between conservatives and left parties, the country politics had been stable over the time. On the other hand the citizens have a positive attitude regarding the police as they see them as reliable and the least corrupt public institution.[10] As consequence, corruption is not perceived has a problematic factor for doing business in Italy, in opposite to the high tax rate, access to financing, inefficient government bureaucracy, restrictive labor and tax regulations.[11]

---

[9] Bribe Payers Index 2011: http://bpi.transparency.org/bpi2011/results/

[10] Business Anti-Corruption Portal Italy (July 2014): http://www.business-anti-corruption.com/country-profiles/europe-central-asia/italy/snapshot.aspx

[11] The Global Competitiveness Report 2013-2014, page 226

"Rome 2012"

With this background (including the two World Wars) it is not surprisingly that Enzo Ferrari not turned out being a political person. Starting as a child, his passion became car racing: *"Racing is a great mania to which one must sacrifice everything, without reticence, without hesitation."* As team manager, he had been forced to become a business man, as he had to finance the racing team. *"The demands of mass production are contrary to my temperament"*. In this role he took pragmatic decisions, including to integrate the Ferrari company into the global Fiat company: *"In Maranello, I created a factory that made cars known all over the world. Fiat turned it into a real industrial concern."*

1.2 *Il Cavallino rampante*

The prancing horse became 1932 the famous logo of the Ferrari racing-team. The symbol was originally on the plane of the Italian World War I hero Count Francesco Baracca, who used it as a tribute to his former cavalry regiment.[12] Five years after his death, his mother met Enzo Ferrari at a race week-end and offered him the symbol as a talisman. Enzo

---

[12] Franks, Norman (2000): Aces of World War 1

accepted it proudly, just changing the original white background to yellow, as respect to his birthplace Modena.

This instinctual behavior had a strong psychological effect, as Carl Jung investigated in his earlier "Theory of Symbols" that symbols are the key to understand the human nature.[13] So what can tell us the prancing horse about Enzo as person?

- In sports and transportation the car is the successor of the horse. Not only regarding getting from point A to B. *"I enjoy feeling the car's reactions, becoming part of it."* Especially a car as a Ferrari is not a simple machine, but personalized; a character implicated. This similar to a stallion, the car has to tamed by an experienced driver. The prancing position represents the start of a car race, where the drivers keep up the engine speed, to have enough "horse powers" available to accelerate as fast as possible. Besides this, an expensive horse can be compared to an exclusive car, as not just the inner values are counting, but also the esthetics. *"My cars must be beautiful."*

- The Ferrari logo includes two hints of Enzo's home, the thin Italian flag and the yellow background. Even if Enzo was Italian, he was more strongly related to his home region Modena and seldom left to other areas or even outside the country.

The logo was not only important as a talisman, it communicated Enzo's philosophy and dream to potential fans and customers, but also to drivers and other employees. As group members require something that everyone can approve, a positive and emotional loaded symbol as a prancing horse is ideal to unify employees from mechanics up to the drivers. For this the logo became an important part of his leadership tools, as all employees could identify with horse and company. Enzo created in-group-effects and reached to create a homogenous employee group, which had been highly motivated to give their best for the company and its idea. It also made them different to other companies. As the out-group[14] concept predicts, Ferrari

---

[13] Cowgil, Charles (1997): Carl Jung

[14] Tajfel, Henri (1974): "Social Identity and Intergroup Behavior"

employees had a highly competitive thinking and wanted to beat the competitor on the track, just as it was Enzo' philosophy.

Further using a strong logo corresponded to Enzo's introversive character, as his ideas, values and vision got symbolized by the picture of the horse. This way the public's attention went to logo, he as person had been known, but was not in the center of the daily news. On the other hand this did not stop him to symbolize his idols as unreachable heroes. It is recorded that he mentioned to all young and talented drivers that they remind him a little bit to the legendary Tazio Nuvolari. For example to Gilles Villeneuve, who later also should become such a hero. Not only for the Scuderia, but Formula One in general. Montreal's Formula One track received the name "Circuit Villeneuve" and especially Ferrari's later driver Jean Alesi took the iconic "27", Villeneuve's preferred number, to honor his idol. Also as his driving style had been similar to him. Today the Gilles Villeneuve Museum in Berthierville, around one hour driving from Montreal, honors Canada's most famous Formula One driver.

Photo with friendly permission from the Musée Gilles Villeneuve

After his tragically race accident, there should had been always a photo of him in Enzo's office. This special relation was not only based on Gilles' talent and spectacular driving style, but also his team oriented behavior in the 1979 Formula 1 season. Thanks to this, it was possible for the Scuderia's number one driver Jody Scheckter to win with just 3 Grand Prix victories the annual championship and for Ferrari the Constructor's Championship. Gilles believed in the importance of the team and hoped to get the next year the number one status with the team's unrestricted support. With this, for a race driver untypical, attitude he gained Enzo Ferrari's full respect and recognition.[15]

As logos and symbols are emotionally loaded, they get larger than life. When they are properly installed, they are strong and have a higher protection against negative news and allegations. A circumstances which the company helped to overstay without problem the tragic accident at the '57 Mille Miglia, where one tire of Alfonso de Portago's Ferrari 335 S exploded and as consequence not only the driver died, but also the co-pilot and 9 spectators, including 5 children. After this event, there had been legal allegations against the person Enzo Ferrari, including negative statements from the Catholic Church. Even if he had been liberated from these allegations, this experience should shape Enzo for the rest of his life. But also in times that critics had been against the person, the Cavallino Rampante stayed shining. Also the 335 S continued its career and won later the same year the Venezuelan Grand Prix.

1957: Ferrari 335 S, 4.0L, V12, 390hp @ 7400 rpm, 300km/h, 880kg.

---

[15] Benetton, Lorenzo (2014): "Enzo Ferrari and Gilles Villeneuve"

Only in high age Enzo revealed why he chose "Scuderia" as term for the racing team. It was simple, near his first workshop had been a stable (English for the Italian "Scuderia").[16] He associated the noble animals with sophisticated race cars. As conclusion, he understood his team as a stable. The right place for the prancing horse.

1.3 Creating a myth

Even if the pure facts of the Ferrari story, starting from Enzo's first steps as a driver until becoming the world's most famous sports car manufacturer, could had been enough to create a myth, Enzo actively promoted this development. He had a propensity for epic histories. This already started in younger years, where he amplified his narrations, so that sometimes the borders between fact and fiction blurred. With this, he was part of a long tradition. Already in the Roman Empire the official communication channels exaggerated with the descriptions of their enemies. This had the effect that the population got distracted from internal topics and later the Emperor could sell his victories more glorious, if the enemies had been illustrated as huge and strong barbarians. Kings and nobility used later fictive family histories to justify their claims to rule. A local example comes from the Milanese noble family Visconti. Their famous arms shows a giant snake, which is eating a man. Due to the family legend, a dragon lived in the fifth century near Milan and many citizens became victims of its appetite. A real plague for the city, until a heroic member of the Visconti could kill the beast. Another interpretation says that the snake is a symbol for a Saracen leader, who dueled with Ottone Visconti in the First Crusade.[17] Alfa Romeo took the snake and included it into their famous badge. Through the time it should receive several updates, the original version from 1910 was still including a traditional illustration with a clear recognizable man. In 1972, the badge received a new version, and from that one on it is more abstract, until the victim is hardly recognizable as human, for what many viewers today just see a fire-spitting dragon. This stayed the same also with the

---

[16] Dal Monte, Luca (2018): "Enzo Ferrari"

[17] The Alfa Romeo Logo History (fetched 22.08.2014)

latest update from 2015.

2016: The Visconti arms at the Castello Sforzeco, Milan

Some of Enzo Ferrari's stories sound too epic as that could have happened exactly as described, although it is not possible to disprove them, as based on the facts, it could had been the case. One example was his description of his first Targa Florio participation in 1919, where he claimed to get delayed by the cars of the president, who gave a speech in one of the little towns, where the race was passing by.[18] But also the trip to Sicily, where the Targa Florio took traditionally place, should become an adventure, as Enzo and his racing colleague Ugo Sivocci got stocked by deep snow in the Sicilian mountains. They had to stay several hours inside the car, as outside waited a group of wolves for them.[19] Again, the story was possible, as there existed wolves in Sicily, but trapped in deep snow in the south of Italy, sounds surreal. Nevertheless historic weather data confirmed precipitation in Palermo for November 18 to 20, so right before the Targo Florio in that year.[20]

---

[18] Lehbrink, Harmut / Schlegelmilch, Rainer (1995): "Ferrari"

[19] Motor Trend (2007): "The Secret History of Ferrari: Outtakes"
[20] Geographic.org / Weather Data (fetched 06.03.2019): "Palermo"

Even if Enzo had known the background story of the Alfa Romeo badge, it can be assumed that he did not decorated his narrations on purpose to build up a myth. It may look strange that Enzo on the one hand was the down-to-earth engineer, who admired hard honest work and on the other hand liked big epic stories, but it makes clear that he was a very complex person and also appreciating and creating of big stories is a part of the Italian culture. Either way, the Ferrari myth got included into the symbol of the prancing horse and fostered its strength.

In a tragic way, Ugo Sivocci initiated another famous race symbol, Alfa Romeo's "Quadrifoglio" (Italian for: "four-leave clover"). He was a talented driver, often leading a race around mid-time, but hardly ever be able to win it. To attract good luck, he decided to paint the four-leaf clover as symbol of luck on his Alfa Romeo before the 1923 Targa Florio. And really destiny changed as he won the famous race. Even though, the symbol may have had a second more practical reason. As cars looked similar and the streets had been often unpaved and dusty, the big green clover was easy to spot from the distance and made it possible for spectators and competitors to identify Ugo. Since that day, the symbol became his trademark and he let it paint on all of his race cars. Later in the same year, Ugo Sivocci died tragically, while he was testing an Alfa Romeo P1 in preparation for the Italian Grand Prix. As it was no official race, the symbol was not yet painted to the car.

We have seen that symbols can represent an emotional loaded product / company or uses as psychological protection. The Ferrari logo not changed with the time, but other companies adapted theirs. This to update it to new tastes and fashions, or also as the company itself changed. It could be that mergers & acquisitions took place or simply that the company grew alone.

1970: Alfa Romeo Giulia 1750 GTAm, 2.0L, Straight 4, 220hp @ 7200rpm, 220km/h, 920kg, design by Bertone

Superstitious or not, people saw this as a sign and since then, the Quadrifoglio became a the official logo of the Alfa Romeo racing department.[21] Similar is not limited to motor sports, but can be found often in factories or other productions sites. Such work environments include a more or less given risk for life and health, people not only want to rely on health & safety regulations, but additional to this, include traditional symbols of protection, for example there is no factory in Mexico without a statue of Virgin of Guadalupe, the country's saint.

1.4 *"I want to build a car that's faster than all of them."*

As for the director its own company is more than a just way to earn money, also employees are not just in to earn a living. Of course in most of the cases it is the main reason, but not the only one. Especially key-employees,

---

[21] Banovsky, Michael (2015): "More than Luck: the Story of Alfa Romeo's Quadrifoglio Badge

which we want and need to have inside the company, are more complicated. Two examples:

- 1891 born Vittorio Jano was one of the most talented automobile designers. He started his career in Fiat and changed 1923 together with his manager Luigi Bazzi to Alfa Romeo due to an offer by Enzo Ferrari, as Enzo became responsible for the official Alfa racing team. An interesting fact is that Alfa Romeo wanted to hire Vittorio several times before and made him financially attractive offers, but he did not joined the company before Enzo convinced him. For the Milanese company he designed the famous P2 and later in 1932 also its successful successor, the P3, which should win the Italian, French and German Grand Prix in the same year, besides the "Targa Florio" in the next two ones. A famous open road race, organized since 1906 near the Sicilian city of Palermo.

1932: Alfa Romeo P3, 2.7L, Straight 8, 215hp @ 5600rpm, 232km/h, 703kg, design by Vittorio Jano

Until Enzo left Alfa Romeo in 1937, they worked together in the racing team. The same year Vittorio joined Lancia, as they offered him the position as chief development engineer. For his new employer he developed 1954 the revolutionary D50. In the '55 Formula one season Alberto Ascari won two non-official races with the D50, but had a deadly accident later in a testing session. This tragedy together with financial problems led to the situation that Lancia sold their complete racing team to the still young Ferrari team. As Ferrari's '55 racing cars, the 555 Supersqualo and the 625 F1, not brought the hoped success, they updated the D50 and used it for the '56 season. Result: the championship for Juan Mario Fangio on the Ferrari D50. Together with the cars, also Vittorio joined to work with Enzo again. We can assume that these two times he not went to him because of the money, but Enzo's vision and dream: *"If you can dream it, you can do it."* Both men's ideas and goals had been similar, Vittorio believed in the Ferrari team and company, so he took twice the risk to work for them, instead of staying in a safe place, as the well-known Fiat company in the beginning of his career.

1956: Ferrari D50, 2.5L, V8, 285hp, 620kg, design by Vittorio Jano

Because of the Ferrari myth, Formula 1 drivers have normally two big goals: 1) winning the championship and 2) winning the championship with Ferrari. After Michael Schumacher won 1994 and '95 the championship, he decided to leave his comfort zone and change for the next season to the Ferrari team, even if they had not been competitive at that time. *"I will do everything I can to bring the Number One to Ferrari. The whole team and all the fans deserve it."* He gave up his established position at Benetton, with a very good forecast to win the championship again, but to start a long term adventure with Ferrari, being aware that the first years he might not be able again to win the season, but step-by-step had to develop the team together with other key-employees. *"When you start out in a team, you have to get the teamwork going and then you get something back."* Result: Five championships from 2000 to 2004. Of course Ferrari offered him a high salary, but the main reason for Michael's choice to change the employer was that he wanted to be part of the Ferrari myth. As Jean Alesi said before: *"That was my dream, to drive for Ferrari"* and Kimi Räikkönen later: *"If I could have won five or six titles with another team, I would still take this only one with Ferrari"*. Eddie Irvine resumed it: *"To be a Formula 1 driver is one thing, to drive for Ferrari is to be a Formula 1 driver on a magnitude of 10."*[22]

2001: Ferrari F2001, 3.0L, V10, 600kg, design by Ror Byrne and Ross Brawn

These two examples show that employees not just work for the money. A phenomenon that Herzberg's "Two-Factor-Theory" wants to explain. According to the scientist, there are two independent factors, one can explain the motivation of the employee and the other one the job dissatisfaction. As result Herzberg argued that in the working environment exist "motivators" and "hygiene factors".[23] As each human being is different, there exist distinctive factors which can motivate you, as for example challenging projects, recognition, responsibility, an office with a view, or maybe just an additional plant. In opposite to this, the hygiene factors bring not additional motivations, but cause demotivation, if they are not given, for example regular unpaid overtime or missing job-safety. The salary is a special factor. It can be seen has hygiene, but also as an indirect motivation factor, as money gives the employee the opportunity to buy their personal motivation factors.

This theory has a high relevance for the manager, as he or she should be aware what are the employees' motivators, the reason why they are inside the company and what are their personal goals. If possible, a manager

---

[22] Van Osten, Phillip (2019): "Humble Irvine: 'Not many out there better than me - except Schumacher' "

[23] Herzberg, Frederick (1964): "The Motivation-Hygiene Concept and Problems of Manpower"

should have at least semi-annual one-on-one interviews with the employees to understand their needs and ideas. For Enzo, he answered this question alone: *"Racing amuses me."*

An established brand does not only motivate the own employees, but revalues the whole industry and makes it an attractive place to do business. It even motivates its competitors. Fair and free competition, including respect for the competitor, does not force employees to deliver their highest efforts, but motivates them to do so. Thanks to intrinsic motivation, the expected award is not the primary motivator, but the process itself. Enzo once said that races amuses him. Decades later, in 2017, Mercedes Benz Formula One head Toto Wolff confirms that after three years where his team reached extraordinary results and practically drove in their own league, he rediscovered this year his love for Formula One again, as Mercedes and Ferrari drivers had been close to each other and bother teams won races. *"I love the intense competition. It means you won't be winning easily – you'll have to fierce fight"*.[24] To develop such a flow of emotion, the competition could be intensive and go to the limit, but nevertheless have be based on values and respect to each other.

In an extreme case, the employee's motivation can turn against the company, as David Cressey's Fraud Triangle wants to illustrate.[25] A renegade employee, internal fraud or sabotage can be reasoned with missing motivation- and hygiene factors at work or in private life, as actual or potential debts. Open communication between manager and employees can help to reduce such fraud risks, but also this cannot bring down such risk to 0%.

---

[24] Benson, Andrew (2017): "Toto Wolff: Mercedes boss says this year's battle with Ferrari has revived his love for F1"

[25] Crassey, David (1973): "Other People's Money: A Study in the Social Psychology of Embezzlement"

1.5 *"I am an agitator of men."*

As his company became bigger and more complex, Enzo hired additional employees, which meant for him to step out of his comfort zone, what was being engineer and technical expert, now he had to be the responsible general manager. According his practical character, he was well aware of this change right from the beginning, so he installed key positions with known and trusted people, whom he gave freedom to take their own decisions, even if he used his right to have the final word, as with the D50, when he declined Vittorio Jano's technical suggestions. An example, which we will see later in the book. Enzo never got caught in the trap of "micromanagement", but surely it must had been a temptation for him. As driver he could have explained in details how to drive the cars, especially as he was keen on that they not got mistreated. As engineer he could have spent hours in the factory and demonstrate his employees, how he wanted to have cars and engines being constructed. Here helped his humble attitude: *"Who am I in this world?"* Even if he was good in the things he had done, he never reached the level of Nuvolari as driver or Jano as engineer.

Micromanagement can be seen as the opposite of leadership, as the manager loses important time in using too much of it to explain unimportant details to the employees, time he or she would need to concentrate on the real important topics.

As director and manager, Enzo was not the best engineer, nor the fastest race driver. Enzo was well aware of his limitations and saw his key strength in bringing the right people together. As he had general knowledge about these topics, he could judge who are the right people for his projects and if they work adequately together. The advantage of being a generalist versus a specialist can be illustrated by the life of Giotto Bizzarrini.

He was born in 1926 as the son of a rich landowner and inventor. Due to this, since an early age he came into contact with mechanics and technology. No surprise that he attended the University of Pisa, where he received in '53 an engineering degree. After graduation he stayed at the university to teach, but then changed to Alfa Romeo. In short time he joined the experimental department, not only as engineer, but also a test driver: *"I became a test driver who coincidentally was also an engineer, with mathematical principles. I always needed to know why something fails, so I can invent a solution.*"

In '57 he left to join the ascending Ferrari company, one year earlier than his friend from Alfa-times, Carlo Chiti. Giotto continued with this double position as chief engineer and test driver until five years later, where in an infamous event eight employees left the company, one of them being him. At this time he worked on the new Ferrari 250 GTO. Already while still working for Ferrari, Giotto became friend with the rich gentlemen driver Conde Giovanni Volpi di Misurata. As the "night of the long knives" not had been a sudden explosion, but the result of raising disagreements, the former Ferrari employees started to have a still diffuse vision of founding their own company. For this after the leave, everything went fast, the 24 years old Giovanni connected the group with the two business people Giorgio Billi and Jaimi Ortiz, who had been interested in financing a Formula One team. The original name of the new company became "Automobili Turismo Sport Serennissima" (ATS), a company with the goal to produce GT and also monoposto race cars.[26] But already few months later, Giotto and Giovanni left this new company. Giotto opened his own design studio and realize his ideas from the former GTO-project with Giovanni's help and his new racing team Scuderia Serenissima. Based on a 250 SWB chassis he designed the "Breadvan", a creation, which looked very similar to the Ferrari 250 GTO, but in opposite to this one, featured a "shooting back", which should give the car an aerodynamically advantage against its conventional competitors. After working as freelancer for different companies, he founded in '64 Bizzarrini as a car manufacturer. Despite its attractive car, the GT 5300 (formerly known as A3/C produced by Iso), the company had to close its doors already five years later. Giotto himself explained it that he only concentrated on the technical issues, but not the commercial book keeping, so that financing and logistics broke together. Further views on the topic present also other factors, which caused problems for the Bizzarrini company, as the Italian bureaucracy or the limited financial resources.[27]

---

[26] Lazzari, Michael John (2014): "A.T.S. - The Italian Team that challenged Ferrari"

[27] Koobs de Hartog, Jack (2011): "Bizzarrini P528 Anniversario"

Due to the company's books it could not flawless said how many cars the small company had produced, due to Jack Koobs de Hartog's Bizzarrini register it had been 139. A direct comparison of the Ferrari 250 GTO, the 250 SWB "Breadvan" and the Bizzarrini GT 5300 show clearly one continuous line.[28] A possible picture of how the 250 GTO could have evolved under Ferrari, if Giotto Bizzarrini not had left, or even how the car would have looked, if he had the opportunity to finish it based on his original ideas.

1964: Bizzarrini GT 5300 Strada, 5.3L, V8, 365HP, 1150KG, design by Giotto Bizzarrini and Giugiaro, photo with friendly permission from Jack Koobs de Hartog

Even if he came from a rich family, there had been parts of his life, where he had to live with his wife in the company's workshop. Nevertheless he never gave up and found other possibilities to bring him back into the game, as working as independent consultant for the car industry and later going back to his roots and giving lectures at the University of Rome. As manager and leader he never reached Enzo's success, but due to his

---

[28] Gulett, Mike (2013): "Giotto Bizzarrini – A Body Designer? – Oh Yes"

preferences and character, this never had been his goal. He went his way, staying true to himself and with this, found satisfaction with creating outstanding automobiles.

1.6 *"Divide et Impera"*

Besides its Latin name, the expression "divide and rule" is not based on the Old Romans, but on the Italian philosopher, politician, poet, diplomat and historian Niccolo Machiavelli and his famous book "Il Principe" (Italian for "The Prince"), a book about the philosophy of politics and government, especially written for the Medici family, which ruled Firenze and had been the most important family dynasty at this time.

"Ponte Vecchio", Firenze

Using a principle from this text shows again that even if Enzo Ferrari originally not received strong formal education in his childhood, he used his time later to read and understand literature and history.

Divide and rule stands for the principle to divide a big group into smaller sub groups, to make them easier to rain. This not just through pure dividing, but also a construction that the new sub-groups are not having relations with each other, but the relations are limited to the one leader. A strategy, what was not Machiavelli's invitation, in fact he received the inspiration for this by the foreign politics of the Roman Empire, already used by Emperor Cesar himself. Enzo Ferrari had to manage several groups, the most obvious ones have been the racing team and the factory, but also he took time to select new drivers and organize an annual press conference. Independent from his management style, he always took the important decisions and respectfully gained the title "Il Commendatore".

1.7 *"I am a cop, not a racing driver"* (Armando Spatafora)

Psychology knows two different learning theories; behaviorism and cognitive learning. The first one can be described as "learning by doing", as every action provokes a reward or punishment. For example you are driving with you car, ignoring the traffic sign to reduce the speed (stimulus), get stopped by the police and have to pay a fine (punishment). Due to this experience, the likelihood for the behavior (ignoring speed limit) will go down, as you are learning from the situation. In the beginning you may adapt your behavior just in the situations, where you see a police car, known as "classical conditioning". As it is not always possible for you to spot them or their cameras on time, you still will receive fines or other punishments as temporal prohibitions to drive. When you have received several punishments for repeated negative behavior, you will start generally to comply with the speed limits, as soon as you see the related traffic sign, independently if you spot a policeman or not. The classical conditioning has evolved to "operant conditioning", where reward or punishment are not needed anymore, just the original stimulus (in our case the traffic sign).[29]

The theory of cognitive learning is going a step further. You are not just learning from rewards and punishments, which you have received yourself, but also can observe others and study what are the results of their behavior. We are now adapting our original example: As a child you are sitting in the back-row of your father's car. He is ignoring the sign announcing a speed-limit and gets stopped by a police-car. This time the punishment is not for yourself, but for a third person. Due to this experience you recognize that

---

[29] Myers, David (2008): "Exploring Psychology"

your father has adapted his future behavior and from now on is complying with the traffic rules. Years later you finally received your driver's licence. At the beginning you are driving with caution, but step by step you are taking this off and start to drive a bit faster than allowed. Based on the "self-efficacy"-theory[30] you assume that you are now in a different situation than your father had been, as you observed him. You are younger, and your faster reflexes allow you to react in time to not get caught by the police. Based on this, your shown behavior is against the originally learnt, you "have to learn it yourself".

Important is the expectation of the outcome, which is determined by two factors the possibility of the outcome and the outcome itself. For example a sales employee has 5 possible business cases.

1) Offer (Price + Quality) = 100 USD
2) Offer (Price + Quality) = 100 USD
3) Offer (Price + Quality) = 100 USD
4) Offer (Price + Quality) = 100 USD
5) Offer (Price + Quality) = 100 USD
→ Expected Value: 500 USD

As alternative the employee can support the offer with a bribe:

1) Offer (Price + Quality + Bribe) = 200 USD
2) Offer (Price + Quality + Bribe) = 200 USD
3) Offer (Price + Quality + Bribe) = 200 USD
4) Offer (Price + Quality + Bribe) = 200 USD
5) Offer (Price + Quality + Bribe) = -200 USD (getting caught and fined)
→ Expected Value: 600 USD

From a pure economic point of view (and not including the general costs of corruption), the second alternative is more attractive. Paying a bribe or not is no question of culture, but calculation. If the Government wants to foster ethical behavior, as clean business or correct payment of taxes, there are two possibilities.
    a) Raise the fines: If getting caught means -400 USD instead of -200, the total changes to 400 USD. Inferior to the perceived outcome of clean business. If the fines raise to 800 USD, the total outcome

---

[30] Bandura, Albert (1993): "Perceived Self-Efficacy in Cognitive Development and Functioning"

would be 0 and with this a serious threat to the sustainability of the business.
b) Raise the controls: If you are getting caught 3 times, instead of only once, your total would change from 600 USD to -200 USD. Again a serious threat to the future of the company.

Individuals do these calculations, but based on missing information and psychological biases do not stick completely to the statistic rules. If you got caught once, you perceive in many cases the general possibility of getting caught higher than it is. The same is valid for the other way around. If you did not get caught, you are tempted to perceive the risk lower than it is in reality.

1962: Ferrari 250 GTE 2+2, 3.0L, V12, 240hp @7000rpm, design by Pininfarina

With this learning experience you could have met one of the most famous police cars, Rome's Ferrari 250 GTE. The Italian president Giovanni Gronchi visited in the early 60s the city's special police unit "Squadra Mobile" to appreciate their merits in combating the crime. In this event he asked the policemen how he could support them and one, half as joke, answered with a Ferrari. The president took this surprisingly serious and went to Ferrari. Enzo saw an opportunity to become a supplier of the numerous Italian police departments and gave two 250 GTEs to the Roman police department. One of the cars unfortunately got destroyed in the first police trainings, but the other one got put in service. It became famous, as one of its drivers, Armando Spatafora, not just declined the possibility to become a Ferrari racing driver with the simple sentence: "I am a cop and not a racing driver", but also chased a gangster and his Citroen right over the Spanish Steps. The car surprisingly survived this and other operations. From 1962 to '68 it was actively used and today can be seen at the Roman police museum.³¹

The Spanish Steps at Christmas, Rome

According to social-psychology there are 4 different steps of socialization. It is not that the replace each other, more that they the human being steps into a new phase of life, new peer-groups get important and others get less frequented.³²

- Stage 1: A new-born child has a natural sense of basic trust regarding its parents. For this it starts copying their behavior and learns their values and attitudes. In the case of Enzo Ferrari he clearly took his father's values and attitudes, what should determine his relation to hard work and appreciation of diligent, dedicated employees. Also it was his father, who took him in 1908 together with his brother to see his first car race and so started his passion for the sports.³³

---

³¹ Petrolicious Productions (2013): "Ferrari 250 GTE on Special Assignment"

³² Berger, Peter L. / Luckmann, Thomas (1966): „The Social Construction of Reality"

³³ Hyde, Justin (2014): „February 18: Enzo Ferrari was born on this date in 1898"

- Stage 2: With entering kindergarten and school starts a new stage for the child. Being Mondays to Fridays away from the parents, friends are getting a new peer-group. The human being is executing learnt behavior, while being separated from the parents, but also learns new values, attitudes and behavior through teachers and friends. Enzo's school career was not too long due to the economic and political situation at that time. Nevertheless he understood the importance of education and practiced continuous learning in his life. A fact, which he had proved in all his interviews and press conferences.

- Stage 3: The move from education to work is the next big step in human life. Typical the human being builds up a new peer-group and the importance of previous ones slowly declines. The loss of his father's workshop was a liberation for the young Enzo, as his future was not determined anymore, but now it was up to him to write it himself. As he was determined to become a famous race driver, he sold his parent's house and bought himself a race car from that money. In his first event, a hill climb in Parma, he finished on the fourth position. In total he participated in 47 races and won 13 of them. He got recognized for his talent and with this became part of a circle of drivers, his new peer-group.[34] In 1932 he gave up his active racing career, mainly in favor of his family, but another reason was his meeting with Tazio Nuvolari. Enzo accepted that he never could drive on the same level as "The Flying Mantuan". As his personal philosophy not included second places, it was not too hard for him to step out the cockpit and to concentrate to lead and manage the racing team, as he knew that here he could win. Including that Tazio later joined the Scuderia. Unforgettable was Tazio's 1935 "Impossible Victory" as he won with a, at that time inferior, Alfa Romeo P3, against the dominating German competitors form Mercedes Benz and Auto Union, on the most difficult Nürburgring. A key moment for Enzo, as this should be later known as the greatest win in history of motor racing and

---

[34] History.com (fetched 26.09.2014): „October 5, 1919: Enzo Ferrari makes his debut as a race car driver"

he identified Tazio as the perfect driver. A framing effect as in later times Enzo's compared all of his drivers with him and mostly they failed this aspiration. Talented ones, as Gilles Villeneuve, received a *"I see a little Nuvolari in you"* as a compliment.

1930: Alfa Romeo 6C 1750 GS, 1.8L, Straight 6, 55hp @ 4400rpm, 125km/h

In the same period he also joined a second peer-group, a one with young engineers, where he met Luigi Bazzi and Vittorio Janos, who both should join Enzo later in 1923 at his employer Alfa Romeo. In 1919 happened another occurrence, which should become important for the Ferrari company: Italo-American driver Ralph dePalma won the Indianapolis 500 with a Packard V12. Seeing and hearing this car in the Italian TV strongly influenced Enzo, and from now on the V12 was the perfect engine for him; for racing, but also production cars.

- Stage 4: The last stage of socialization is the phase where the human being retires from work, leaving these peer-groups and again find new ones. *"Work is something I give, never seek."* According his own philosophy, work kept finding him, even when officially retired. For this he practically worked all his life and never entered in this fourth stage. As he never took holidays, nor had much leisure time, he would not had an idea what to do with this time. So he associated the loss of work with death: *"One must keep working continuously; otherwise, one things of death."*

2 INTEGRITY BASED LEADERSHIP

2.1) *"I have yet to meet anyone quite so stubborn as myself and animated by this overpowering passion that leaves me no time for thought or anything else."*

2.2) *"Stand-up"*

2.3) *"A car maker must be someone who loves his passion for cars and he must be someone who knows a lot about human beings."*

2.4) *"Managers do things right; leaders do the right thing."*

2.5) A car that flies

2.6) Tone from the Top

2.7) *"Consistency is the most important thing in business."*

2.8) *"I have always given the public the least possible about myself"*

2.9) *"Aerodynamics are for people who can't build engines"*

  2.9.1) How to build a strong engine?

  2.9.2) The importance of aerodynamics

2.10) The Impossible Victory

2.11) *"I think of myself as constantly realizing a childhood dream."*

2.12 Countach, Conformity Pressure and Change Management

2.1 *"I have yet to meet anyone quite so stubborn as myself and animated by this overpowering passion that leaves me no time for thought or anything else."*

First of all we have to analyze what "integrity" means. The US American author and philosopher Ayn Rand defined it once: *"Achievement of your happiness is the only moral purpose of your life, and that happiness, not pain or mindless self-indulgence, is the proof of your moral integrity, since it is the proof and the result of your loyalty to the achievement of your values."*

This complex statement is based on psychological theories and can be interpreted as this:

- We have two given variables: "values" and "behavior". Normally the behavior should be motivated and based on one's own values. But this does not automatically has to be the case. The strength of the values (and derived attitudes) determinates how easily behavior can be distracted from the values, for example through temptations or urgent needs. Values and attitudes are learnt in the different stages of socialization.
- If we have such a situation that values and behavior are not compatible anymore, the individual feels being outside its normal state of harmony. Based on Leon Festinger's "theory of cognitive dissonance"[35], the person perceives now an inner pressure to get back into harmony again.[36] For this he or she can adapt the two variables "values" (= "cognition") and "behavior". Of course, normally the values should be stronger and so resistant to a change, but if the person took a non-value based decision several times or in an important decision, the individual is not sure anymore if this is really a value and furthermore decides from the observed own behavior that there must be a complete different value behind, from which this action is related from. With this logical process, the human being is with the new assumed value in harmony again, as this new one is compatible with the own behavior.

---

[35] Festinger, Leon (1957): „A Theory of Cognitive Dissonance"

[36] Fischer, Lorenz / Wiswede, Guenter (1997): „Grundlagen der Sozialpsychologie"

- As each person feels the need of having a positive iamge of him or herself, values and behavior get compared to the assumed peer-group's ones and if they are not consist with the ones of the peers, the person perceives this as negative and feels a pressure to develop assumed positive moral values and regarding behavior.
- **Integrity is defined as value based behavior. If values and behavior are in harmony, also the human being is, and with this feels inner happiness.**

These are more than just theoretical conclusions. A controlled experiment confirmed the philosopher's idea that an emotional arousal is related to an active ethical decision, as for example to deny the acceptance or offering of a bribe .[37]

Strong inner values and attitudes prepare a person to resist external temptations and hostile environments. Attitudes only get effective if a person enters in a relevant situation. For example the attitude "not to steal" (derived from the value "honesty") just gets relevant in the situation of an opportunity to do so. This is especially important as employees are not always in the safe environment of their group and offices, but sometimes alone, as for example in home office or field work.

Enzo described himself as a stubborn person, what have been confirmed by the people who had regular contact with him. If stubbornness is been seen from the positive side, it can be interpreted as having strong values and acting accordingly, or shortly said as integrity. Enzo confirmed this idea with his quote: *"You have to have courage to stand up to your critics."*

---

[37] Jaber-Lopez, Tarek / Garcia-Gallego, Aurora / Perakakis, Pandelis / Georgantzis, Nikolaos (2014): "Physiological and behavioral patterns of corruption"

2.2 *"Stand-up"*

Especially for the founder, a company is much more than just a machine for earning money.[38] In many cases it is a dream, including that the world becomes a better place with the offered products and solutions. Feeling this high identification with the company, no one would jeopardize it with unethical actions. Of course it is very difficult to keep this vision and passion up through all levels of employees. To nevertheless ensure a "stand up"-culture, the standing up must be made as easy as possible. If an idea turns into action or not, depends on several variables: motivation, situation, ability and expected output. Let us say an employee witnessed a non-ethical situation inside the company. As such actions are against the best interest of the company, management is interested to know about it. There are ways to positively influence the variables:

- Motivation: The higher the identification of the employee with its company, the more likely he or she will report any wrong doing. A positive working atmosphere is imperative to ensure a "stand up"-culture. Besides that, employees should learn and understand why anti-corruption and anti-trust laws exist. Corruption is not a faceless crime, society is paying a high price for it. Furthermore fines for wrong-doing get higher each year and can become an obstacle for the survival of the company, and with this the vision and dream of its founder and other employees. Related Compliance workshops are easier to conduct in high-risk countries, as employees know corruption not just from the news, but face its consequences in their daily life, for example through ineffective public education or missing infrastructure. But as most companies are working globally, also employees in low risk regions, have to understand the cost of corruption, for the society and the own company. Corruption is a risk-factor and for a company, risk means cost.

---

[38] Moss Kanter, Rosabeth (2011): „How Great Companies Think Differently" in Harvard Business Review

- Situation: Perception is subjective to the observer. An employee has to be able to identify a risk situation. It is not always easy to understand from the first moment, if something is legal, illegal or in a grey area. Values are learnt, so the perception of the same situation can be different based on the culture and education level. The best way to learn this, is through interactive workshops. For this it is important that the applied case studies are as real as possible. With this the employee can identify later the learnt situation and act according the learnt solution.

- Ability: *"You have to have courage to stand up to your critics."* As a leader this is easily said. But most employees are dependent on their work, and especially if management is involved in potential wrong-doing, have to consider, if they will report something that could lead to reprisals. The probability to report a potential wrong doing depends on the possibility that the expected outcome will occur and what the expected outcome would be. For a corporate ethics program trust is a key-factor, as the company is dependent that for the case that an employee has knowledge about a wrong doing, he or she would address it, maybe to the manager, a compliance officer or an anonymous whistleblower-hotline. General trust levels vary from society to society. Especially countries with an unequally distributed income tend to have low trust levels between its citizens.[39] First measure for the company is to implement a whistleblower-hotline, depending of the company structure, this can be managed internally or out-sourced to a third-party company. Additional to this hotline must exist a robust process to ensure that reporting employees are protected or better, that also anonymous reports are getting invested. Depending the local culture, people are more or less trustful to anonymous tools as telephone or email hotlines. For this the Compliance Officer must be known to the whole organization as trusted advisor. To achieve this, he or she cannot limit him or herself on being expert in Compliance matters, but has also to have profound business knowledge. If the Compliance Officer does not know, how the company is really

---

[39] OECD: Society at a Glance 2011: OECD Social Indicators: Trust

earning the money, there is no ability to give relevant answers to the employees' questions. Beside the expert-figure, the Compliance Officer must be a trusted colleague. This makes it imperative for him or her to leave the office and meet and interact with the employees to reach a positive impression. Compliance cannot be a part of the top-management, but must be perceived as an independent function. With reporting an incident, the employee is leaving his or her comfort-zone, for this it is relevant to communicate the output of such investigations. Only if the employees understand that the using of the whistleblower hotline will lead to a positive and relevant action, they will include it in their mind-set of possible actions.

Enzo Ferrari was known for his stubborn character, open words and fighting for his ideas. Something which he has learned in his childhood and youth, as it was definitely not an easy time, but on the other hand his efforts brought most of the time positive results.

That self-confidence, but also the opposite helplessness are learned attributes confirmed an experiment by Martin Seligman and Steve Maier. They took dogs and separated them into three groups. The second and third groups got treated with electrical shocks. The dogs of group 2 had the possibility to stop the pain by pressing a button. The group 3 dogs had no possibility to stop this by their own behavior. For this they perceived the electrical shocks as randomly and inescapable.

In a second step both scientists changed the setup of the experiment. Now all dogs of the three groups had the possibility to escape the shocks by jumping over a low partition. As it was an easy task, the dogs from the first two groups had in general no problem with it. Only the participants from the last group showed a different behavior. As they perceived the pain as something inescapable, they not even tried to escape, but stayed in their place and gave their selves in to the pain.[40]

---

[40] Seligman, Martin / Maier, Steve (1967): "Failure to escape traumatic shock"

Self-confidingness or perceived helplessness are a result of classical conditioning. Not all groups or societies have the same importance for "standing up". Similar to the presented dog experiment, also humans learn helplessness. According action and re-action, impunity is a treat to the implementation of a "stand up"-culture, independent if in society or a company. The Mexican UDLAP university published "The Global Impunity Index 2015", where Italy can be found on position 22, behind the Netherlands and Germany, but still before Switzerland and France. As statistical inaccuracy can apply, it can be said that all these countries are more or less on the same positive level.[41] Such a positive environment favors a stand up-culture, as the inside culture would be compatible with the general outside one.

To ensure an adequate and desired company culture, it some cases the internal company culture must be different than the external society one. A difficult and long-term task, but working with the three variables (motivation, situation and ability), should it make possible to reach the goal to implement a culture, where employees stand up for the company and their values.

---

[41] UDLAP (2015): "Índice Global De Impunidad (IGI) 2015"

Vinci, Italy

Leonardo da Vinci, talented artist and curious in all aspects, became the ideal of the Renaissance time. In his famous "Vitruvian Man" he realistically pictured a man from different angles, but Leonardo not only understood the outside, also human psychology, as his quote *"It is easier to resist at the beginning than at the end"* shows. Being in the beginning of a potential Compliance risk is the best time to contact your Compliance Officer. An individual will do this if his or her benefit will be higher than the investments.

Definitions:

r) Estimated Compliance Risk: The estimated negative impact for company

b) Anticipated Benefit of Compliance: The estimated positive impact of the Compliance to solve the problem

c) Cost of Information: The estimated cost to contact the Compliance Officer and / or to involve him or her. This includes also an estimated negative or positive impact for the employee, for example potential disciplinary action or an award for whistleblower. For the last case the cost would turn into benefit.

$(1/r) > b - c =$ no Compliance contact

An employee, who received Compliance training, will guess how big a Compliance risk may be. As he or she is not an expert on the topic, this estimation can be right, but also wrong. If the Compliance department will be contacted depends now, how the benefit of this is anticipated by the employee and how cost-intensive is receiving relevant Compliance information and decisions. If the 1/"estimated risk" is assumed to be higher than the anticipated benefit minus the costs to receive this information, the employee will not seek to contact Compliance. As the risk estimation can be wrong, this can lead to a Compliance problem; a relevant risk for the company.

$(1/r) < b - c =$ Compliance contact

On the other hand, if benefit minus costs is still higher than the 1/"estimated risk"; Compliance will be involved. So these are the four factors, with which can be worked on:

- Foster employees' Compliance knowledge so that they able to judge correctly potential risks.
- Make the Compliance department a trusted advisor which can offer relevant information. This maximized the anticipated benefit of Compliance involvement.
- Lower the cost of information. Compliance must be close to the business and easy to reach. Additionally an award for positive behavior up to for whistleblower can be implemented. If possible tools as smart phones and apps should be used to ensure communication availability 24 hours and 7 days a week.
- Connect Compliance with company and personal values. With this a potential wrong-doing will lead to pressure inside the employee,

as (potential) actions not are compatible with own attitudes and values. Lowering psychological pressures (as for example "must win projects") would be another benefit of Compliance involvement.

Just as Leonardo predicts, the longer you are walking down on the wrong path, the more difficult it gets to resist the future wrong doing, as with the time the cost of information gets higher. This includes that first of all, the employee has to admit his personal failure and also has to assume that now the correct behavior will be paired with a smaller or bigger disciplinary action.

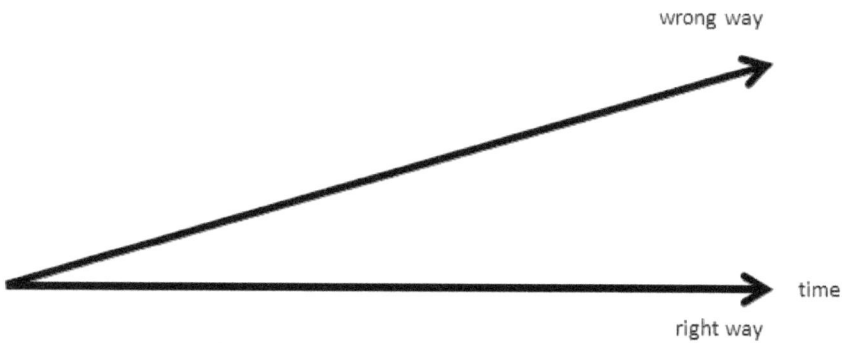

Perception is important. The employee has to understand that he or she is on the wrong way. In many cases this is not the case right from the beginning. The employee perceives him or herself as on the right way, but then more or less suddenly understands that this is not the case. Hereby can perception be everywhere in between the absolute black and white. Through the employee's eyes he or she can be on any imagine imaginable path on or above the right one, even above the wrong way.

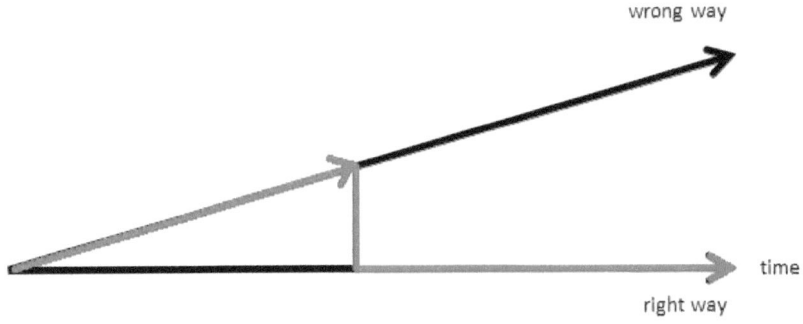

Again, Compliance trainings support employees not just to stay on the right way, but also if they left this path, to recognize this as early as possible. Here such a workshop cannot limit itself on pure teaching of information, but must include real-life case discussions and psychological stress situations, which may lead to the ethical blindness-phenomenon.

According to Leonardo, it is easier to resist a future wrong-doing (=continuing to walk down the wrong path), if you are still in the beginning, at or soon after a decision. This because the longer you are on the wrong way, the bigger gets the gap and the more difficult to jump from the wrong to the right path. Meaning, if you want to return on the right way, you have to communicate with your Compliance Officer and a) commit your wrong-doing to yourself and b) to the company. Most organizations have a range of disciplinary actions, which starts from nothing, if it is plausible that the deviation was a pure accident, up to separation of the employee from the company, if it is a sever case. The cost of information gets higher with the time. But there can be also negative costs, if there is an whistleblower ward.

Based on Leonardo we include "g = gap" in our calculation:

$$(1/r) < b - c - g$$

Herby the gap is defined as:

v) Own perceived responsibility for wrong-doing

s) Severity of the wrong decision (the angular degree between both paths)

t) Time

$(1/r) < b - c - (v * s * t)$

According to mathematics, if any of these values would be 0, g become 0:

v=0 : The employee feels not responsible for the deviation, it was an accident.

s=0 : The employee does not perceive a negative impact for the company

t=0 : The employee is still in the process of decision making.

If 1/"anticipated compliance risk" is lower than the benefit of possible compliance involvement, minus the costs of information and the gap, the employee most-likely will continue on the wrong path without making the situation transparent, as it is easier to give in the temptation to follow the wrong path than to resist it and return to right one.

Further Compliance can work with these factors:

- Responsibility: Workshops can discuss the responsibility of employees, especially regarding approvals and signatures.
- Severity: A good Compliance training is not limited on laws and regulations, but explains also what is behind, like cost of corruption. Further Compliance can be presented as part of the company's sustainability strategy. It is not just important to sell today, but also to sell in the future.

As the flow of time is still no value, which we can influence, the race is on; and Compliance should make it for the employee as easy as possible to get reached and support them.

This formula is not meant to be a mathematical equation, but should explain the relation, which have the single factors on each other.

In business psychology literature, group pressure is often presented as a risk factor, but it can be used also for the benefit of the company. The classic experiment to demonstrate group pressure is the conformity experiment by Solomon Asch. The experiment leader presented three lines to the participants, each with a different length. Then the students saw a second card with just one line. Their task was to tell, which of the first three lines had the same length as the one from the second card. A basic task, as the differences had been quite obvious. But just the last student is really a participant. The other ones had been involved in the experiment and consciously gave a wrong answer. Interesting in Asch's experiment, in most of the cases, the independent last participant repeated the earlier wrong answers.[42] This behavior could be interpreted in several ways. Sometimes the participant gave consciously the wrong answer, as he or she was afraid to discuss this with the group and defend the own point of view. In other cases the independent participant observed the earlier answers from the group and started to doubt his or her own perception. Now the participant gave the same answer as the other participants, but with the idea that this was really the correct one.

This effect can be used to create a positive group pressure. Communication, trainings and workshops are not only to be used to inform and train employees, but also are an ideal channel to communicate a positive message. If a certain number of employees are reached and convinced, so that they really live a stand up-culture, these employees commit a positive peer pressure to the still not convinced ones. Of course the tone from the top is most relevant, but the group pressure works from all levels, also lower level employees can influence higher ones. For this a positive and open corporate culture is a mandatory first step to create a stand up culture.

---

[42] Asch, Solomon (1951): "Effects of group pressure on the modification and distortion of judgments"

2.3 *"A car maker must be someone who loves his passion for cars and he must be someone who knows a lot about human beings."*

Enzo had been in two different management positions, head of the racing team and director of the car company. Two different tasks, which require other management styles. There are different management models available, but to demonstrate Enzo's tasks we will use the classic managerial grid model, which was elaborated in 1964 by Robert R. Blake and Jane Mouton. This model is working with two dimensions: 1) concern for people and 2) concern for production. With this there are 5 management styles possible:

- People low / production low: "Impoverished style", this style can be found at managers, which have internally resigned from company and position. For this they do not show interested in their employees, nor their tasks. This style supports them to concentrate on them-selves and to avoid short range problems, before they leave their position and / or company.

- People high / production low: "Country club style". These managers care a lot for their employees and give them a lot of space and freedom. They have the philosophy that happy employees are more productive.

- People low / production high: "Authoritarian style". These kind of managers have only their tasks and results in mind and the employee is just another resource. Similar to a machine, if the employee is not functioning, he or she has to be replaced.

- People high / production high: "Team leader". The manager is concerned about projects and production and want to reach the highest possible output. He or she is convinced that these tasks can only be reached, if all employees are motivated and feel them-selves as a part of company.

- People medium / production medium: "Middle-of-the-road". These managers try to use a bit from everything to reach their results and so to find a middle way.[43]

Management style, of course, depends on the character of a person, but more than that it is learned. This is why each person has more than just one style and is able to vary it, according the involved people and the situation.

Management style depends on the employees

Enzo Ferrari was born in a small town as second son of an engineer. With this he came early in contact with technics and mechanics, including that earning money meant hard work. *"We were awakened in the morning by the ringing of hammers."* This young age experience should influence him and his management style. You had to show knowledge and dedication to be included into his circle of confidence. This characteristic was not always for his best benefit, as two examples around Paul Frère demonstrate. Paul was automotive journalist and racing driver. He gave priority to his family, that is why he denied becoming full time driver, but always had been available, if a substitute was needed or an additional team-member for long distance races. With this attitude Enzo Ferrari continuously employed him as a driver, but nevertheless because of their different philosophies, Paul became not a member of Enzo's closer circle:

- 1956: The Scuderia Ferrari deployed the D50, which they took from the last year's Lancia team. The performance of the car was quite changing and the engineers tried to make it more stable. As part of the efforts, they took away the typical side-tanks, but this brought not the hoped positive effect. Paul Frère mentioned this topic again, but got ignored, as he only participated as guest driver. Result: The car stayed unpredictable until the end of the season, but nevertheless Juan Mario Fangio could win the championship.

---

[43] Blake, R.; Mouton, J. (1964): The Managerial Grid: The Key to Leadership Excellence

- 1960: As presented in another chapter, Paul was also critical to the 250 TR and its aero dynamical attributes. He got ignored again and the result: The cars stayed fast even without having the best aerodynamics, but the team underestimated the high fuel consumption (due to the missing aerodynamics), so that 2 from 4 started cars ended up on the track with empty tanks. Nevertheless a Ferrari car won, ironically the one driven by the two Belgians Gendevien & Frère.

Enzo had a high opinion of hard work and that you have to dedicate yourself 100% to achieve success, on the other hand he had no good opinions of employees, which had other priorities. For employees, who not had been in his circle of trust, he was a more authorial leader, for the ones inside, he used a more team leader style. If you made it once into his group of peers, you normally stayed there. Loyalty was appreciated in the Italian culture and Enzo was no exception to the rule. Several of the key-employees in the early Ferrari corporation had been former co-workers of him, as Giocchino Colombo, who was responsible for the legendary Alfa Romeo 158, also known as "Alfetta" and should became famous for his Ferrari engines; or the Fiat technician Luigi Bazzi, who worked with Ferrari until the 1960s.[44]

Trust was a key factor not only for Enzo Ferrari, but also it was the Italian way to conduct business. There are two different philosophies how to receive the trust of your manager or business partner:
- You have to earn trust.
- You are trusted from the beginning, but have to work to stay in this preferred situation.

Due to himself, Enzo preferred the second definition: *"I give my collaborators a great trust."* He explained this as the good employees would feel motivated by this received trust and give their best effort to justify it. Other kind of employees would start creating mistakes. An ideal way to support the employees' self-selection. By analyzing Enzo's decisions, you can say that he

---

[44] Formica, Piero (fetched July 29, 2014) : Enzo Ferrari – The Making of the Motor Racing and Sport Cars Knowledge Cluster

gave employees the mentioned trust from the beginning, but nevertheless you had to work hard to reach the small circle of people, who earned his highest level of trust.

Rosenberg's and Jacobsen's "Pygamalion Effect" supports Ferrari's philosophy, explaining a self-fulfilling prophecy: If employee A treats employee B with respect, this confirms B's positive self-esteem that he/she is a respectful person. By imposing this value, in return B treats A respectfully. A now perceives B's respectful behavior and concludes that B is a respectful person. A cycle is created. If this does not yet exist, it is up to the management, including its Ethics & Compliance department, to treat the employees of the company respectfully to start this cycle.[45]

Management style depends on the situation

Enzo had been in two different situations:

- 1929 he founded the Scuderia Ferrari, which until 1939 should be the official Alfa Romeo racing team. 1946 the Ferrari team constructed their first car, and from this moment on, acted as independent team. In 1974 Enzo stepped back as sporting director and Formula 1 team manager, but stayed involved until his death in 1988. In this role as team manager he was strongly focused on the technical site and was known that in the case of victory he underlined the importance of the car and in the other case, blamed the drivers. Or to say it with the words of Niki Lauda: *"When we won, then it was Ferrari who had won, not the driver, because Ferrari was the best car. When we lost, it was always the driver's fault."*[46] This included the fast replacement of drivers and key-employees in the case of missing success or accidents.

---

[45] Rosenthal, R. / Jacobsen, L. (1968): "Pygmalion in the classroom: teacher expectation and pupils' intellectual development."

[46] Motor Trend (2007): The Secret History of Ferrari Outtakes

1958: Ferrari Dino 246, 2.4L, V6, design by Vittorio Jano and Carlo Chiti

Regarding the managerial grid model, his management style could be quite matching defined as authoritarian. In racing sports, not only the cars have a fast pace, also the success. To ensure a competetive car and infrastructure, teams need to find sponsors, which bring in the needed money. As such companies want to use the sport as communication channel, they are depending on the success of the car, as a fast car receives more attention in the media and with this again, the logo of the sponsor reaches a larger group of potential customers. For this a team seldomly can allow itself the luxury to develop over three years, but quick success is needed. Time to develop employees is rare, employees, including key-employees as drivers must function from the beginning. On the other hand, as team manager you have the luck that your employees are normally all self-motivated and self select them for tasks, even if this means taking risks and minimilze private life. A part from his normal strict appearance, Enzo was aware of the drivers' importance and credited them: *"It's because of you, ... that we are what we are."*

- In 1947 Enzo founded "Ferrari S.p.A." the luxury sports car manufacturer, as we know it from today. Main reason for its existence was the need to sell cars to fund the racing team. First street car became the 125, even if especially in this early time the difference between street and racing cars was not strong. Ferrari's unique selling proposition was to offer street cars with the latest racing technology. Based on this, many clients used their cars to utilize them in different kind of races, as we still had the time of the "gentlemen drivers". Others used their Ferrari to see and be seen, or just to enjoy the machine.

1947: Ferrari 125, 1.5L, V12, 90hp @ 6000rpm, 750kg, design by Carozzeria Touring

The situation of a car company is significant different to the one of a racing team, as a street car can stay several years on the market, in opposite to a racing car, which has to be completely overworked for each new season. Due to this, also the development of a new car can take several years, while the development of racing car has to be done in months. This differences have as result that a car manufacturer has much larger planning and production circles as a racing team. A different situation, requires other management styles, or as Enzo defined himself: *"His job is to harmonize the ambitions of his collaborators."* This is the description of a team-leader style, but based on is numerous quotes, he always set the importance of the car (product) higher than the human factor. Even though he came close this to this style, as the production of high quality products with low motivated employees is not possible. *"What we do at Ferrari is elite work,"* he said, well aware about the motivation and capacity of his employees, as without this it would not be possible to manufacture the world's leading sport cars.

2012: Ferrari F12 Berlinietta, 6.3L, V12, 730hp @ 8250rpm, 340km/h, 1525kg, design by Centro Stile Ferrari (Flavio Mazoni); photo with friendly permission from David Lee

So in general as a car maker Enzo maintained a more team leader style, while as direct manager of the racing team he was more the authorial one. One key factor, which style to use is the limited resource "time". If plenty of it is available and you have a skilled and motivated team, you should give them space to find the best decision. If there is no time, it is up to the leader to make decisions quickly, based on his or her best knowledge at that time.

Enzo's goals always had been to win races and championships. For this he was not afraid to integrate the best and highest talented people inside his team, starting right from the beginning with Vittorio Jano. A business philosophy, which goes back to Niccolò Machiavelli: *"The first method for estimating the intelligence of a ruler is to look at the men he has around him."*[47] As the best team wins, but not automatically the team with the best single players, this strategy can work out, but also has its risks.

- 1988 the Ferrari Formula 1 team hired the British race car designer John Barnard. Due to his success with McLaren he had the image of a wunderkind. As Ferrari at that time was already a long time without titles, they not just offered him an attractive salary, but also

---

[47] Machiavelli, Niccolò (ca. 1543): "The Prince"

the possibility to open his office in England and not working from the factory in Maranello. In the 1980s all successful Formula 1 teams beside Ferrari, had the headquarters in the UK, for this he wanted to stay inside this creative and competitive region and not move to Italy, where he felt being far away from the center of motorsports. Apart he not spoke Italian, what was an additional reason why he preferred to stay in his country. This geographic separation was not well perceived by everyone in the team, especially as he later forbade the mechanics to have wine at lunch, while Ferrari had its testing sessions. Barnard's input helped Ferrari to get on the right track again, also with the introduction of the semi-automatic gearbox, but beside single victories, the big goal of winning championships could not be reached.

- The Scuderia was traditionally a team, what focused on team and car. As this strategy brought no success for the teams, they felt pressure for a change and introduced a radical innovation, 1996 came with Michael Schumacher the dominating driver. In opposite to John Barnard, he learnt Italian, integrated himself into the team and used this starting point to become a respected leader. As both, former Ferrari Formula One team-manager Jean Todt and former Ferrari president Luca di Montezemolo confirm, already before Schumacher the Ferrari team tried to get the leading driver. In 1993 there had been meetings with Ayrton Senna. The talks had been open and promising, even one of the meetings took place in Montezemolo's private home in Bolonia. Nevertheless Senna decided to stay with the Williams team. Further ideas to finish his career at the Scuderia had been destroyed by his tragic accident.[48] Less known, already in '89 and '90 had been non-formal contacts between the Brazilian star and the former Ferrari team manager Cesar Fiorio. Both already signed a pre-contract and Senna asked, similar to Schumacher later, to get the best technical experts, as the McLaren technical manager Steve Nichols, for the team. Even further than that, he wished to have the fastest available driver as his team-mate. This to ensure that we would have to deliver his

---

[48] Noticias-F1.com (2016): "Todt: Ayrton queria venir a Ferrari y lo queríamos"

maximum performance, just as it was the Enzo Ferrari philosophy that the drivers would push themselves to the limit. Information about these negotiations leaked inside the Ferrari team and let to the situation that especially the relation between Alain Prost and Cesare Fiorio got complicated and finally in '91 the manager had to leave the team, soon to be followed by Prost.[49]

As team manager Enzo Ferrari underlined the importance of the car in case of the victory, on the first view this looks as he would have preferred the machine over the person. But in reality he had personalized his creations and saw the cars as an output of the complete team, starting from the designer, going over to the engineer, until the person who cleaned it before the race. *"A man builds something, a beautiful machine"*, in interviews Enzo always used a colorful language to express the special relation to his creations. As his driver Phil Hill remembered later, the only situation where Enzo got angry with him, was as he criticized the car once in 1961. He took it quite personal and just responded: *"Maybe you ought to just put your foot down harder."*[50]

With the car having the highest importance for his work, he avoided a cult around his drivers, but made a statement that the team is the star, which was, of course, also including the drivers, as they are the ones, who supported with the technical set up of the machines and at the end, made the car shine on the track. With this his he achieved that the drivers stayed a part of the team and that there had been positive working atmosphere in the team. *"I have really enjoyed my time at Ferrari, not just because of the successes."* (Michael Schumacher)

---

[49] Papadopoulos, Dimitris (2014): "Senna & Ferrari: Wie es beinahe zur Traumehe gekommen waere"

[50] Levin, Doron (1988, in The New York Times): "Enzo Ferrari, Builder of Racing Cars, Is Dead at 90"

BUSINESS PHILOSOPHY ACCORDING TO ENZO FERRARI

2002: Ferrari F2002, 3.0L, V10, design by Rory Byrne, Ross Brawn & Paolo Martinelli

In the race is the driver alone in the car. In Enzo's active time as team manager the only contact was the shown signs at the finishing line. And even with today's technology the contact is limited to one radio message per round to not disturb the driver's concentration. This situation is compatible to the business life, where employees also are not in the same time, nor the safe environment of the office, but working more and more in home offices or are even travelling around the world for the company. As we will see later in the book, this situation can have its risks. A racing driver gets prepared by learning the rules and so receiving the necessary racing license. Furthermore each weekend before the qualifications and the races, there is a meeting with officials and drivers, to repeat the most important topics and discuss the particularities of this special racetrack. Beside the preparation, there are the controls to ensure that nobody is too fast in the pit lane or taking somewhere a short-cut. Depending the characteristics of the track, such controls can be more or less effective.

1967: Ferrari 412 P, 4.0L, V12, 420hp@ 8000rpm, 792kg

If we take instead of the racing driver a global sales-manager, the situation is quite similar. The manager is flying alone to different countries and cultures. For him or her this can include risks for health, safety or even lead to temptations as forgetting to play by the rules. As attitudes are learnt, there is a risk that we forget them. In a new and unknown situation this can happen quickly, as we maybe have to understand that our known behavior is not leading anymore to a, for us, positive result, and without these rewards or even with receiving punishments, we will stop with our normal behavior after a while, and try out another kind. This can start with ignoring a red traffic light and can go up to deviate more serious laws, as paying a bribe to ensure business. If we take the concept from the motorsports, solution for the business can be preparation workshops before the employees start to their trip. This with the idea that they are better prepared for being in the foreign country, understand its culture and with a more detailed insight, know already before the trip how to behave in the country. A "loss of control"-effect gets minimalized and with this, the risk of misbehavior. The employee gets protected against him or herself. According to Julian Rotter's "locus of control"-theory[51] the employee stays in control thanks to better knowledge. Individuals who feel in control of the situation, in average behave based on their personal values. Other ones, who are feeling helpless are tempted to behave against such values and attitudes, this because of an inner force to get as fast as possible out of this

---

[51] Rotter, Julian (1954): "Social learning and clinical psychology"

unpleasant position and back to a situation, where he or she feels in control again.

Another way to reduce such risks is to make the distance felt shorter. Today's modern racing cars can be nearly completely technical controlled by the crew at the command stand in the pit lane. Passively that they receive all information and tell the driver what to do, for example to use less speed to save fuel and look after the tires. Actively that the crew can remotely change engine preferences or restart the software of the car. These possibilities are reducing the possibilities of the driver and have two effects on him: 1) He feels less special and more part of the team and 2) he perceives more control, which would make it more difficult to ignore orders.

Again, these solutions from the track we can apply also in the business. With technologies as smartphone, tablet, laptop, internet and global roaming package, employees maybe are on a different continent, but their communication is as if they would work just around the corner. Decisions do not have to be made alone, but can be discussed with the team. Such technology plus the preparation workshops are supporting, but of course, they are not reducing such a risk to 0, also because not all misbehavior can be explained with the "loss of control"-effect. Such an example we can see in the next chapter.

2.4 *"Managers do things right; leaders do the right thing."*

In 1967, the Austrian-born management consultant and philosopher Peter Ferdinand Drucker defined: *"Efficiency is doing things right; effectiveness is doing the right things."*[52] Nearly 20 years later, Warren G. Bennis y Burt Nanus took this phrase and re-modeled it to: *"Managers do things right; leaders do the right thing."*[53] But what we really need and want is "efficient effectiveness" or a leading manager, who does the right things right. Was Enzo this ideal model? Surely he acted according the two roles:

---

[52] Drucker, Peter Ferdinand (1967): "The Effective Executive"

[53] Bennis, Warren G. / Nanus, Burt (1985): "Leaders: The Strategies for Taking Charge"

- Leader: He was very charismatic and especially in his earlier time able to inspire people around him. He could explain his passion and start the same fire in his employees, independent if engineers or drivers. Also he had the capacity to resist the offer by Ford, as the result would had not been compatible with his personal values. Due to the deaths of Tazio Nuvolari (1953) and Alberto Ascari (1955), who not just had been highly talented drivers, but also personal friends; and later of his son Dino (1956), he changed and became more introversive; what had a negative influence to his ability to lead and inspire. A visible symbol for this became his sunglasses, which he used now nearly all the time, independent if being in- or outside. Nevertheless he always stayed a man of values.

- Manager: Enzo started being engineer and driver and later had to learn management skills, as he had to finance his racing team. Even if he never had a formal business education, he instinctively made the right decisions, so that he built up the Ferrari company, including sold it to Fiat, as it was necessary to do so.

2.5 A car that flies

According to Kendra Cherry, Emotional Intelligence is the ability to perceive, control and evaluate emotions.[54] EI is partly based on the character of a person, but mostly learned. Even if the reader may think that it is a new topic, in fact EI is based on Edward Thorndike's social intelligence-theory and first published in the 1930s. Based on this concept, Daniel Goleman developed later his 6 Leadership styles:[55]

- Visionary: *"I want to build a car that's faster than all of them."* Enzo started as a racing driver, but as he not came from a rich background, in opposite to the gentlemen driver at that time, he always had to take care to have a car to drive, and prepare it himself. Due to this, he discovered early his passion for cars and

---

[54] Cherry, Kendra (fetched 23.06.2014): What is Emotional Intelligence?

[55] Murray, Alan (fetched 26.07.2014): Leadership Styles, in The Wall Street Journal

technics. He had his vision to build cars himself and had been able to convince potential key-employees to join him. Even if Enzo always stayed in control, these employees had a lot of freedom to develop their own ideas to reach the big goal of the perfect race car. *"If you can dream it, you can do it."*

- Coaching: As his style was more to explain people his vision and goals, he expected them to understand and work independently to comply with the given tasks. A coaching approach he only used once, for his first son Dino, whom he had with his wife Laura. He was also the reason, why he retired being racing driver and concentrated on his role as team manager for Alfa Romeo. Alfredo (as Dino's full name was), studied economics in Bologna and then later engineering in Switzerland. After his studies he was involved in the company's development of the V6-engine and could convince his father to use it, even if Enzo was known for his preference for the V12: *"I married the 12 cylinder engine and I never divorced it."* The company used it for the Formula 2 race cars and later for the Dino street cars.

1969: Dino 246 GT9, 2.4L, V6, 196hp @ 7600rpm, 238km/h, 1080kg, design by Pininfarina

Enzo took his son already in early age to the races and with this introduced him to motorsports. Later he ensured that he could get the, for the company necessary, formal economical and technical background; and as he saw that Dino had the required talent and interest, he coached him and introduced him slowly to the different parts of the company and gave him the opportunity to work with Vittorio Jano on projects as the 750 Monza and a V6 engine.

1954: Ferrari 750 Monza, 3.0L, Straight 4, 250hp @ 6000rpm, 260km/h, 760kg

Giving his son these tasks should pay out, as the 6 cylinder engines made career within the Dino, Fiat and Ferrari cars, further the 750 Monza reached its goals to win important races. If Dino's career not got stopped by his much too young death with the age of 24, he surely would had been his father's successor as company leader.

- Affiliative: Enzo always emphasized the importance of the team in opposite to single persons. This had the advantage that he activated the strongest team performance, but the disadvantage that he not always had the best relation with his star pilots. For example the Argentinian driver Juan Mario Fangio joined 1956 the team, but already one year later he left Ferrari again to return to Maserati. With him he took the start number 1, as despite their difficult relation, both men had a successful year and Fangio could win the Formula 1 championship with the D50.

- Democratic: Enzo used a democratic style, especially in his earlier years, where he gave employees of his circle of trust freedom to make their own decisions and actively listened to their ideas. Especially in his time as race driver he studied other drivers and cars and used these ideas for himself, including he tried to adapt the driving style of his later friend Tazio Nuvolari. Surely his ability to use a democratic leadership style became limited with the time, especially after the death of his son. This was to see in his relation with Niki Lauda, who had won the championship with the Ferrari team and was known for his technical expertise. Starting after his infamous accident, Enzo Ferrari disagreed with Lauda's decisions, as coming back too early or quitting the rain race of Suzuki. Even if both still won the 1977 championship together, it meant the end of their collaboration that year,[56] and Lauda started 1978 for the Brabham Alfa Romeo team.

1977: Ferrari 312 T2, 3.0L, V12, 500hp @ 12200rpm, design by Mauro Forghieri

- Pacesetting: Enzo was a perfectionist, who wanted to develop and build the perfect race car. This was not just the target for him, but also for his employees. Even if in general he underlined the importance of the team, he had one exception, between the different drivers he wanted to have a competitive atmosphere, as he believed that just in competition drivers would go to their limits and so activate their best. Due to this believe he accepted an aggressive atmosphere inside the team, between the different drivers, but what also affected the internal teams, which had been supporting the drivers. The most extreme example of this inner team rivalry was the 1982 Formula 1 season and the relation between Didier Pironi and Gilles Villeneuve. Both pilots pushed their selves to the limits and beyond, as several of their actions showed.

---

[56] Roebuck, Nigel (2013): Lauda's falling out with Ferrari

1982: Ferrari 126 C2, 1.5L, V6, 650hp, design by Mauro Forghieri & Harvey Postlethwaite

For many fans this continuous battle, at and over the limit, was the ultimate reason for Villeneuve's deadly high speed accident at the Belgium race track. His team-mate should have a serious accident later the season, where he broke both legs, what meant not just losing the championship, where he was on the best way to win it, but also the end of his Formula 1 career.

- Commanding: As stated before, for people, who had not between in his inner circle, he got often perceived as commander, "Il Commentatore". The decision of a group is not automatically better than the one of an individual. James Arthur Finch Stoner concluded in his experiment that decisions which had been taken inside a group tend to be significant higher than decisions which had been taken by an individual.[57] Even if his work does not give an answer to the question why, it can be speculated. If a group decides, there is no person who takes 100% of the responsibility. In the case of a negative result, responsibility is shared, so no one loses his or her face. In opposite, if an individual takes a decision, in the case of a negative result, it is him or her alone, who takes

---

[57] Finch Stoner, James Arthur (1959): "A comparison of individual and group decisions involving risk"

the consequences. This is not only true for the financial impact, but also the potential loss of status. This means that an individual with a lower status, in the company or society, in average takes more risky decisions as there is less to lose, but more to win. Traditions get important for long-term leaders. For Enzo Ferrari this meant the focus on the engine, especially the 12 cylinder one. This had the advantage that the company achieved a technological leadership in the topic, but had on the other hand the disadvantage that other technologies got too late adapted, as for example aerodynamics or the introduction of the turbo engine in Formula 1.

Enzo Ferrari's example verifies that these six leadership styles are based on the emotional intelligence-theory. As due to the experiences of live he was not able anymore to feel and perceive the whole spectrum of emotions, especially positive ones, he lost also the ability to execute the different leadership styles. A sign of this change had been his famous sunglasses, which he began to use day and night starting in the early 1960s. To be more precise, he wore a model by Pernol, the number 2762.[58] This Italian manufacturer had been founded 1917 in Turin. Originally the company made sunglasses especially for pilots and race drivers before it extended its market to the rich and wealthy. One of its famous clients had been actor Steve McQueen.[59] Enso Ferrari understood self-promotion and the value of the myth. He actively used the sunglasses to underline his character and suffering. For interviews he always wore the dark glasses, even inside closed rooms. After the official events, back in privacy or in his close circle of trusted friends, he switched back to his normal eye-wear.[60]

It was not only the death of his son, in 1957 he was alleged of manslaughter as at the Mille Miglia Ferrari driver Alfonso de Portago due to a flat tire tragically drove into a line of spectators, killing them and himself in the accident. Already earlier the Vatican newspaper L'Osservatore Romano called him a "Saturn", one of the mythical titans who was devouring his

---

[58] YellowBirdRS on FerrariChat (2007): "Strange Question - Enzo Ferrari's Glasses"

[59] Persol History (fetched 21.4.2019)

[60] Di Montezemolo, Luca (2019): "Beyond the Grid"

own children.⁶¹ As Enzo believed in his innocence, he came without a lawyer to the court and contended his statement. He felt prejudiced as murder and stated this at court: *"Why should I continue in an activity whose only reward is being branded a murderer?"* As result of the trial, Enzo Ferrari was rehabilitated as innocent, as it was seen as a race accident. Before this disaster, the Mille Miglia was a source of happiness for Enzo, but this was lost now. For the several accidents that year, '57 was the last year of the original race, it should get resurrected 20 years later as a race for classic cars. Due to all this happenings, the '50s changed Enzo and he became less and less seen in big public events, as he became very skeptical against unknown people. He fled into his work and his commanding leadership style. This appearance made people think that he was always this hard person, but Enzo thought differently about himself: *"I consider myself weak and so I put on a kind of mask"*, with this he followed again Machiavelli: *"Everyone sees what you appear to be, few really know what you are."*⁶² As additional strategy he avoided now and in future to hire Italian drivers, so the local press could not claim anymore that he would risk the life of young Italians.⁶³ Through this inner process, Enzo lost an important part of his emotional intelligence.

An example for the loss of empathy was his relation with Carrol Shelby. From the early 1950s to '58 Carrol drove several Ferraris, mainly in endurance races. As gentlemen driver he gained positive race results and beside that enjoyed the atmosphere of the events and the friendship with fellow drivers. For this the deaths of several Ferrari race drivers, including his friend Luigi Musso, had a major impact on him. The tragedies together with Enzo's short statements, Shelby perceived as cold behavior. Similar to the press, Carrol blamed Enzo for the drivers' death, as in his eyes, Enzo's believe in competition without compromise over-motivated the men that then went to their limits and beyond. For this it was not understandable that Enzo not showed more emotions after the accidents and took further consequences in the management of the racing team. As consequence

---

⁶¹ Mc Cafferty, Hugo (2013): "Enzo Ferrari: A driving passion"

⁶² Machiavelli, Niccolo (ca. 1543): "The Prince"

⁶³ Walthert, Matthew (2014): „Ferrari, Italy and Formula 1: Where Have the Italian Drivers Gone, and Why?"

Carrol never wanted to drive for the Scuderia again, build up his own car and bet Ferrari, where it hurt most, on the track. The famous AC Cobra became the result of Shelby's ideas. As driver he recognized the potential of the British AC Ace-cars. Three years later he offered AC to update the car with a Ford V8 engine. As AC were struggling at this time, they gladly accepted the offer. The original Cobra was built from '62 and '68, and especially in the Le Mans races strongly supported by Ford. From 1963 to '65 the Ferraris still stayed unbeatable, but after this came Shelby's time. With the gained experience and the new Ford GT40, the Shelby team won in '66 and '67. Important races, also as the '66 victory should end Ferrari's successful Le Mans history, as the company never again won this classic event.

1955: Ferrari 375MM Shelby, 4.5L, V12

This example underlines the importance of empathy, for clients and employees. If you cannot understand these stakeholders, including their needs, they can leave your company from one day to another. If it is a key-employee or –client, it can have a relevant impact on the company. The topic stays actual, as today's millennials are less loyal to brands and employers than earlier generations and expect not only a material wage, but also satisfaction of their emotional and social needs. Empathy is needed to understand them and to keep with the company.

Daniel Goleman divides Emotional Intelligence into five components.[64] Using these systematics, it is clear how the circumstances in the 1950s limited Enzo's abilities:

- Self-awareness: All his life Enzo understood himself has the *"aggregator of men"*, the manager and leader who kept the company together. But further than that he we was aware that motorsports is only a small part of the world: *"Whom am I in this world?"*

- Self-regulation: Even with a growing wealth and financial independence he stayed a humble person and expected similar from his employees, independent if they had been technical engineers or famous drivers.

- Internal motivation: *"Racing amuses me"*, after personal tragedies Enzo concentrated on his childhood's passion, other motivational triggers had not been required.

- Empathy: To not further hurt himself, he reduced social contacts, especially with his drivers. As this is not a one way relation, with shutting himself off, he lost in several cases also the ability to understand key-employees. Confrontations and separations had been the result.

- Social skills: Enzo strongly focused on the technical and financial part of the business and avoided participating in social events, he even stopped the travels to the racing events. Traditionally he only attended the Monza Grand-Prix and the additional Imola race. In an environment where connections can lead to business, a relevant limitation.

Emotional Intelligence is effective, when the five components work together as one. Limitations in one factor cannot be compensated with stronger abilities in one of the other ones. Of course, nobody has the same

---

[64] Rampton, John (2016): „Here's How to Know for Sure if You're Emotionally Intelligent"

quality of skills for all requirements, but it is important to work on all, including the weakest component.

2.6 Tone from the Top

Companies can have well defined values, but at the end employees are looking at their top management to see how they are acting and leading. A good leader should motivate the team, but also being conscious to not to over-motivate the employees. That this can go wrong shows an example from "Juventus di Turin". Their motto is *"Winning isn't important, it's the only thing that matters!"* This is a line by one of their most famous players, Giampiero Boniperti, with 182 goals in all competitions, he held the club record for more than 40 years. After his active career as a player he stayed in responsible positions for Juventus, including becoming their president. This personal motto, became the philosophy for the whole club, until you can find it printed inside the tricots. The idea is to motivate everybody to give the best and win the title. But on the other hand this high pressure can make people think that they really should do everything for winning the title or project, even if it means bypassing laws and policies. Especially if the business is operating in high risk-markets and / or project business, it is mandatory to have a robust Compliance system implemented, as employees must know where the clear red line is, so that they push not too far to win the "must win projects". From this point of view, a compliance program is not just a tool for risk mitigation, it is furthermore ethical necessary, so that beside the business pressure the employees have a clear statement, what is expected and what not, what is possible and what not according the internal policies.

2013 Tricot of Jueventus di Turin

Compliance, of course, comes from "to comply". This can be misinterpreted being a program, which is limited to control that the employees are complying with the internal and external policies. If it would be just this, a Compliance department is not necessary, as these functions are covered by Internal Audit. Compliance is much more, it is an integrated idea of pro-active and responsive tasks working together. Due to its closeness to legal, Compliance's core is to avoid that employees (and with this the company) are breaching laws, what would lead to fines and further official actions against the firm.

An important part of a Compliance program is the tone from the top. For this, management should be well aware how to use their words. Business means pressure and there are projects, which are definitely more important to win than others. We cannot take completely the pressure off the employees, but it is imperative that the message has to more detailed. An employee cannot just think in the today, but has to include tomorrow and beyond. Based on the sustainability philosophy, it is not just important to win today the important projects, but still be able to do so in 10 years and later. Ex-territorial laws like the FCPA and the UKBA are risk factors, as fines are easily going into millions of Dollars and limit the positive future development of the company. As mentioned, the tone from the top is key for the company culture and with this for the Compliance program. Giving this message is the preventive part to avoid wrong-doing from the side of the employees. As this is such an important action, regarding the seize of the company, it is to analyze if there should be implemented a special policy and / or process, how this tone should be given. Finally there should be a regular control in place to understand, if the tone is adequate and understandable. This can be pure statistics, how such a communication was given, but can include also a regular survey to learn, how this message was perceived by the employees.

For Juventus it came, as it had to come. To reach their only goal winning, some people crossed the line and the team had been involved 2006 in a huge soccer scandal (also known as the "Calciopoli"). A couple of mayor teams, beside Juventus also AC Milan, Fiorentina, Lazio and Reggina got accused of rigging games. As a result, Juventus received the following sanctions:

- Relegation to Serie B

- Stripping off 2005 and 2006 Serie A titles

- Excluded from UEFA Champions League in 2006 and '07

- Playing three home matches behind closed doors

Apart from these fines, which in numbers mean lots and lots of million Euros, several key players left the team, as Favio Cannavaro, Lilian Thuram and Zlatan Ibrahiovic. This is a corruption risk, which is normally a little bit forgotten, but the image of the company is directly related to how easy it is to find and keep their employees. A big part of the reputation is regarding the business area, where the company is active. For example in Germany most of the engineering and business student would like to work in their local automotive industry. But also companies, which are known for their flexibility and their services for the employees, as for example Google, are quite at the top of the list.[65] On the other hand, companies, which are in the news with (potential) corruption cases loose attractivly. Going there means

---

[65] Buchhorn, Eva (2014): " Beliebteste Arbeitgeber – BMW schlägt Google" (in Spiegel)

accepting the risk to not have a safe position, as million Dollar fines are questioning the future effectiveness of the company and also the idea, that if a company is corrupt in the external dealings, they function the same way internally, meaning you are not advancing due to your capabilities and hard work, but because of your connections. For this a non-transparent company has the serious problem that they are not getting the employees, which it wants to have (or have to pay higher salaries for them) or have the employees, which it does not want to have.

Especially in sports there have been several cases of over-motivated people crossing lines, just to name some examples:

- 1989: Ayrton Senna had to win the second-last grand-prix (Suzuka) to not lose all possibilities to still win the championship. Before a chicane he tried a risky maneuver to overtake Alain Prost (both on McLaren Honda). Knowing that it had to come to an accident, Prost closed the way and it came to the collision. Prost stepped out the car and Senna first tried to continue the race, but later got disqualified. Title for Prost.

- 1990: the pay-back. This time Prost (now with Ferrari) had to win the Grand Prix of Japan to still have hopes for the title, but inside the race Senna provoked the collision. Result, the championship title for the Brazilian pilot.

1990: Ferrari F1-90, 3.5L, V12, 680hp @ 12.750rpm, design by Enrique Scalabroni & Steve Nichols

- 1997: The European Grand-Prix is the season's final. Both Jacque Villeneuve (Williams) and Michael Schumacher (Ferrari) could win the championship, if they win this last race. Schumacher was leading most of the race, but then slowed down due to technical problems. It was clear that it was only a question of time, when Villeneuve would overtake. So round by round he came nearer and as he finally started the overtaking, Schumacher closed the way, as a collision with both cars out of the race would had been the only possibility that he still could win the championship (the first for Ferrari since 1979). The plan just partly worked, both drivers had to abandon the race after the accident, but Schumacher got disqualified later, not just for the race, but the whole season. Title for Villeneuve.

1997: Ferrari F310B, 3.0L, V10, design by Rory Byrne and Ross Brawn

In sports and business, concentrating on the one big goal has the risk of developing a tunnel vision. Due to human nature, we all want to have a positive self-image. The easiest way to achieve this is through competition, as a victory is the official confirmation that we had been better than the rest. In the stone age this instinct has ensured the survival of our group, as food was a limited resource and we had to give our best in the hunt. Enzo Ferrari always played with this human characteristic to ensure competition among his drivers about being the internal number one. As he framed it: *"Being second is to be the first of the ones who lose."* Today Formula 1 teams are in-between the strategy to have 2 drivers competing about being the internal number one or having a clear number one driver and a supporter. Both philosophies have their pro and contras. As discussed, competition and over-motivation can provoke people crossing lines, and provoking accidents and disqualifications, so the idea of having less competition in the own team and with this more cooperative drivers, who support better the technical development of the whole team, can have its advantages. These thoughts are not just limited to sports teams, but can be valid also, for example, a sales team. In general, the manager wants to support competition through commission based payments and titles as "sales person of the year", but on the other hand also needs the group act as a team. For this soft skills are most important to ensure that people are motivated, but not over-motivated. That is why the manager must know how to speak with each person, what can depend on the different characters, but also the actual situation in life and with this, the dependence on the job. Employees must be clear, what is expected and where are the limits, instructions as *"you are the best"* or *"be creative"* should be avoided.

As seen in the several examples, over-motivated employees can overstep the red-line, which separates legal from illegal, even if they are people with strong personal values, as for instance both, Senna and Schumacher, had been active for different social projects. Ayton's team-mate and later Ferrari driver Gerhard Berger described Senna once: *"Before the race he read the Bible and in the race he drove over your head. The super successful are all like this."*[66]

As the risk is identified and also the possible risk-group, the question is, what can be done to mitigate it. Regular trainings should create awareness for the topic and also get the employees out of their daily routines. The clear message must be that every person is 100% responsible for its own actions and for this should execute an adequate decision making process. Different case discussions can work as an "ethical vaccination", maybe the employee was not yet in such a situation, but may face it in the future. He or she will remember later the example cases and can use them as blueprint or pattern for his or her actions. As employees appreciate a positive self-image, they welcome an adequate vaccination. As Michael Schumacher said in an interview: *"It matters how I achieve something".*

---

[66] Gute Zitate (fetched 09.09.2014): "Gerhard Berger"

As defined in the beginning of this chapter, attitudes get only effective in the relevant situation and are deduced from the person's values. Most drivers had the value "fairness", as they had been good sportsmen and as they all are benefiting from it. Being fair means also that others are fair to you, and if not, there is a process to escalate the topic. So the value is given, but the attitude "not to drive in each other cars, if it is the last race of the season and you still can win the championship" is not existing yet. As most of the drivers not had been in this situation before (and likely never will be), they not thought about what would be fair to do in this duel. After a long season it can be seen that it is fair for me to win even with this maneuver, as you can find easily arguments for it:

- The championship is not just for me, but for the whole team, who did a great work to support me.

- My opponent had the stronger car and I am the better driver.

- My opponent did the same to me last year.

- ...

But there are surely more arguments against such a maneuver, which may not had been included in the driver's first thoughts:

- Millions of motorsports fans invert money and time into their passion, they deserve a fair race.

- The other driver is in the same position as me, so also would have deserved the victory.

- Due to the speed, accidents are always dangerous, for drivers, but also spectators.

- Unfair maneuvers are weakening the credibility of the sports, everybody is losing.

- All drivers have to comply with the rules, if not there are consequences.

- Around the race-track are a lot of cameras. Surely the race stewards would analyze the maneuver and disqualify me.

- ...

A discussion or a role-play about such pros and contras should lead to the result that the driver will develop a (hopefully) positive attitude to not provoke accidents, if one day he would be in a similar situation. For this a Compliance training can work as an "ethical vaccination", as the positive attitude will not be activated now, but stays as "antibodies" inside the person and help to make him immune to the regarding temptations. To ensure an effective protection, such vaccinations have to be repeated from time to time.

This theory gets confirmed by Oliver Sheldon's study for the Rutgers Business School: *"If people want to avoid unethical behavior, it may help to anticipate situations where they will be tempted and consider how acting upon such temptations fits with their long-term goals or beliefs about their own morality."*[67] This idea can be resumed as *"think before you drive"*, even if this is the claim of a campaign by Bridgestone and the FIA ("Fédération Internationale de 'Automobile", English: "International Automobile Federation").[68] Its goal is promote the usage of seat belts, child seats and to review regularly the tire conditions. The Formula 1 drivers supported the message, as for example the Ferrari team Michael Schumacher and Rubens Barrichello formed a pit crew and demonstrated for the attending press the basic activities, which all drivers should execute.[69] As Bridgestone left Formula 1, both parties continued separately. In 2014 you could read along the race tracks: *"Bernie says: 'Think before you drive.'"* As discussed, both, the race driver and the company employee have the required positive values, but if they perceive a potential situation as not relevant and / or not likely to experience, required attitudes are not formed yet. If they should face this situation, there is not enough time to conduct an extended decision making process and the needed attitudes cannot be activated, as they are not yet existing. To avoid such

---

[67] Science Daily (2015): "Anticipating temptation may reduce unethical behavior, research finds"

[68] Bridgestone (fetched 29.05.2015): "Think before you drive"

[69] Crash.net (fetched 29.05.2015): "F1: Ferrari duo back 'think before you drive' campaign

situation, in Formula 1 there are the driver meetings before the trainings and race. In business it can be done via interactive workshops. As attitudes are derived from values, it is imperative that such a training not only explains what to do in the theoretical situation, but also explains the why, for example the negative impact on the company and the general costs of corruption.

"Being second is to be the first of the ones who lose." is only half of truth. Of course it is no victory and no project won. But for the spectators it is important to have good competition, the most remembered race seasons are the ones with good fights; not just one leading driver, but two or more are battling about victory. This way the sport receives more attention and creates more revenue. Even teams & drivers which get second or less still receive attractive sponsoring contracts and, via a complicated key, revenue share from the championship organizer.[70] Also in business life being second has a certain value:

- For the market: As second you supported chasing the winner and ensure that the winning company really made their best effort to convince the client. A competitive market means that best products and prices are available. As result, a stronger economic grow means a bigger market for all companies.

- For the client: Similar offers support the client to reduce prices of their suppliers and give them the possibility to change suppliers for different projects. With this the company not gets dependent to one supplier only.

- For the company: Even if you not won the project, with being a strong second you reached to minimize the margin for the winning company. Further you are in a good position for the case that your competitor gets problems in the execution of the project and / or cannot deliver the solution's promised quality.

---

[70] Arshad, Sameer (2014): "How money is Generated in Formula 1 and then Distributed?"

With all business pressures, an adequate tone from the top has to communicate this and include the possibility to lose projects. And why not celebrate a good second position? Even if it has not direct positive impact on the company's numbers, there may positive aspects to it:

- You had the second best offer, so if the winner get into problems with the execution of the project, it will strengthen your company's position for the next tender.

- Often the decision which offer to take does not only depend on pure numbers and specifications, but on the decision maker's experience. A change of employees inside the potential client company can lead to a different starting position for the next tender.

- With the elaboration of the offer you gained important information about potential technical solutions and client acceptance.

Ferrari Formula 1 driver Sebastian Vettel knew very good Enzo's quote that the second is the first of the loser, as he said this several times before.[71] Nevertheless he celebrated the second position at his first Monza Grand Prix for the Scuderia: *"It's an incredible day, it's the best second place I ever had in Formula One. … In terms of emotions it's more than a victory."* Of course this had been mainly based on the special atmosphere of Italian Grand Prix, but also due to fact that the updated engine meant a good step into the right direction and gave the car the required speed to keep up with Mercedes powered competitors.[72]

As risks and temptations are known, the Italian soccer league is working on innovations how to foster ethical behavior. One idea is to use the implemented card-systematics and add to the yellow & red one a new green card. In opposite to the first ones, the new green one is not meant as a disciplinary sanction, but to foster ethical behavior. Also it will not be showed inside the playtime, but after the match. Serie B president Andrea Abodi defined that players would have to perform an "extraordinary act" to earn such a green card. This is not only to foster positive behavior for itself,

---

[71] GP Update (2009): "Second is the first loser – Vettel"

[72] Ferrari.com (2015): "Italian Grand Prix – Best second place ever"

but Abodi understands that non-ethical behavior of the teams and players *"drives people away from the stadium"*. The actual concept defines the green card as a symbolic act, for this has no direct countable advantage, but nevertheless the soccer league hopes that the concept has a positive effect for the sports.[73] An idea which gets discussed also in companies and similar organizations. Positive behavior is defined in the corporate values and the related code of conduct, so you may argue that this is what the company expects from its employees. On the other hand, not everything can be defined inside the guidelines. Via bonus payments the employees get motivated to maximize their efforts on measurable output. For this, if an employee "goes the extra-mile" regarding ethics & compliance, the employer should recognize such. Similar to the Italian soccer league, this is in the interest of the company, as a human being normally things in shorter circles than a company. Transparent business is an advantage on the long-run and may face obstacles on the short one. It is for discussion, if a corporate green card should be a pure symbolic act or include a higher financial factor.

To close the circle, Juventus fought its way back into the first division and had in its 2013-14 season Jeep as tricot sponsor, a company which got mentioned by Enzo like this: *"Jeep is America's only real sports car."*

2.7 *"Consistency is the most important thing in business."*

Due to the mentioned direct leadership-style, it was no surprise that some of his employees suffered from it. 1961 it should came to an internal management crisis, as the long-term sales manager Girolamo Gardini left the company after several discussions with Enzo Ferrari. Originally he made Enzo an ultimatum that either his wife Laura should back off the company's business or he would leave. Enzo gave not in to this demand, but proactively separated him from the company. But it was not only the sales manager who left, also 5 other employees, who supported him had to leave, followed by two others only weeks later.

---

[73] BBC (2015): "Green cards: Italy's Serie B to reward positive player behaviour"

This decision was communicated at Ferrari's annual press conference, Enzo's traditional event, where also the company's important partners, as for example Luis Chinetti, participated. Even if it was a mayor discussion and an important cut for both parties, until today, the detailed reasons for the dispute never went public. A sign that even in this difficult situation both sides not completely lost the respect for the other one.

Even if most of the authors concentrated on Laura to explain the massive walkout of employees, there are also reasons:

- Enzo changed in the middle of 1950s, there had been two tragic situations, who took away happiness from him, first the death of his son Dino in '56 and then the later deathly accidents of several Ferrari drivers, especially the '57 accident of Alfonso de Portago at the Mille Miglia, what led to the end of the traditional race event and Enzo facing a court hearing, including the comparison of him with Saturn. Since then he tried to minimize human relations and concentrated on the work. Due to these circumstance the work atmosphere at the company notable suffered, and everybody perceived the tension.

- The later dismissed employees perceived their-selves as the future leadership of the company, especially as Enzo was close to the general retirement age. To do something against the common deadly accidents in motorsports, the group around Carlo Chiti developed a fuel tank for race cars, which consisted of two separated tanks, which are inside another, one for the fuel and the other one with reducing fluid. In the case of an accident and a damaged tank, both liquids would leave, but the fluid should avoid the fuel to create a fire.[74] Doing so, the employees had not taken into consideration that none of them had been inside Enzo's inner circle of trust. So it came, as it had to come, Enzo was not open to support a further development of this idea and with this, the project was stopped inside the company.

---

[74] Chizzola, Gianni (2004): "AUTODELTA and surroundings"

As at beginning of 1960's Enzo lost parts of his emotional intelligence capacities, it can be assumed that he would not jeopardized the sustainable development of his company, due of problems with his wife, so maybe it was the spark for the explosion and the massive separation of key employees, but not the only reason. A confrontation that potentially could had been avoided by including an intermediate, who was part of Enzo's circle of trust, as Vittorio Jano for example. But as this was not the case, the two groups went separate ways.

In detail these key employees left:

- Geralamo Gardini, commercial director
- Giotto Bizzarrini, director controlling and testing
- Carlo Chitti, director design and racing
- Ermanno Della Casa, administrative director
- Fausto Galazzi, director foundry and metallurgy
- Romolo Tavoni, sport director
- Enzo Selmi, HR director[75]

One of this eight employees, Giotto Bizzarrini, had been developing at this time the new 250 GTO, which should be introduced in the next year. Instead Giotto, Carlo Chiti, his friend from Alfa-time, and several other key people formed a new company called ATS (Automobili Turismo Sport Serenissima, later: Automobili Turismo e Sport). At least for a few months, until he left to realize the 250 SW for the Scuderia Serenissima. Carlo stayed and developed the ATS 2500 GT. The car had limited success, nevertheless it became important because its V8 engine had been the base for Alfa Romeo's new motor, which got used later in the famous Tipo 33. The ATS 2500 GT conquered its place in history as it was in '63 the first mid-engine gran turismo. Enzo Ferrari was for a long time afraid of this technical concept, as such cars are more sensible and require a higher concentration of the driver. Even if Ferrari used the mid-engine in motorsports, the first street car should became the Dino at the end of the sixties.

---

[75] Auto Italiana (1961): "Perche' si sono dimessi gli otto dirigenti della S.E.F.A.C.-Ferrari"

1964: ATS 2500 GTS, 2.5L, V8, 220hp, design by Bertone (Franco Scaglione). / 2017: ATS GT, 2.5L, V8, 650hp @ 7250rpm, 331 km/h, 1300kg, design by Emanuele Bomboi. Photo with friendly permission from ATS Automobili Turismo e Sport.

After the leave from Romolo Tavoni, Eugenio Dragoni took the open position of the Ferrari sport director. He was not only Enzo's friend, but supported also his philosophy that the race drivers should not achieve a too outstanding position inside the team. Based on his skills, the Ferrari team could win, for example, the '64 Formula One World Championship and several times Le Mans, but on the other hand based on his hard line, champions as Phil Hill and John Surtees left the Scuderia. Phil joined the "rebel" ATS team, after at the '62 Targa Florio he requested a change of the gearbox and Romolo just answered that a real champion should know how to shift. Carlo Chiti could convince the, at that time, still raining F1 champion to change to the new ATS F1 team. The ATS 100 car was based on Carlos' Ferrari 156, but because of the small budget, the car never became competitive. The team only participated in five of ten '63 races and from these Phil only could finish once, at the eleventh position in Monza. The end of the ATS Formula One dream.

After ATS had to close its doors, Carlo Chiti founded together with the Alfa Romeo dealer Lodovico Chizzola. Autodelta S.p.A., which developed, constructed and tuned racing cars.[76] Three years later Alfa Romeo bought the small, but innovative company and Carlo Chiti had been back at his former employer. This time, he became responsible for the successful

---

[76] Collins, Peter / McDonough, Ed: "Tipo 33"

prototypes and touring cars. After Alfa Romeo ended its Formula One engagement, Chiti again moved on; left Alfa in 1984 to found Motori Moderni and together with Minardi come back into Formula One. But this is another adventure…

1969: Alfa Romeo 33/3 Spider, 3.0L, V8, 420hp @ 9400rpm, 650kg

In total ATS only finished twelve GT cars. Even though, the car stayed a part of Italian car history, this due to its driving performance and the timeless design made by Bertone. So it is no surprise that the ATS brand got reactivated 50 years after the founding of the original company. The new ATS Automobili Turismo e Sport stays true to the original philosophy and creates small exclusive cars to offer a direct driving experience. Beside a protype racer and a classic roadster, ATS has also a new GT in their portfolio. Was a first show car from 2013 still powered by a four-cylinder engine, included the 2017 model an adequate 2.5L V8, just like the original. In opposite to the original and actual competitors, ATS not only had a focus on the driving experience, but also included latest high tech into the cockpit, as a navigation system with 3D touchscreen and a hi-fi sound system.

1964: ATS 2500 GTS, 2.5L, V8, 220hp, design by Bertone (Franco Scaglione). / 2017: ATS GT, 2.5L, V8, 650hp @ 7250rpm, 331 km/h, 1300kg, design by Emanuele Bomboi. Photo with friendly permission from ATS Automobili Turismo e Sport.

Thanks to his knowledge, creativity, entrepreneurship and attitude, Carlos Chiti stayed an inspiration. The independent designer Marco Procaccine created in 2012 the "Alfa Romeo Carlo Chiti". A potential small sports car with front-engine and traditional rear-wheel drive. With this, the car would be positioned below the more extreme 4C.

2012: Alfa Romeo Carlo Chiti, design by Marco Procaccine. Photo with friendly permission from Marco Procaccine.

BUSINESS PHILOSOPHY ACCORDING TO ENZO FERRARI

Back in 1961, for Enzo Ferrari it was a difficult situation, as he lost important employees, and this put on risk the development of the prestigious GTO-project, but he believed it was crucial to stay hard on the topic, as the employees had criticized his company strategy and with this his overall leadership claim. There had been several discussions going on and due to the concept that if you cannot change the people, you have to change the people, he had to take this step. It helped Enzo in this situation that he had a good eye to discover talents, so two young engineers, Mauro Forghieri and Sergio Scaglietti climbed up the internal hierarchy and became responsible to develop the 250 GTO. It became a big success as the car won its class at the 1962 12 Hours of Sebring. Both stayed in responsible functions and should guarantee Ferrari's prosperity in the 1960s.

1962: Ferrari 250 GTO, 3.0L, V12, 300hp@ 7500rpm, 280km/h, 1050kg, design by Ferrari Gestione Sportiva (Giotto Bizzarrini, Sergio Scaglietti)

Another example for this described consistency experienced Alain Prost as he 1991 criticized car and team: *"I underlined the defects of the Ferrari throughout the season, but no-one has listened to a word."* As such public words were against the Ferrari philosophy, he got separated from the team and replaced until the end of the season by the Italian driver Gianni Morbidelli. A consequent decision, what not came cheap for the Scuderia, as Prost received a high compensation payment.

1991: Ferrari 643, 3.5L, V12, design by Steve Nicols & Jean-Claude Migeot

From 1971 to '73 the Ferrari Corporation built only 500 units of its 365 GTC/4. For this the car received the nickname "the lost Ferrari"; a missing link, but nevertheless an important one. Even if the car technically based on the 365 GTB/4 "Daytona", its mission was to replace the 365 GTC, a luxurious 2+2 coupe.

Its design makes the 365 GTC/4 to an important link. On the one hand it reminds strongly to the classical 60s design of the Daytona, but including new style elements, which announces the more decent Ferrari line of the 70s and early 80s, later seen in the 308 GTB or the 512 BBi. With this the car connected two eras. For itself it was not a huge success, but nevertheless it had been an important intermediate-step in the change process of the company.

BUSINESS PHILOSOPHY ACCORDING TO ENZO FERRARI

1971: Ferrari 365 GTC/4, 4.4L, V12, 340hp @ 6200rpm, 1730kg, design by Pininfarina (Filippo Sapino)

Peter Drucker once said that *"culture eats strategy for breakfast."* Enzo Ferrari was a firm person, who always stayed true to his beliefs. Even if the values stay the same, from time to time is a change in corporate culture required to adapt to changed markets. Doing so, it is not enough to plan this and adapt the corporate rules and guidelines. Culture does not exist on papers, but has to be lived by humans. It is imperative to prepare the employees and accompany them through a certain transition time. Such a process includes two main steps:

1. Raise employee's involvement for the change: The majority of individuals do not like changes, as these bring them outside their learnt comfort-zone. The employer has to communicate the needs for the change and that this is not just in the benefit for the company, but the whole organization including its internal individuals and the outside stakeholders. The last group is not limited to the stock owners, but can include also the neighborhood school, which depends on local taxes. If the employees understand the advantages, they are open for the change.

2.   The Change itself: The new processes and tools have to be tested and then implemented, this to be accompanied by adequate trainings.

Both steps are not separated from each other. The raise of involvement must be first, but has to be continued in the second step and beyond. Culture change is not an easy process and includes a risk that not all employees are able or willing to adapt. The company has to be aware that a smaller number of employees will leave the company.

Several of Enzo Ferrari's contemporaries described him as "machivallic", not surprisingly as he himself took *"divide et impera"* as personal philosophy. The consistency philosophy comes from the same Niccolò Machiavelli, his *"Hence it comes that all armed prophets have been victorious, and all unarmed prophets have been destroyed."*[77] (Later reduced to the simple: *"Before else, be armed"*) is not just relevant for business negotiations (see chapter 3.6), but also for ethics.

A known problem in still many societies is the impunity of public cases. If the company wants to ensure that values and guidelines get followed, it must ensure that violations to them not only get identified, but also remediated. Nobody in the company stands over its code of conduct (on which guidelines, policies and tools are set up on) and a remediation must be adequate to the deviation, there can be no different answers for different levels of employees. If the deviation indicates it, the company has to take the hard decision to separate the employee from the company, even if this means a loss of important knowledge and complying with the difficult local labor laws. Just this way you can earn the respect of the employees. Ferrari Formula One driver Kimi Räikkönen thanked the team after his first tests of the new 2015 car that they gave them, the drivers, a reasonable starting point. This is similar to a company, where tone from the top and implemented tools and guidelines only can be a starting point for each employee, as each individual has to decide form him or herself, if this can be accepted or not. If not, the employee should pro-actively take the step to leave the company. If the individual cannot or want to take this step, there

---

[77] Machiavelli, Niccolo (ca. 1543): "The Prince"

is a risk that sooner or later he or she will commit violations to company values and guidelines. As each person is different, including different personal values and attitudes, it is practically impossible to eliminate the risk to have such a person inside the company. It is in the best interest of the company to identify them, to protect itself, but also all other employees.

Macchiavelli wrote further: *"...when they depend upon their own resources and can employ force, they seldom fail."*[78] An ethics, compliance or internal audit department has to be independent, adequately stuffed and financed; reporting to the CEO and / or a global department.

2.8 *"I have always given the public the least possible about myself"*

Most of the people associate a leader as an extrovert character, Enzo Ferrari was definitely not this kind of man. He avoided big groups, so especially in his later years he not attended anymore personally the races and reduced his contact with the press to the famous annual conference. In his rare interviews he was surprisingly open, about the company, but also himself as person. Even the most standard questions he replied passionately, with technical or business information, but sometimes also until going into history and philosophy.[79] For these events he had prepared declarations, but was also able to reply eloquently to all following questions from the audience or a single interviewer. As he correctly received himself as myth, he even fostered this in presenting himself as in the role of a classic tragic hero. *"The world creates idols only to destroy them."* As it was his ambition to build the fastest race car of them all, in these moments he was anxious to explain in the best possible manner the relevant news around Ferrari and especially its racing department.

Enzo was an introverted person and avoided big events, including attending the race week-ends. But there was one regular event, where he confronted a group of journalists and answer their, sometimes critical, questions. Just as

---

[78] Machiavelli, Niccolo (ca. 1543): "The Prince"

[79] Botsford, Keith (1977): "The pride and passion of Enzo Ferrari"

Machiavelli wrote: *"Nothing causes a prince to be so much esteemed as great enterprises and giving proof of prowess."*[80] The annual Ferrari press conferences are an ideal example of the four qualities, which make an introvert a respected leader: [81]

- Enzo obviously PREPARED very good these rare events. Another attitude which can be found already in the Roman Empire. The philosopher and politician Marcus Tullius Cicero (106 BC – 43 BC) taught: *"Before beginning, plan carefully."*

- He actively listened to the gathered press and was PRESENT to give them unique and relevant answers.

- As he was an empathic person, he understood what journalists wanted and needed to know for him. As he perceived the results of his company as elite work, he wanted to enable the present journalists, who took the time to attend the press conference and prepared questions, also to deliver later such elite work. He PUSHED himself to give them the required (what not always had to be the same as the asked for) information for this task.

- Enzo was selective, who is entering his circle of friends and trusted colleagues. One criteria to earn his respect and get inside this groups was the ability to discuss with him about the important topics. For this he gained the needed PRACTICE to discuss with the journalists.

---

[80] Machiavelli, Niccolò (ca. 1543): "The Prince"

[81] Tartakovsky, Margarita (fetched 03.09.2014): "4 Things Introverts Do that Makes Them Effective Leaders"

BUSINESS PHILOSOPHY ACCORDING TO ENZO FERRARI

2.9 *"Aerodynamics are for people who can't build engines"*

We are in the middle of June 1960 and the 28th "24 Hours of Le Mans" was on the calendar of all racing fans. After the poor results from last year, the Ferrari racing team came back to France with four new TRs and just one goal, to win this classic. Car starting number 9 with its pilots Wolfgang von Trips & Phil Hill, no. 12 with Ludvico Scarfiotti & Pedro Rodriguez, no. 10 with Willy Mairesse & Richie Ginther and no. 11 with Paul Frère & Olivier Gendebien.

Belgian pilot Paul Frère was first not convinced about the new TR ("Testarossa" as Italian for "red head", named due to its red valve covers), as its windshield looked quite inelegant and much too steep.

1960: Ferrari 250 TR 60, 3.0L, V12, design by Pininfarina / Medardo Fantuzzi

As always, Enzo Ferrari was not open to any kind of critics regarding his cars and answered with the famous quote: *"Aerodynamics are for people who can't build engines."*

The qualification underlined his statement, as due to their powerful 12 cylinder engines the TRs could easily outperform their competitors. But later in the race, the luck should change and already in lap 22 it looked like a disaster for the Scuderia. Even if the cars had no problem with the speed, the missing aerodynamics affected the fuel consumption, what was not correctly forecasted by the team. As a direct result, car no. 9 and 12 run out of fuel in the middle of the racetrack. Luckily the two remaining cars could prevent the same bitter fate. For car no. 10 came then the end in round 204, but car number 11 made it all the way until the finish line and won with 4 laps advance to the second, a privately deployed last year's TR. So even if the team had several problems the week-end, Enzo Ferrari kept right, at least with hiring his doubting pilot Paul Frère.

This is a not just a real life story, but furthermore we can take this quote to use it as philosophy how to run a corporate Compliance program, as "integrity is our engine and controls our aerodynamics."

2.9.1 How to build a strong engine?

To answer this question, we have first to understand what "integrity" really means. An easy definition is: "Value based behavior". As values are very top-level, humans have to interpret and break them down into "attitudes". One of racing drivers' normal values is "individualism", for this they have chosen a sports, when on the track, they are alone against the opponent and the difficulty of the machine.[82] These values and attitudes are learnt, mostly in early age.

An easy attitude model explains a an direct relation: stimulus → attitude → action.[83] But it has to be accepted that life is not that easy. Circumstances can intervener, as group-pressure, experience of stimulus (situation) or temptations. What can be done to tune our engine? The best option are trainings:

- Experience of stimulus (situation): Regular trainings should be not limited to the presentation of the company's processes, tools and policies, but furthermore have interactive workshops, where employees have to solve potential risky situations and discuss them in the group. With this the employees get to know different kind of stimuli. If they never have been before in a similar situation, they get to know it, at least theoretically and learn what would be the desired action. This is an appropriate approach and can be

---

[82] Hofstede, G. (1980): Cultures consequences: National differences in work-related values.

[83] McGuire, W.J. (1969): The nature of attitudes and attitude change, in Lindzey, G. & Aronson E.: The handbook of social psychology, Vol.3

executed by companies of all sizes, as potential discussion cases can be found for free on the internet, as, for instance, in the tool-kit "Resisting Extortion and Solicitation in International Transactions" or short: "RESIST".[84]

- Attitudes: As the employee will most probably face these temptations not inside its office, they have (or better: think they have to) solve the problem alone. For this beside pure knowledge, Compliance trainings have to include a motivational component, so that the trainees understand that you have to comply because of the given laws and policies, but also what stands behind this, what are the costs of compliance: externally (for the market and society) and internally (for the company, including the employees). This way employees (hopefully) not just comply because they have to, but because it became part of their attitude and they want to; the attitude becomes stronger.

- Temptations: Temptations will always exist and this is a topic for the aerodynamics, as internal controls should be effective and so limit uncontrolled situations. But regarding the engine-part, possible temptations can be included and also analyzed, why they maybe look on the first view as a temptation, but on the long way, the honest way is more successful (sustainability).

Integrity must be the heart of the company's code of conduct, which is directly linked to the company's core values. To live and control these values, most of the global enterprises and each time more medium sized companies have installed a Compliance program and department. At the start of its implementation, employees must be prepared to this, as such a change is easily perceived as a threat, as a first step towards George Orwell's 1984. Clarification is needed to explain the corruption risks for the company, for example the US Foreign Corrupt Practices Act or UK Bribery Act. Furthermore employees should not just learn about anti-corruption laws, but what stands behind them, as the cost of corruption for the society, individual and company.

---

[84] http://www.iccwbo.org/products-and-services/fighting-commercial-crime/resist/

The top management functions as role-model and communicator. Only if they are acting by the values ("walk the talk"), the desired integrity culture has a chance to be lived by the whole company. This is even more important than their verbal or written messages, as nonverbal communication represents two-thirds of the total communication.[85] Clear body language is needed, and for this part of all management workshops.

Only if really nobody is above the company's rules and policies, the rest of the employees will follow. Further, top management is needed to be the first communicator of the compliance program. Directly to all employees, for example via mass media as newsletter or company magazine, but also in management meetings, so the message will go slowly through all levels.

A special focus has to be on the middle management. For most employees they are perceived as leaders, known from daily work. More than the absolute top, they are facing the details of the company's policies, tools and general bureaucracy. This can be a stress factor, so they have to understand the purpose of the compliance program's policies and tools and keep communicating this in a positive way to their co-workers.

If the company has no key values, mission and vision in place, it is a perfect opportunity to let all employees participate in a process to elaborate and establish them. Involving employees in this process is the best way to ensure that the company culture is compatible with their personal values. These key values have to be interpreted and transformed into a code of conduct, a set of basic rules, which are mandatory for all employees, nobody can be above this code. The here manifested rules cannot be broken, under no circumstances, as they define the core of the company, its philosophy; or as Enzo Ferrari said once: *"It's not negotiable!"*

---

85 Hogan, K. / Stubbs, R. (2003): Can't get Through 8 Barriers to Communication

2.9.2 The importance of aerodynamics

As he also stated, *"aerodynamics are for people who can't build engines"*, we have to be honest that we cannot expect that our integrity message will reach the complete company. We estimate that more than 99% of the employees are good and honest people, giving their best for the company and working not just based on the company values, but their own ones. On the other hand, there is always a "black sheep" around. So as we are not able to build the perfect engine, we need aerodynamics, which in this case are the internal controls. Adapted to the reality of the company, they must reduce the risk that a renegade employee could harm the company to a minimum.

As car design is advancing fast, new cars are featuring better aerodynamics. So it is for a Compliance system most important, that there are audits and regular reviews. The gained insight has to be used to update the program, to ensure that it is as user-friendly as possible and as robust as necessary. To reach this result, beside the mentioned audits, a stress test can be conducted to see, how a group of potential internal fraudsters could bypass the controls of the company.

As Compliance employees are in the risk of getting "blind" regarding their own system, such internal audits should be executed by a separate department. Also possible are audits by colleagues from other countries, this to get a new and fresh input.

Ferrari 312/68 F1, 3.0L, V12, 410hp @ 11000rpm, 507kg, design by Mauro Forghieri

In several companies a compliance program got implemented after a corruption case. If time is the key factor in the implementation, a control based approach can temporally work. But employees are creative, even the best compliance controls can be outflanked. So it is crucial that at least the second step of the implementation is concentrating on values and integrity, as a compliance program always needs the two parts, integrity & values. But if you ask which of the two factors is more important on the long run, the answer is integrity. As all Ferraristi know, the engine is the heart of the car.

Here lies another risk in implementation phase, to ensure a real robust control system, companies may go too far and introduce too complex policies and procedures. With this you have, yes, strong controls, but on the other hand, they are a bottle-neck for the business and demotivate even the integer employees. With other words the aerodynamics are not supporting the engine, but are braking the car. Is not possible? Unfortunately yes, as the example of the F92A later in the book shows. Compliance controls have to be as strong as needed, but also as less bureaucratic as possible. We have to see "the cost of information" for the employee:

- If the cost of getting the answer to the question or following the process is higher than the perceived value of the answer, business or personal risk, the employee gets tempted to ignore company rules and policies, but to do whatever he or she thinks is best to do.
- If the cost of getting the answer to question or following the process is lower than the perceived value of the answer, business or personal risk, the employee most likely sticks to the rules.

As cost and risk are no objective values, but depend on the perception of the employee, the company can work with them:

- Cost: Processes have to be regularly reviewed to ensure that the same security level cannot be reached with a less bureaucratic design or the usage of additional software. Further the reachability of the responsible employee, for example a Compliance Officer, is a cost factor. Here is not just included the direct reachability, but also the perceived competency level and his or her openness to discuss the topic.

- Risk: Employees may not always be aware of the risk-level that they are operating in. Corrupt actions may lead not just to fines for the company, but can also include a black-listening or charges directly against the employee, including prison. As the legal system can change rapidly, it is the duty of the company to inform their employees about such risks.

"Ferrari Heart"

No need to say that also Enzo Ferrari understood later the importance of good aerodynamics and explained his quote that if you have the strongest engine, aerodynamics are not important, but if the competitors have similar strengths, aerodynamics are, of course, important. Similar to that also integrity and controls are highly connected:

- Acceleration: A lower aerodynamic drag leads to a faster acceleration of the car. The internal controls have to support employees that they are able to act confirm personal and company values. Internal controls ensure a proper tone from the top and adequate internal communication. This is one source of inspiration for the employees to live by the values, including that they would use the anonymous whistleblower-hotline, if they witness a violation to them. The aerodynamic drag does not only determine a positive change culture, but also lead to a higher maximum speed, so the total quality of corporate culture.

- Endurance: As seen in the 24 Hours of Le Mans in 1960, because of the unfavorable aerodynamics, the Ferrari team calculated wrongly the fuel consumption. As result, two TRs ran out of fuel and had to abandon the race. We can assume that we have good people working for our company, nevertheless they are no saints. For this our internal processes and controls have to ensure that all tasks can be executed as smoothly as possible and our engine does not have to work on maximum over the complete distance of the race. Surely employees have their values, but effective internal processes allow that decisions can be taken without tempting the employees' values too often.

- Air supply: Integrity is not a fix parameter, but can raise or fall. If the aerodynamics of the car are not able to lead enough air to the engine, sooner or later it will overhead. An overburden of bureaucracy demotivates. In a country this can lead to corruption and inside a company to violation of Company policies.

- Brakes & Handling: Aerodynamics support in two ways, first that the brakes receive sufficient air not to overhead and second, wings and downforce are stabilizing the car, so that the driver can control the vehicle also on difficult roads. This is important as ethics can get outside control and lead to biases as "Ethical Blindness".[86] Sometimes controls and process have to protect the employees against their selves. Especially on difficult roads, as regions with a higher perceived corruption level.

---

[86] Palazzo, Guido / Krings, Franciska / Hoffrage, Ulrich (2012): "Ethical Blindness"

As the management has integrity, they will implement controls; this especially to avoid leading their employees into temptations. Imagine that you are given the keys to shiny "599 SA Aperta". Your manager told you not to use the car, but there are absolutely no controls. You could resist not to take it for a short week-end trip? You really could?

2010: Ferrari 599 SA Aperta, 6.0L, 661hp @ 8250rpm, 1605kg, design by Pininfarina

Maybe, maybe not. Most people have their price or as the Irish poet Oscar Wilde said: *"I can resist anything, but temptation."* Knowing that humans have their weak points, it is only ethical to have to implement a control system, as it takes away the temptation or also the objective and / or subjective "pressure to be corrupt". In our business life we are always in competition, this can be with our colleagues and, of course, with other companies. What is expected from us is winning. If there are no clear rules in the game, you cannot be sure what your management is expecting from you. Stay by the rules or maybe also to include some smaller or bigger "strategic foul", if needed? With the implementation of a value- and control-based compliance system, it is clear to all employees, what is expected from you and what not. As shown before, the individual acts now in a known surrounding, what is more pleasant and for the whole company should lead to a better working atmosphere.

Paul Frère was not the first pilot who was unhappy about missing aerodynamics. Already one decade earlier, the young and rich gentlemen driver Giannino Marzotto complained to Enzo Ferrari that his cars where too heavy and lack modern aerodynamics. As usual Enzo was not open to this kind of critics and roughly replied that his cars were the most successful and efficient to date. Giannino and his brother had not been satisfied by this and decided to create their own car, based on a Ferrari 166 they used the engine from the Ferrari 212 and designed their own bodywork. As wind tunnels where not existing at that time, they used their knowledge and experience for the design. The result was the 212 Ouvo (English for "egg").

1952: Ferrari 212 Ouvo Export Berlinetta, 2.6L, V12, design by Marzotto

Enzo was not happy about this competitor and inscribed strong cars and drivers to the races, where the Ouvo appeared. Nevertheless the car presented favorite results thanks to its specifications. The Marzotto brothers even let races, but got stopped by technical problems. In '52 they finally won the Giro di Toscana. This success brought them Enzo's respect and one year later Giovanni became again driver for the Scuderia and won the Mille Miglia with a Ferrari 340 MM Spider.[87]

2.10 The Impossible Victory

Under the lead of its team manager Enzo Ferrari, Alfa Romeo launched in 1932 the Alfa Romeo P3. The first genuine single seated race car had been created by Jano Vittorio and with this can be seen as the origin of modern Formula 1 cars. The first version included a 2.7L V8 engine, what should be changed to 2,9L in '34 and finally 3,2L for the '35 Nürburgring Race. In its

---

[87] Grandprix History (fetched 31.05.2015): "Horribly Beautiful – Ferrari 166/212 Ouvo at the Mille Miglia"

introduction year the car was the state of the art and dominated the racing world. In 1933 Alfa Romeo restructured its racing activities and the team got known as "Scuderia Ferrari". In this time, Alfa continued to deploy the successful P3s. With the updates on the engine, the P3 was still the car to beat, but one year later, even with other updates, the P3 was outdated and over the year without chances to beat its German competitors from Auto Union and Mercedes Benz; Belgium, Switzerland, Italy and Spain, nearly all official European Grand Prix races had been won by these cars.

1935: Alfa Romeo P3, 3.2L, Straight 8, design by Jano Vittorio

The Germany of 1935 was a totalistic state ruled by the National-social party NSDAP and its leader Adolf Hitler. Italy at that time was also a totalistic state, led by the fascist Benito Mussolini. As common in non-democratic countries, sports had been seen as a field to demonstrate technical and philosophical superiority. Starting in '34, Germany used public funds to finance the development of new race cars.[88] The engineers of Auto Union and Mercedes Benz had good use for this additional money and delivered new generations of race cars, which should dominate automobile racing for the next years: the Auto Union B and the Mercedes Benz W25. Besides focusing on the engine, both companies understood the importance of aerodynamics and developed here a strategic advantage. In opposite to this, Alfa Romeo, financially supported by the Italian government, went

---

[88] De Graaf, Mia (2013): "Mussolini's magic motor sells for £6million: Legendary Alfa Romeo which was built to beat Hitler can still do top speed of 165mph"

into another direction and developed the Bimotore, a special version of the P3, with two engines, in the front and back.

With his famous quote *"Aerodynamics are for people who can't build engines"* Enzo Ferrari brought later in 1960 his philosophy perfectly to the point. By this means he was in best Italian tradition, as much earlier in 1911, Fiat presented the "S76", a car built with a 28.5L engine and 300 hp. Its only mission was to set a new speed record.[89]

Knowing Enzo, it was not surprisingly that Alfa Romeo tried to gain lost ground with a double-engine car. Former Fiat engineer Luigi Bazzi let the project as chief designer. Although its revolutionary concept, beside a second place in the '35 Berlin Avus race (a race-track practically consisting of two long straights, connected via 180 degrees curves), the car only had limited success. Due to its weight and power, it consumed too much fuel and tires, so that in most of the races it was not competitive. For this the Scuderia dropped the project in favor of "8C 35". In opposite to the Bimotore, the 8C 35 featured just one conventional engine (first a V8, then a V12), but therefor had better aerodynamics and drivability.[90] The car brought success back to Alfa Romeo, but in 1936, so too late for the '35 Nürburgring Race.

In opposite to the Avus, the Nürburgring included long straights, but also numerous curves and gradients. For this it made no sense to use special aerodynamically packages, as the manufacturers used in Berlin race. The Italian team travelled to the mountain race with a new 3,8L engine, but still inferior to its German competitors. The Alfa was rumored to produce 330 hp, the Auto Union Tipo B and the Mercedes Benz W25 both 375 hp[91], on the paper the P3 was without chances.

---

[89] Marjoram, Stefan (2014): "The Best of Turin trailer"

[90] Melissen, Wouter (2013): "Alfa Romeo 8C 35"

[91] Wikipedia (2014): 1935 German Grand Prix

As racetrack and cars were the absolute state of the art, high NSDAP government officials came for the race week-end to see an impressive victory of the local drivers and celebrate the achievements of German engineering. The only unknown factor, the changing Eifel-weather seemed this time only to be a detail. Alfa Romeo driver Tazio Nuvolari started from the second position, but directly lost positions due to a slow start, but this should change. Even in the rain he drove 100% on the limit and after 10 laps took the lead. A broken pump seemed to destroy all hopes, as Nuvolari had to stand over 2 minutes in the box, before he finally could re-join the race. Nevertheless the bitter setback, he continued pushing hard and drove on the absolute limit. In the beginning of the last lap, he was already on the second position again, but still 35 seconds behind the leading Mercedes Benz of Manfred von Brauchitsch (who also set the fastest race lap with 10:32,0), in motorsport half of eternity. But the political elite and 300.000 spectators could not believe their eyes, as they saw which car took as leader the chequered flag, as it was not the silver Mercedes, but the dark-red Alfa Romeo. Destroying the planned propaganda, the governmental officials refused the applause, but the present spectators celebrated the winner. They had seen what experts would call later "The Impossible Victory", as Nuvolari drove all the 500km distance on the absolute limit und with perfection.

1935: Alfa Romeo P3 Tipo B, 3.8L (German GP), Straight 8, 330hp, design by Vittorio Jano

For companies there are several lessons to be learnt. The most important one: One person can make the difference! To develop such an achievement, on the long run employees do not comply with company codes and values because of existing controls and guidelines, but because they believe in them!

In 1929 Enzo could convince Tazio to join the Alfa Romeo team, as both men shared the same passion for car racing. As both had strong characters their ways separated, but also came together several times. Until 1932 Enzo Ferrari was not only team manager, but also active driver. Motorsports was his competition. As Tazio showed him clearly his limits as driver, it can be concluded that he was one factor (beside his family), why Enzo stepped down as driver and concentered on his management responsibility. This opens up speculations what would have happened, if both men did not met, may be Ferrari as company would not exist in the same way as it does today.

To become a successful Compliance Officer it is not enough to follow procedures and execute controls in his or her closed office, but instead the CO must meet the employees at their places. The goal for a Compliance

Officer should be to become recognized as a "trusted advisor". This includes two sub-roles, being a trusted expert, but also a trusted colleague. It makes no sense being the biggest Compliance expert, if you have no idea about the business and how the company is earning the money. Also visibility is needed so that employees can perceive their Compliance Officer as a trusted colleague, who is not just talking about Compliance, but living it as a good example. For this it is helpful not to see everybody as a potential risk factor, but starting from the idea that more than 99% of the employees are good and honest people, making daily their best effort for the good of the company. These people are to be protected and prepared so that they will not get into trouble via accident (or through a case caused by the less than 1% black sheep, which you may have).

(Adapted from the Communicator Model (Market Psychology))

Trust is a relevant topic. According the OECD study "Society at a Glance 2011", the level of trust varies from society to society. There are countries which present a high level of trust as Denmark, Norway or Finland and also ones with a low level as Mexico, Turkey and Chile. According to the statistical information, the study found a significant negative relation between the two factors "trust" and "equally distributed income".[92] As Compliance Office you always have to trust the employees *("I give my collaborators a great trust. Complete trust.")*, if you not want to become paranoid, but you have to be prepared that in the beginning you will not receive the same level of trust back from them. For this as a Compliance Officer you have to be prepared to earn trust, for example with visibility, accessibility,

---

[92] OECD (2011): "Society at a Glance 2011: Trust"

perception as efficient problem-solver and walk the talk. It is not enough to be at the own desk, but you have to meet the employees in their place; could be in office, factory, at the project site or race-track. This investment is important as you need the employees to build trust in you, as only with this they may come forward to you for difficult topics or would use the offered whistleblower hotline.

The company has to find equilibrium between relying on employees' personal values on the one side and controls on the other one. It is a very sensible topic as a Compliance department may calibrate regularly to stay in balance or come back to this point. Controls, guidelines and tools have to be as strong as necessary, but not going over this. If not, bureaucracy can interfere with doing business and further destroy the employees' motivation.

European Championship Grand Prix Season
- July, 14, Belgium (Spa Francochamps): 1st Rudolf Caracciola, Mercedes Benz W25
- July, 23, Germany (Nuerburgring): 1st Tazio Nuvolari, Alfa Romeo P3
- August 25, Switzerland (Bremgarten): 1st Rudolf Caracciola, Mercedes Benz W25
- September 8, Italy (Monza): 1st Hans Stuck, Auto Union B
- September 22, Spain (Lasarte): 1st Rudolf Raracciola, Mercedes Benz W25[93]

The successful Alfa Romeo P3 was designed by Vittorio Jano, who was one of the best engineers of its time. The Alfa Romeo Company wanted to hire him already a long time ago, but Jano always refused. Only in 1923 he changed his mind to the company to work for Enzo Ferrari. It was not the salary which motived him to change, but his friend Luigi Bazzi. Originally he had followed Bazzi to Fiat and as Bazzi later changed from Fiat to Alfa Romeo, he could finally convince Jano to do the same step. Ferrari met Bazzi earlier in Turino, as he tried to get a job in the well-known Fiat

---

[93] Wikipedia (2014): 1935 Grand Prix season

Company. It did not work out, but at least Ferrari could enter the local engineer circles and do some important networking there. Here he met Bazzi, a crucial contact, which he kept alive over the time. So as Ferrari entered to work at Alfa Romeo, he convinced his old friend to work for him. Then it was Bazzi who made the contact to Jano.

2.11 *"I think of myself as constantly realizing a childhood dream."*

Business founders started their companies mostly not first to ensure as source of income, but to follow their vision or dream. Enzo Ferrari expressed this as: *"I think of myself as constantly realizing a childhood dream."* He founded his first company Auto Avio Costruzioni in 1939, as he was 41 years old. The company developed and produced the AAC 815. Already in 1938 Enzo left Alfa Romeo, but the agreement with Alfa Romeo forbade him to use his own name for the next 4 years. For this he has founded, together with other formal Alfa Romeo engineers, Auto Avio Costruzioni, first to produce parts for the Italian air force, but then soon to get back to automobile racing. Today exits just one original 815, it can be found in a private Italian car collection.

1939: Auto Avio Costruzioni 815 Coda Lunga, 1.5L Straight 8, 75hp @ 5500 rpm, 170km/h, 625kg, design by Carrozzeria Touring

Even if the separation itself was not in friendship, Enzo had been for 18 years an Alfa Romeo employee; first as race driver, later also as team manager and general responsible for the company's motor sports activities. In this time, the company offered him enough liberty to grow inside its structures; up to that the "Scuderia Ferrari" became the official Alfa Romeo racing team. The company structure and Enzo's contract allowed him to execute his tasks on a high motivation level. Only as a new management started to reduce Enzo's liberties, he preferred to leave and open up his own company.

As each individual is different, it is imperative for a company to find the employee's motivators, as individuals try to maximize the output in relation to their input.

Employee's input: Working Hours / Employee's output: Salary + further Motivators

People who like their work are less tempted to participate in an internal fraud or an external corruption case to not risk their actual position.

Employee's motivation is not only determined by the relation from his or her in- and output, but also how the individual is doing in comparison to others. A balance is reached if:

$$E1\ Output\ /\ E1\ Input = E2\ Output\ /\ E2\ Input$$

John Stacy Adam's Theory is no mathematical equation, but a social psychological theory, which wants to explain the individual's behavior inside a group, especially a work-group.[94] Individuals prefer to be inside the equilibrium, if not this can lead to different forms of behavior:

E1 O / E1 I < E2 O / E2 I: Employee 1 receives a lower output related on his or her input that Employee 2. The situation is perceived as unfair and will trigger counter measures by E1, as the individual

- tries to reduce its input, as quantity and quality of its work.
- tries to achieve a higher output. This can be on the official way to request a raise of salary or additional secondary motivators. If this gets declined or the employee perceive that it would be, there is a

---

[94] Adams, John Stacy (1965): "Inequity in social exchange"

risk of "self-service", beginning with minor thefts and can lead up to higher value frauds.
- searches for other job positions, what can be inside the same company, but also outside.
- is not satisfied with actual position, for this less motivated to protect it. As its input should be reduced, shortcuts through internal processes and external laws are tempting.

Further, input and output are no measurable units. As people want to be inside the equilibrium, changes can also occur inside the head. The individual can re-evaluate the input as lower as originally perceived or on the other hand, perceive the actual output as high than in the beginning.

Some people have the goal to start their own-business, but nevertheless most individuals stay inside a company or even prefer this dependency, as it offers a perceived security. Here it is important that the company can communicate the founder's vision, ideas and dream, so that hopefully, the employees can understand this and feel the same. With raising their motivation level, fraud and compliance risks can be lowered.

2.12 Countach, Conformity Pressure and Change Management

The mid 1950's saw a revolution in Formula 1. The position of the engine changed from the front to the middle of the car. As many new tendencies in motorsports, it was only a matter of time, when this would be implemented also for street-cars. But it should take some time.

The 1968 Alfa Romeo Carabo, the 70s Ferrari 512 Modulo and Lancia Stratos Zero had one thing in common, they had been futuristic styled mid-engine prototypes, but never made it into production. From today's point of view, they represented the beginning of Italy's edge design; clear straight lines, which influenced coming car appearances, mostly for sedans.

What Alfa Romeo, Ferrari and Lancia could not do, was done by another Italian manufacturer. Lamborghini presented 1971 the LP500 at the Geneva Motorshow and in opposite to the other prototypes, already three years later the first clients received a very similar car: The Lamborghini Countach hit the roads. Marcello Gandini, who already designed the Alfa Romeo Carabo and Lancia Stratos Zero received the opportunity to create finally a buyable super sports car and the result was an unique automobile, only comparable to earlier prototypes.

1982: Lamborghini Countach LP500S, 4.8L, V12, 375hp @ 4500rpm, 257km/h, 1480kg, design by Bertone (Marcello Gandini)

But why Lamborghini, a company with only eleven years in business when the Countach went do the dealers? Maybe be just because of this!

Conformity pressure had been confirmed by different famous experiments, as for example by Asch or the Stanford Prison experiment. Different social levels perceive more or less pressure.

- Leaders feel less pressure than lower levels inside the group. Often it is quite the opposite; they see the position as self-realization and like to show individualism. Fiat's long term leader Gianni Agnelli was famous to wear his watch over the shirt cuff. He himself explained it once that he had not time to peek back his shirt cuff to check the time. Nevertheless it became a fashion statement, often copied, not only by Italian emerging managers.[95] A different example from the same company, the CEO Sergio Marchionne never wore suits, but always

---

[95] Gallagher, Jake (2013): "Gianni Agnelli's 10 Top Best Style Moves"

black sweater and pants. Another fashion statement, but the same reason. According to Marchionne, it saved him time in the morning, as he did not have to decide what to wear.[96]

- Another group, who feels less conformity pressure, are the outsiders, which are no direct part of the main group. In the beginning of the 1970s, Ferruccio Lamborghini was such an outsider. After a discussion with Enzo Ferrari, he decided to build his own sport cars. He used a complete different strategy than his Italian competitors. For him, motor-sports was no topic, not for promotion, nor for technical progress. Instead he wanted to focus 100% on street cars. Accordingly, even if the Lamborghini Countach was a breath-taking super sports car, it never officially got deployed for racing.

The conformity pressure normally works that the individual adapts to the behavior of the main group, but the effect can also get reversed. Then the individual or the small group can influence the big group and can trigger a change of behavior, including attitudes or values. This applies for the situation that the individual or the small group is higher involved in the topic than the main group. Thanks to its small size, knowledge and involvement, they can work more efficient than the big group. With this they are able to convince more and more of the other group's members, at least if they have logical arguments.

These findings we can apply for a company's internal change management, as to be successful it requires to have
- top management as sponsor,
- a convincing and strong concept,
- the tasks be driven by a small effective group and
- this group acts independent from other departments.

The Countach became Lamborghini's most successful model so far. With only minor changes it stayed for 26 years in production. Even if its design is based on late 60's and early 70's prototypes, especially in the 80's the extraordinary design met the taste of the rich Wall Street-bankers and other

---

[96] Spears, John (2011): "Why Chrysler boss Sergio Marchionne always wears black"

Yuppies. In 1990 Lamborghini presented the Diablo. In opposite to its name, its design was already less unique and aggressive. At that time the company had already 27 years on the market and became an established player, less opportunity to escape conformity pressure.

3 THE CUSTOMER RELATIONSHIP

3.1) *"The Client is not always right!"*
3.2) *"The Ferrari is a dream"*
3.3) *"I never tell a lie."*
3.4) *"No, you must drive a Ferrari"*
3.5) *"If you like this car, we'll make it."*
3.6) *"If it goes badly, I'm not going to spend money on this kind of motorsport anymore."*
3.7) *"I believe most things can be said in a few lines"*

3.1 *"The Client is not always right!"*

Similar to Enzo Ferrari, Ferruccio Lamborghini was no son of rich parents, but made his fortune based on his own work and company. His best known products had been tractors and other agricultural machines. As hobby he had a big collection of luxury cars, including, of course, Alfa Romeo and Ferrari. Due to the legend, he liked driving his several Ferrari vehicles (including 250GT Coupe, 250GT SWB and 250GT 2+2), but was unhappy with some of the car's behaviors, like being too hard and noisy for a weekend's drive. Especially he had a problem with the clutches and had to bring the cars several times to the workshop. After several discussions with his dealership, he gave a list of ideas what to change to Enzo. As Ferruccio did not received an answer, he finally decided to speak personally with him. *"Ferrari, your cars are rubbish"*, he complained. Of course not a diplomatic start of the conversation and Enzo answered accordingly: *"Lamborghini, you may be able to drive a tractor but you will never be able to handle a Ferrari properly."* Angry about this reply he decided to build his own sports car, which should be able to compete with a Ferrari or even being better.

First he started with his existing 250GT, implemented a bigger clutch and exchanged the original Ferrari cylinder heads with more sophisticated ones. Due to Ferruccio, the countable result was that his personal 250GT was 25km/h faster than the unmodified 250GTs. A circumstance, which he enjoyed on the motorway near Modena, as sometimes he could play out this superiority against other Ferrari drivers.[97]

1966: Lamborghini Miura, 3.9L, V12, 350hp @ 7000rpm, 277km/h, 1292kg, design by Bertone (Giugiaro & Gandini)

---

[97] Thoroughbred & Classic Cars (1991): "Interview with Ferruccio Lamborghini"

If you enter "customer orientation" today into the Google search-engine, around 1 second later you will receive 20.7 million hits. Most of the pages will tell you how to understand better your client and so to maximize your profit. Most employees will learn "the client is king". So it just must had been based on his known less openness for criticism that Enzo Ferrari acted that way, right? Of course we can only speculate, but if we analyze the situation, he is right and furthermore there had been other business leaders with the same opinion:

- Steve Jobs, Apple: "*A lot of times people don't know what they want until you show it to them.*" 2001 Apple introduced the first generation of the iPod, not being the first mobile digital media player, but revolutionary because of its direct link to Apple's music store. If Apple would have asked before, what their clients wanted to have, most probably the answer would not had been that a mp3-player including connection to a music-store and so giving Apple a nearly monopoly where to buy the content. Companies are a think-tank, gathering different kind of experts, as pure visionaries, but also experienced engineers. Sometimes they know much better what the client wants, even much earlier than the client itself. Of course, sometimes not and then the new product will become a failure. Meanwhile the development of the original iPod carried on and produced additional versions as the shuffle, nano and touch. But even with this variety the product became a smaller part of the total Apple portfolio, mostly replaced by the iPhone, which can be seen as an iPod including a telephone application. An actual task for Apple is the further integration of its products into other already established products. First step here was the AppleTV, which got followed by the Apple CarPlay, a more functional implementation of the iPhone into today's cars. With this system the driver is not limited on music, podcasts and eBooks, but additional has access to a selected number of apps, this can include your favorite radio station, messaging services or maps. One of the company's partners to include this system into its cars is the Fiat company, including its different brands. As a result the world's first car featuring this new system was 2014 the Ferrari FF.[98] A good

---

[98] Ferrari.com (fetched 09.09.2014): "Discover the first car ever featuring Apple CarPlay"

choice as FF stands for "Ferrari Four", the "four" here with a double meaning, there are four seats, but also it is the first Ferrari with a four-wheel drive. So the car can be seen as an answer to the world-wide rising demand of bigger luxury cars.

2011: Ferrari FF, 6.3L, V12, 651hp@ 8000rpm, 1880kg, design by Pininfarina

- Henry Ford, Ford: "*If I had asked people what they want, they would have said faster horses.*" The company presented 1910 their famous Model T, the first car aimed to a new target group, which until now could not afford an automobile, but still used horses. As cars in that times still had been quite exclusive, Ford's target group could not imagined that the introduction of automation would made it possible to produce an affordable car.

Like Henry Ford's idea, also Enzo Ferrari's proper philosophy let to a new car manufacturer and we would have lost some incredible products if he would had acted differently. Just with the difference to Ford that these products came not from his own factory, but the new Lamborghini one. So his opinion led not just to new products, but also to more competition.

If you analyze your client portfolio, many times you will detect the "20 80"-rule, meaning that 20% of your clients are creating 80% of the turnover. For this you may implement an ABC-classification to ensure a VIP treatment for your best clients and maybe a more basic one for the B and C ones.

You also will detect that a small percentage of your clients are natural trouble-makers, having wrong expectations, continuously bringing one unreasonable claims, and keeping your service hotline busy. It has to be analyzed if it is worth to keep these customers, the decision can be different if they are an A or C client.

1959: Ferrari 250 GT Berlinetta SWB, 3.0L, V12, 240hp @ 7000rpm, design by Pininfarina

Ferruccio Lamborghini on the one hand liked Ferraris. His first one was a 250GT and it should not stay the only one. But since the beginning he found the cars too noisy and hard for being a street car. He mentioned this several times to his local dealer, without getting a further reaction. As Enzo was tired of Ferruccio's continues claims, he roughly answered that he was just a tractor maker and had no ideas how to build sport cars. Due to his buyer's history and budget, Lamborghini was a A client, but on the other hand he was difficult and opened several technical claims. Accordingly, he was not A anymore, but perhaps a B client.

"I slammed the door and vowed I would build my own car." Since Ferruccio's quote we have competition between these two manufacturers and we can be thankful for this. Two examples how perfect competition leads to the best results:

- The 80s brought back the interest in super sports cars of Porsche, Lamborghini and Ferrari. The race for the fastest and most exclusive car started again in 1986 by Porsche and its 959, a 2.8 liters V6 car and a potential maximum speed of 314 km/h. Just one year later Ferrari celebrated the 40th company anniversary with the F40, a 2.9 liters V8 and a maximum speed of 324km/h. Later in 1990 Lamborghini presented the Diablo with a 5.7 liters V12 engine and on the paper 1 km/h faster than the F40. Of course most of these cars never got used to such limits and some of them got bought less to use them, but as object for speculation and sell them later for the double or triple of their original price. With a strong limitation to just 1315 cars, the official price of 400,000 USD easily got tripled for used F40s. At a smaller format the same effect had been noted for Bburago's 1:18 version of the F40. Not just that you had to enroll at our model car- or toy-store, some of the cars got bought by smaller speculators, who sold them later for the triple of its original price. Beside the general tendency to super cars. The value of the explosion of the F40 had another reason. The car was created to celebrate the company's 40th birthday and one year after its founder died at the age of 90 years. Many believed that this would mean the end of the traditional company, as it not only had his name, but also was a result of his work and vision. Enzo had arranged his succession already over a decade ago, when Luca de Montezemelo became director of Ferrari's road car division in 1971. He let Ferrari since 2014 and ensured that the company continued operating based on Enzo's spirit and values.

1987: Ferrari F40, 2.9L, V8, 471hp@ 7000rpm, 324km/h, 1100kg, design by Pininfarina; photo with friendly permission from David Lee

- If the competition is not limited due to (legal or non-legal) monopolies and corruption, every company has to optimize the use of its resources (employees, experience, patents, machines, money) to produce the best possible products and solutions, to convince the potential clients. This is similar to a Formula 1 season. Before the season all participating teams can sit together and discuss rules and technical specification, as long as it is in the best interest for all (for example cost reduction, attracting of additional competitors or new safety features) and not limiting the competition, as implementing of barriers to keep new potential teams out of the race. Enzo Ferrari was not very political, but a believer of the forces of a free market. As car racing is nearly the ultimate competition, it was only logical for him to implement the technology, which got proved through racing and winning, later in his street cars. Something which you can see in all Ferrari cars, then and now, but maybe easiest to be discovered in the F50, as the car not just features aerodynamics, which one makes automatically think of a Formula 1 car, furthermore its 4.7 liters V12-engine is a direct development coming from the F92A.

1996: Ferrari F50, 4.7L, V12, 520hp @ 8500rpm, 325km/h, 1350kg, design by Pininfarina; photo with friendly permission from David Lee

BUSINESS PHILOSOPHY ACCORDING TO ENZO FERRARI

Much less known than the rivalry between Ferrari and Lamborghini was the short business relation between Ferrari and Cunningham. Its owner Briggs Cunningham was a racing driver and further constructor of racing cars, some few even with permission to be driven on normal streets, but in opposite to Enzo, Briggs came from a wealthy family. In events as the 12 Hours of Sebring and the 24 Hours of Le Mans, the Cunningham team focused on their own constructions, but also deployed other cars. In 1954 the team entered their Cunningham C4-R, but also a Ferrari 375 MM.

1954: Ferrari 375 MM Cunningham street version, 4.5L, V12, 340hp @ 7000rpm, design by Pininfarina

1954: Ferrari 375 MM Cunningham Le Mans version, 4.5L, V12, 340hp @ 7000rpm, design by Pininfarina

The Le Mans version was truly unique, as at the front of the elegant Pininfarina body got two additional huge air intakes to cool down the brakes. The main task of the car was to test the Ferrari engine under race conditions. It was Brigg's idea to change for the next season his cars' engines from the Chrysler V8 to the Ferrari V12. Unfortunately in the race, the Ferrari 375 had to give up after 120 laps, the reason was a broken rocker arm. Due to the legend, Briggs visited Enzo in his factory to discuss the engine failure. As expected, Il Commendatore defended his product and denied that his engine was the reason why the car did not made it to finish the race. Similar to Ferruccio Lamborghini, Briggs was upset about Enzo's stubbornness and the two men never should do business again with each other.[99] But was it really just this? Besides Cunningham's 375, there was another private one at the '54 Le Mans race, driven by Luigi Chinetti. The same year Luigi agreed with Enzo to become the official Ferrari agent for the US. Four years later he founded the North American Racing Team (NART), which deployed Ferrari race cars to promote them for the US market. For this, the team used the official Ferrari logo, on top the US flag instead the Italian one. A logo which represented NART's official status as US Ferrari team. Why this official status?

Luigi Chinetti started his career, similar to Enzo Ferrari, at Alfa Romeo, where he entered 1917 as mechanic, but soon became a race driver for the company. In 1932 he won for a first time the 24 Hours of Le Mans with an Alfa Romeo 8C 2300LM

1932: Alfa Romeo 2300 8C Le Mans, 2.3L, Straight 8, 155hp @ 5000rpm, 205km/h, 980kg, design by Touring

---

[99] Before it's news (2015): "the Ferrari 375mm owned and raced by Briggs Cunningham in the 1954 Le Mans, the two huge air intakes on its hood cooled the heat exchanged for the water cooled brakes"

With the outbreak of World War II, he immigrated to the United States and became later an US citizen. After the war he returned to sports and won in '49 Le Mans again, this time on a Ferrari 166 MM Barchetta. Due to the legend, Luigi visited Enzo three years earlier in an office in Modena and convinced him to build his own cars. Not just race cars, but also street cars, as Luigi understood the United Staates as a big potential market for them. Luigi promised to buy 20 or 25 cars and sell them there. He could do that, as he used the time oversea to create a net of connections, including to Briggs Cunningham, who was the first, whoever imported a Ferrari car into the US. As Luigi was not only a talented racer, but also salesman, he knew how to promote the cars in the US: via racing. Not only inside the country, but also south of the border.

1949: Ferrari 166 MM Barchetta, 2.0L, V12, 140hp @ 6000rpm, 220km/h, 650kg, design by Carrozzeria Touring (Carlo Anderloni)

The Mexican part of the Pan-American Highway, which more or less complete connects the north of Alaska with the south of Argentina, had been completed in early 1950. To communicate this accordingly and attract foreign investors, the Mexican government implemented an open streets race, similar to the Italian classics Mille Miglia and Targa Florio. As the target group had been mostly inside the US, the race was organized together with the American Automobile Association. The first event the same year went from the country's north to the south border and won by an American Spanisch driver team on an Oldsmobile 88. Already in its first year, the Panamerica called the first fatal accidents. A sad tradition, what should lead years later also to its end. But before this, the Scuderia Ferrari entered as first factory team into the event. The predicting result, a victory for the Scuderia and its drivers Piero Taruffi & Luigi Chinetti on a Ferrari 212 Inter.

1951: Ferrari 212 Inter Vignale, 2.6L, V12, 170hp @ 6500 rpm, design by Giovanni Michelotti

The event became more attractive for manufactures, so that the '52 and '53 events had been won by Mercedes Benz and Maserati. By 1954, the event was already highly professional and gave no more opportunities for amateur teams. Several categories ensured opportunities for different car concepts, while the overall victory went to Umberto Magliolo on a Ferrari 375 Plus. The same time, this should be also the last Panamerica, as the Mexican government gave in to the raising critics that proclaimed that the event is too bloody and that the local streets are not suitable for such an event. The Mexican government announced that the goal to promote the Pan-American Highway had been reached and stopped the annual race.

1954: Ferrari 375 Plus Pininfaria, 4.9L, V12, 330hp @ 6000rpm, 950 kg, design by Pininfarina

Luis Chinetti founded in '58 NART, which competed particularly in the endurance races of Sebring and Le Mans, but then also in Formula 1. In 1964 the Scuderia Ferrari started together with NART as one team, in the European races the cars were painted in the traditional red and in the last two races in the US and Mexico, they participated in the NART colors white and blue.

1964:Ferrari 156 F1 "Aero": 1.5L, V6, 200hp @ 10600rpm, 456 design by Mauro Forghieri

1964: Ferrari 158, V8, 210hp @ 11000rpm, 270km/h, 468kg, design by Mauro Forghieri

1964: Ferrari 158, V8, 210hp @ 11000rpm, 270km/h, 468kg, design by Mauro Forghieri

The decision about the championship should bring the last race of the season, the Mexico Grand Prix. After a strategic decision that the two drivers Lorenzo Bandini and John Surtees had to change positions, Surtees came in on the second position and with this won with just one point advantage the driver's championship. The Ferrari / NART-team won also the manufacturer's championship.

1967: Ferrari 275 GTB/4 NART Spider

As Luis knew the American market, he used his good connection to Enzo and convinced him to create special versions for the US market, as the 275 GTB/4 NART Spyder.[100] But this was not the only Ferrari based on him. Already in the 50s he had the idea together with his partner Jon von Neumann that they would need a car tailor made for their biggest market inside the US. This car should be powerful with all abilities to participate in races, but on the other hand elegant for the use on the streets. Most important, it has to be open so that the driver could enjoy the sunshine state. Thanks to their mutual beneficial business relation, Enzo could be convinced to create such an automobile. In 1957 the company presented the 250 California Spyder LWB (Long Wheel Base). The bodywork not only showed a timeless elegance, big parts of it had been crafted out of Aluminum. Pure race versions had an all-Aluminum body to save weight. Of course Luis Chinetti had been proud of his concept and so took two years later the new SWB (Short Wheel Base)-version to the races. At Sebring his NART racing team reached with the California Competizione the first position in the GT9-class.[101]

1960: Ferrari 250 SWB California Spyder Competizione, 3.0L, V12, 280hp @ 7000rpm, 1050kg, design by Scaglietti

---

[100] McCluggage, Denise (2014): "Ferrari in America at 60: Luigi Chinetti, first Ferrari dealer in US, also a Le Mans champion"

[101] Supercars.net (fetched 5.12.2015): "Ferrari 250 SWB California Spyder Competizione"

The friendship between Luigi Chinetti and Enzo Ferrari started as they got to know each other as they both drove for the Alfa Romeo racing team and met again after the war.[102] This personal relation was the base for a trustful business relationship which let until the victory of the Formula 1 championship and the successful development of today's most important market for the company. With this in mind, Enzo's hard line against Briggs Cunningham's technical complaints maybe had been more than a normal protection of his technology and products, but further a strategic decision to conquer with Luigi the US market and protect his friend against local competitors. NART existed until the 70s and in 1977 Luigi closed his dealership. Based on Italian business culture, earnings & relationship won against the pure business approach. This to ensure sustainability, as friendship meant experience with the partner, and with this made him predictable and trustable for the future.

3.2 "The Ferrari is a dream"

Due to Enzo's philosophy that the Ferrari street cars are an offshoot of the racing cars, for this if the owner would like to, he or she could use them with some minor adaptions also for racing. This possibility explained the high prices of the Ferrari street cars and also fostered their myth. Additionally the company uses their marketing to keep this myth alive and ensure that a Ferrari car always stays a dream, independently if you have the budget to buy one or not. Consciously the company produces less cars than they could sell.

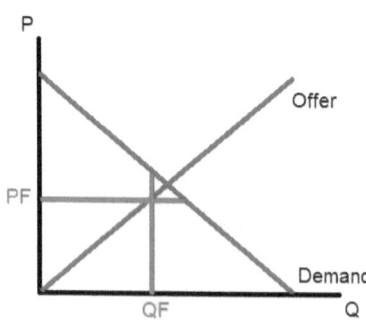

---

[102] Siano, Joseph (1994): "Luigi Chinetti Sr. 93, Automobile Importer and Champion Driver"

The graphic shows they classical relation between offer and demand, while "Q" stands for quantity and "P" for price. In 2014 Ferrari produced around 7000 (QF) units a year.[103] This number was not the result of limited production facilities, but an active decision by Enzo Ferrari's successor Luca di Montezemolo, who always had been aware to keep Ferrari's exclusivity.[104]

As the graphic demonstrates, for this quantity and price the demand is higher than the offer. The company would have had several options to get the relation into equilibrium, including:
- Ramp up production
- Raise prices
- Reduce marketing activities (including motorsports activities) to lower demand

None of them got used, because Ferrari wants to have the situation like this. Thanks to these limitations, on the short run the company sells less cars than they could do, but on the long one they keep the interest high. As generally known, things which are hard to get, are perceived as more attractive. It is the task of the management to let the gap between offer and demand not getting to big, as it must be hard to get the car, for example being some months on the waiting list, but on the other hand they have to avoid that potential clients would get desperate and buy from the competitor. A positive side effect is a high level of planning certainty. Even if based on crisis the demand would get less, it still would need a time until the demand would fall under the offer. It is a continuous temptation for the company not to raise the prices, as it is a relative easy to execute action, which would bring in immediately additional earnings, but on the long run would make the brand weaker and less attractive.

---

[103] Ewing, Steven J. (2014): "Ferrari to launch new model every year, keep production limited"

[104] St. Antoine, Arthur (2015): "Luca di Montezemolo is the Other Enzo Ferrari"

The Ferrari company always had cars and special version in its portfolio, which had been strictly limited, some examples:

- 1948: 166 Sport, total production of 3
- 1962-64: 250 GTO, total production of 36
- 1984-86: 288 GTO, total production of 272[105]
- 1987-92: F40, total production of 1,315
- 1994-96: F50, total production of 380
- 2002-02: Enzo, total production of 500[106]
- 2005-07: FXX, total production of 30
- 2015-today: FXX K, today production of 40

Due to the legend, it was only planned to produce 271 288 GTOs (standing for Gran Turismo Omologato), but the company wanted to honor their Formula 1 Champion Niki Lauda and give the last of the cars to him. To do so, they had to produce one more.

1984: Ferrari 288 GTO, 2.9L, V8, 400hp @ 7000rpm, 306km/h, 1160kg, design by Pininfarina; photo with friendly permission from David Lee

Besides making its peace with Lauda, Ferrari combined two myths, the highly limited car with the successful champion. Similar was done later with the Enzo and the FXX, which had been a gift for its five times champion

---

[105] Monticello, Mike (2010, in Road & Track 61): "2011 Ferrari 599 GTO"

[106] McCoy, Carbon (2002): "Ferrari Road Car Models and Production Numbers"

Michael Schumacher. Only 30 FXX got produced, where the last one was even more special, the only one painted in black and featuring the Michael Schumacher logo on the leather seats.[107] Moreover that the FXX was really more than just a car. It looked similar to the Enzo and of course the car is technically based on it; but on the other hand it is also completely different, as it included Ferrari's latest development and was more than just a car. The FXX was a package, as it was a pure racing car without street approvals; owners can use it only on Ferrari selected race tracks. Further the package included regular meetings and FXX owners are even included in the Ferrari testing and development program. Two years later, the company introduced the evolution package, beside minor aerodynamic changes, it included technical adjusts for faster shifting gears.[108]

2005: Ferrari FXX, 6.3L, V12, 809hp @ 8500rpm, design by Pininfarina (Ken Okuyama)

---

[107] Mihalascu, Dan (2013): "Michael Schumacher's Unique Black Ferrari FXX Could be Yours for EURO 2.03 Million"

[108] Motor Trend (2007): " Ferrari FXX Evoluzione: Maranello's track toy gets even faster": http://www.motortrend.com/auto_news/112_news290710_ferrari_fxx_evoluzione/

2007: Ferrari FXX Evoluzione, 6.3L, V12, 860hp @ 9500rpm, design by Pininfarina (Ken Okuyama)

Receiving one of the super sports cars is a real sign of honor. Ferrari driver Sebastian Vettel won four Formula One World Championships, but all still in his time with the Red Bull-team. For this he had to buy his F40 on his own. In an auction he purchased the car, which belonged before to Luciano Pavarotti.[109]

As seen, the company is very strict with its limitations and also the super-rich cannot buy a better position on the waiting list. But if you want to have a more exclusive model, you still can do what clients did in the beginning of the Ferrari production: going to one of known coachbuilders and buy some of their designs. For example in 1989 Pininfarina presented a show car called "Mythos", a unique design based on the actual Testarossa. It was not planned to sell this car to public, but according the legend, 2 or 3 got produced for the Sultan of Brunei. It was not the first special delivery for him, even more mysterious was the Ferrari F90. Based on the '88 Testarossa, Pininfarina designed it exclusively for this client, Ferrari even denied its existence until 2005.[110]

Ten years later, Ferrari is more open with existence of custom-made models. With the company's One-Off Program, clients can realize their personal ideas together with the Centro Stile Ferrari and external designers like Pininfarina. Such a product was the Ferrari SP12 EC. Guitarist and long-term Ferrari collector Eric Clapton realized his person dream, a new

---

[109] Handelsblatt (2015): "Vettel fährt den Pavarotti-Ferrari"

[110] Owen, Richard (fetched 25.09.2014): "1988 Ferrari F90"

interpretation of the 70's 512 BB. Based on an actual Ferrari 458 Italia, the designers took Eric's ideas and realized a design to only sell once. An unique experience, as the client leaves his passive role as buyer and gets part of the development-team.[111] Of course such a car comes with a price-ticket, estimated 3.6 Million Euro for the SP12 EC. But nevertheless it is not only the price alone, a participation in the one-off program requires a long term client relation.

1989: Ferrari Mythos, 4.9L, Flat-12, 390hp, 290km/h, design by Pininfarina

With the strategy to build less cars than the company could sell, it get reached that a Ferrari car always stays a dream, as even with the required well balanced bank account it is not easy to buy such. We tend to give a higher value to the products, which are difficult to get. For this a Ferrari is more than a simple car, but has a relevant emotional part, as it represents success on the race track and even more, represents Enzo's dream, vision and philosophy.

Offering a dream and not an ordinary product, opens additional opportunities for the business. The client does not want to be limited to the passive role of the product buyer, but to became a part of the dream. This requires a sensible handling of the business philosophy and product portfolio, as the client can distinguish between the short hype and the long-term dream. Thanks to this Ferrari, Star Wars and Apple became part of

---

[111] Ferrari.com (2015): "New stylistic notes for Ferrari: The SP12 EC is born. EC like Eric Clapton"

today's pop culture, while other products, movies and books disappeared after a limited time out of the general awareness.

In 2015 Ferrari re-used the FXX philosophy and presented the FXX K, based on the LaFerrari. K stands for kinetic energy recovery system or short KERS, the car's hybrid system. With this, the power of the engine can temporary boosted from 860 to 1050hp. Like the original FXX, the FXX K has no permissions to be driven on public roads and should further not used for competition. So the car is useless if you need a transportation from A to B or if you want to test your skills directly against other drivers. The owners can use it only for test drives. For 2,5 Million Euro the buyer not only receives the car itself, but a package, including Ferrari organized test events, including a pit-crew and the direct contact with the official company's test drivers and engineers. This for two years, later an annual fee is required. With this Ferrari implemented a super consumer strategy, which requires to identify, listen and engage them. They are a unique source to understand the potential target group, as preferences, emotions and behaviors.[112] 2,5 Million Euro to spend limits the FXX K program only to a small group of people, but nevertheless this is not the only investment the buyer has to do. These highly involved clients have to spend their precious leisure-time and furthermore pay for the travel costs to the different race tracks. In most cases, these clients cannot give technical feedback on the same level as the company's test drivers, but they can express how they feel as they are driving the product. The company understands, how they perceive the interiors, if they like the sound of the engine and many other details, which all together build the overall product. Not only that they are happy to share these precious insights for free, they are willing to pay the company or the experience.

---

[112] Yoon, Eddie (2016): "The Benefits of Hiring Your Best Customers"

BUSINESS PHILOSOPHY ACCORDING TO ENZO FERRARI

2014: Ferrari FXX K, 6.3L, V12, 860rpm @ 9200rpm, design by Flavio Manzoni

As Enzo started at Alfa Romeo and still in his time at Ferrari S.p.A., Gentlemen Driver had been an established part of the racing scene. Rich and some of them more, and some less, talented. One of the first group had been the Vittorio Marzotto. Coming from a wealthy family, he not only enjoyed his life, but also had the required talent. In 1950 he drove, wearing a complete suite with tie, a 195S to victory at the Mille Miglia. He became also a Formula 1 substitute driver and so once could start in '52 at the French Grand Prix for the Scuderia. Enzo's original business concept had been around people as him, as the Ferrari street cars should be a civil version of the successful race cars and further offer the buyers the option to use them with very few changes in local or also global race events. In relation to Vittorio, this meant that he not only bought the cars for his personal use, but also to deploy them in his "Scuderia Marzotto".

1950: Ferrari 195S, 2.3L, V12, 170hp @ 7000rpm, 200km/h, 720kg, design by Carozzerria Touring

Enzo understood that the time of the Gentlemen Drivers was slowly coming to an end. In the beginning, they had been part of the most important events as the Formula One, Le Mans or Mille Miglia. Because of safety issues, many of these traditional endurance events had been stopped and a new athletic type of race drivers did not allow space for amateurs. Today you can find them in lower classes, but normally without access to the latest technology. Concepts as the FXX and FXX K take the original idea of the rich amateurs and give them back the possibility to participate in today's car and race environment. They can experience how a high technology race car can be driven on the limit and how mechanical and electronic changes lead to different car behavior. Beside the pure satisfaction of their clients, it gives Ferrari a second benefit. These amateurs take the role to act as additional test drivers, so the company receives valuable feedback to the car.

But it does not stop there, wealthy and loyal clients can acquire the different racing licenses and with this participate in the company's "Formula One Clienti" program. Every year a Formula One team builds several race and testing cars. As it is impossible to keep them all. In the past the Scuderia recycled them, to use the base or at least parts for the next season's racers. Today they sell such cars, if they are at least two years old. This can include the car alone or a program similar to the FXX, meaning that Ferrari organizes a team of engineers for the car's maintenance and transports it to different race tracks, so that the client can enjoy several week-ends with the professional attendance. 3 Million USD should be the price for such an exclusive membership.[113]

Once Enzo said that *"racing amuses me."* It can be assumed that this thought is shared with most of his clients. This is not only limited to the race track, but also including competition in other aspects of life, as, hobby, art, business and sports in general. Not only that "racing is business", valid is also "business is racing."

American actor Steve McQueen was the proud owner of a 1953 Ferrari 250 GT Lusso. As not unusual for the luxury models, it was not in the traditional red or yellow, but in a more conservative brown metallic.[114] Based on 250 models, this car still had the racing gens, but in most of the cases, never got used for such an event. McQueen not only liked fast cars in his movies, as in the '68 "Bullit", which is still today known for its car chase scenes, further he saw this as a private philosophy: *"Racing is life. Anything before or after is just waiting."* An idea that could had been expressed directly by Enzo.

In 2016 Ferrari presented the "70 Style Icons"[115]. A limited number of the actual models had been painted and equipped to celebrate the company's most famous creations, but furthermore also drivers. Of course this includes different champions as David Piper ("The Green Jewel"), Sterling Moss ("The Sterling") and Michael Schumacher ("The Schumacher"). Besides that some models are a homage to famous clients as Ingrid Bergmann or Steve McQueen. The last is a Ferrari California T with brown paint job and a camel leather interior.[116] The actor had been attracted by the myth and later became a part of it.

---

[113] Road Show (fetched 8.8.2016): "Inside Ferrari's program to turn mere mortals into Formula One racers"

[114] Orosz, Peter (2009): "Steve McQueen's $2.3 Ferrari 250 GT Lusso: What Can Brown Do For You?"

[115] Ferrari.com (2016): "70 Style Icons"

[116] Tracy, David (2016): "Ferrari's 70th Anniversary Cars Pay Homage to Great Race Drivers And Also Steve McQueen"

1953: Ferrari 250 GT Lusso, 3.0L, V12, 250hp @ 7000 rpm, 240km/h, 1020kg, design by Pininfarina; photo with friendly permission from David Lee

Selling a myth or dream is not only valid for B2C (business to consumer), but also for B2B (business to business). A product is never completely examinable. The promised quality cannot be controlled by the potential buyer, but he or she has to relay on past experience and expert opinions. The less a product is examinable, the more important is its positive image. The myth is based on a promise and proven success, for this also in B2B a sales advantage.

Selling an idea goes further, it can be used also for a company's internal processes. If you are organizing an internal employee training or workshop, you are partially informing how processes are implemented and how they need to be used, but on a second level, the presenter is always a salesperson who has to sell the idea and motivate the people not just to know the processes, but to follow them. Due to this, a presentation should not be limited on information, but also include emotional parts. If possible, using the founder's vision and dream is an ideal starting position. An experienced sales person starts the sales pitch with an emotional part to create a positive atmosphere and a perceived relation between the potential seller and buyer. Then he or she switches to the economic or technical part to present the information and advantages; always closing the talks with an emotional ending, so that the other part leaves the contact with a positive feeling.

Selling a dream does not exclusively work for luxury articles, it can be used also for daily-life products. 1971 Alfa Romeo presented the Alfasud, a modern compact car, which should become another milestone in the company's history, as it was its first car with front wheel drive and also became one of the most sold. This is remarkable as for purists the Alfasud is not a "real" Alfa, as it was manufactured in Sicily, not directly by Alfa Romeo itself, but in a joint venture between Alfa (90%) and another public company, Finmeccanica (10%).

1971: Alfa Romeo Alfasud, 1.2L, Boxer 4, 63hp, designed by Giorgetto Giuagaro.

The Alfasud was designed by Giorgetto Giugaro, known for his clear and practical lines. For example, after the Alfasud he designed its main competitor, the first version of the Volkswagen Golf. The whole project was developed by the Austrian automobile designer and engineer Rudolf Hruska, who combined beauty with practical utility. A fresh solution, which needed also a fresh engine, the Alfsud featured the company's new boxer-engines. This heart of the car should outlive the Alfasud and stay in production until the '90s and last used in the Alfa 33.

Even if they company had an attractive model for the market, Alfa Romeo wanted to top it, so that the car not only should be presented at the '71 Turin Motor Show, but there together with an unique sister-model, the Alfasud Caimano. The project to design this prototype went also to Giuagaro. The idea was to create an automotive dream with no possibility of production. The only limitation was that the Caimano had technically to be based on the given Alfasud technology. Doing so, the designer presented a prototype similar to Alfa's earlier Iguana or Carabo; edgy futuristic design like from another planet. Only in opposite to these earlier examples, without the V8, but an ordinary 1,2L Boxer engine.[117]

With this marketing strategy the company made it clear from the beginning that beside its origin the Alfasud was a 100% Alfa Romeo and that they had been proud of their creation. Nearly 900,000 sold units in eleven years had been the positive result.

3.3 *"I never tell a lie."*

Especially in countries with a higher perceived corruption level, you might like to think that doing business in a transparent way may be a disadvantage. On the first view this seems to be true. Not having anymore the possibilities to invite a governmental official to the Formula 1 grand prix in Monaco or send him a nice red car as Christmas gift does not make the life of a sales-person easier.

Having the best product or solution, but working in a non-transparent market, while competitors still are operating with the famous suitcase full of money is like being in Formula 1: you qualified as first, but then got send back and have to start now the race from the fifth row.

---

[117] Pander, Juergen (2016): "Alfa Romeo Alfasud Caimano: Gib Gas!"

BUSINESS PHILOSOPHY ACCORDING TO ENZO FERRARI

1951: Ferrari 375 F1, 4.5L, V12, 850kg, design by Aurelio Lampredi

For the moment this is a clear disadvantage, but over the long season, it can turn into an advantage. Why?

- If you are winning the race with the help of a bribe, you are sending out wrong indicators to management and the development department. Thanks to the victory the situation gets wrongly perceived as too positive, and the pressure on further development is not as high as it would have to be to have a real competitive car, as management is not seeing their real own strengths, but a faked result. For this the car gets perceived as stronger has it is.

- This will lead to the situation that the competitively of car and team (or product and employees) is decreasing, *as* other teams (or companies) are working harder and harder to catch up to the leader.

- Let's be honest, also racing is at the end about money and profit, directly as reward for the good results, but also coming from tv-stations and sponsors. A team what is working with bribes has to pay higher bribes in each race, as corrupt officials tend to ask for higher sums over the time. In the same period the the car is losing competitively (money is not used to for technical development, but partly for bribes). Risk means money (see risk assessment). Pressure is raising on non-transparent acting companies, as anti-corruption laws (local and global ex-territorial ones) are getting more robust. With this the casino-risk (= risk of getting caught) raises. In the following seasons the two cost factors go up for the team, even if they not get caught.

3.4 *"No, you must drive a Ferrari"*

One part of the casino risk is that the individual tend to use and show their received gifts. For example the former Argentinian president Carlos Menem from the Peronist party. In his presidency he received from a business man a Ferrari 348 tb as a gift. At this time he justified himself accepting it with the statement: *"I am going to leave this car as property of the nation. But meanwhile I shall use it myself."* And he did, including in a trip to the Argentinian coastal resort town of Pinamar to attend a meeting, organized by a local BMW club (Quite ironic as Enzo Ferrari was not found of these cars: *"Beh, macchina tedesco – no, you must drive a Ferrari."*). He enjoyed the trip, not paying for any tolls and going up to 190km/h. Later asked for this present, Menem changed his mind and explained that the Ferrari was for him as person and not for him being the president: *"La Ferrari es mia, mia."* (Spanish for *"The Ferrari is mine, mine."*). Later the car ended up in a public auction and for a time the red car got lost and forgotten. Just in 2006 it got identified again, as an Argentinian business man bought it from 97.000 USD.

1989: Ferrari 348 TS, 3.4L, V8, 300hp@ 7200rpm, 275km/h, 1393kg, design by Pininfarina

Due to the legend, this was not the first time that a Ferrari was destined to a member of the Peronist party. Already in 1949 arrived a special Ferrari 166 MM in Buenos Aires. It was unique, not only that the car was painted in the Argentinian national color light blue ("celeste") and yellow, but also it included both available options, the luxury and the competition package. Unusually as luxury means weight, what reduces the car's performance in races. The buyer was the Automobile Club of Argentina (ACA), what created the rumor that the 166 MM should had been a gift the country's first lady Evita Peron. Nevertheless it seems more likely that it was the idea of the Argentinian race driver Carlos Mendi8teguy, who hoped to bypass the high import taxes that way. Similar to European dictators at that time, President Juan Domingo Peron liked motorsports and its image of competition, speed and technological progress. For this, he not only supported local racing events, but also strongly the ACA[118] and a talented young driver named Juan Manuel Fangio, who had later a successful career with Mercedes Benz until the company withdraw from motorsports after the tragic race accident at Le Mans, where more than 80 spectators got killed. The following year he joined for just one season the Ferrari team, where we won the Formula 1 World Championship on a D50.

1949: Ferrari 166 MM, 2.0L, V12, 140hp @ 6000rpm, design by Carrozzeria Touring (Carlo Anderloni)

In 1950 Carlos Mediteguy won the Mar de Plata open race, but already the same year the car had been shipped back to Italy, as the temporal import license never had been made permanent.[119] Evita never got seen with this

---

[118] Dye, Noug (2002): "How Evita helped Fangio to the top"
[119] Coachbuild.com (fetched 24.10.2015): "Touring Ferrari 166MM Barchetta #0024M"

car, but she and her husband had a known preference for Italian luxury cars. President Juan Peron bought in 1953 a Ferrari 212 Inter Ghia Coupe[120] and Evita owned a '50 Maserati A6 1500.[121]

There had been cases, where a shiny Ferrari (other types of cars) had been a business gift. As mentioned, the new proud owners feel a big temptation to use the car, including putting it on the company parking space, where their colleagues could take a look at it. As most of the companies (private and public ones) have today a whistle-blower hotline and / or an internal investigation department, there is a high possibility that someone would report this new car, as it is in no relation to the normal earnings. This can be due to the fact that an employee would report this according its personal values and integrity, or even just thanks to situation that someone got envious.

Especially in riskier countries Compliance can be a sales advantage, as winning a project with a bribe can be the best decision for the responsible procurement employee, but in most of the cases, this means that the client company receives an inferior product for a higher prices. Based on this concept the client should be interested that its suppliers work on an ethical base.

3.5 *"If you like this car, we'll make it."*

Even if Enzo never travelled personally to the US, the Ferrari myth arrived. Already in the 50s the country became an important market. As the target group had been different than in European ones, the company started to develop models, which especially had been targeted for the American market. In opposite to several European countries, including Italy, the US did not raise taxes based on engine seizes. As a result the company offered models with big engines focusing on the US market and especially for Italy, even models with less than 2L engine seize. Additionally to these technical specifications, the company also experimented with US styling elements,

---

[120] Sports Car Market (2000): "1951 Ferrari 212 Inter Ghia Coupe"

[121] The Maserati Enthusiasts' Page (fetched 24.10.2015): "From Giorgio in Italy"

including the for the time typical colors and tail fins. The result was the Ferrari 410 Superfast I, beside its huge 5.0L engine, already on the first look the car was American, even if the design came from Pininfarina. But at the end the car never went into production, as also US customers wanted an Italian car. A Ferrari which looked like a local Chevrolet had no credibility.

1956: Ferrari 410 Superfast I, 5.0L, V12, 340hp, 280km/h, design by Pininfarina.

Another Ferrari, the 250 GT SWB, nickname "Breadvan" was born because of a boycott by Ferrari. Count Giovanni Volpi di Misurata was another member of the gentlemen drivers and so the first target group of the still young Ferrari company. Supported by his father, a financier and politician, who also founded the recognized Venice Film Festival, he was able to buy Ferrari cars and participate in several racing events. In the early 1960s he founded the Scuderia Serenissima, which mainly deployed Ferrari cars. To keep them updated and give them maintenance he employed Giotto Bizzarrini, chief engineer and test driver of the 250 GTO, before he left the Ferrari company in a serious dispute together with other key employees. In this occasion Enzo not divided business from emotion and decided to boycott Count Volip and his racing team, as he employed these former renegade employees. But Giotto knew very well the car and was able to keep it up to date, even without original Ferrari parts. Together with the engineer Piero Drogo they made some significant changes to the original GT. Interesting that the "Breadvan" should race against the GTO, but was not based on '62 GTO, but its sister model, the 250 GT SWB (short wheel base). The two men lowered the car in comparison to the original GT and gave it a similar body to the GTO, but with a complete different back, later called to be "shooting-brake" design, which gave the car the perception of small truck and its nickname "breadvan". Giotto was an admirer of the kammback aerodynamics theory, which promotes a high tail what abruptly cut off. Due to the German automobile designer Wunibald Kamm, this should reduce the drag of the vehicle. It can be assumed that Giotto already had this design idea, while he worked at Ferrari, but as Enzo was known not to be a supporter of progressive design solutions, he could not realize this for the original 250 GTO-design. In a less extreme version, Giotto used the k-tail for the Iso Grifo and Bizzarrini 5300.

1962: Ferrari 250 GT SWB "Breadvan", V12, 935kg, design by Giotto Bizzarrin, Neri & Bonacini; photo with friendly permission from Jack Koobs de Hartog

BUSINESS PHILOSOPHY ACCORDING TO ENZO FERRARI

1962: Ferrari 250 GT SWB "Breadvan", V12, 935kg, design by Giotto Bizzarrin, Neri & Bonacini; photo with friendly permission from Jack Koobs de Hartog

This was a scene from the early 1960s, today most probably it would not had happened this way, the reason for this is the internet. In the decade of the "breadvan" Ferruccio Lamborghini wrote several letters to the Ferrari corporation, including its director Enzo. As he was a successful business leader, he could be sure that his message would be read. But for the average client writing a letter to a company presented an obstacle. Only if you really had been upset, you took the time to write, and even less times it got received by upper management. In the 90s the communication hurdle became smaller, as everybody went online. Companies implemented their own webpages and clients got their own email addresses. Now it was not necessary anymore to find out the postal address of a company, but with just some clicks on the company's website, everybody could send a message in just some minutes. Of course it still was questionable if the email reaches the responsible management or got stopped by some internal filters, but at least clients lost a part of the respect, what stopped them before even to try to send a letter.

Internet evolved and companies now not just use websites, but all other kind of communication channels, including Twitter, Facebook, Instagram and LinkedIn. Under "@InsideFerrari" the Ferrari racing team is sending Twitter messages to its followers, including actual inside information from the races. This offers new communication and marketing opportunities for companies, but the millions of users are also a potential treat, as also negative messages about company and products can spread around the world in just seconds.

As part of the corporate communication, also upper management has to use social media. This is not limited to be online and read feedback, but proactively communicate, send out tweets and write articles on blogs and LinkedIn. With this development the communication between a company and client became again easier, as everybody, can comment on social media about his or her problems with product and company, if it is adequate or not. Such communications can start their own dynamics. In the beginning it can be one unhappy client, but lots of other users may join and the balance of power changes from an advantage for the company to temporal dominance of the clients.

Back in 60s, the Ferrari corporation had no monopoly in motor sports, so from legal side they had been free to stop supporting their client, the Scuderia Serenissima. Even if from a labor point of view, it looks questionable, as Ferrari tried to avoid that their former employees could work again in their field of expertise and gain money, which they needed for ensure a life for themselves and their families. In the 60s the case not received much public attention, which could had been different in the age of social media.

Thanks to the entrepreneur spirts of affected employees, they all found new opportunities and gave the motor world unique creations as the described 250 GT "Breadvan". Also the "shooting back" design should be seen again with Ferrari cars. A first time in 1968 with the unique "Ferrari 330 Vignale GT Shooting Brake" and finally later in the Ferrari FF, which went 2011 into production.

Similar to sixties, also today not all one-off models came originally from the Ferrari corporation. The Pininfarina company reached out to the known US American film producer, collector and racer Jim Glickenhaus with the question if he would be interested in new car. He was, but had one condition, we wanted a modern super sports car, but at the same time a homage to his Ferrari 330 P4.

1967: Ferrari 330 P4, 4.0L, V12, 450hp @ 8000rpm, 320km/h, 792kg, design by Drogo. Photo with friendly permission from SCG Cars.

Pininfarina agreed and started the project using a Ferrari Enzo as platform. As the company had been a long-term partner for the Scuderia, but not designed the original P3/4, the classic separation between seller and buyer had been dissolved and it became a project for both. To support the Italians, Jim sent them his P4 so that the engineers could study design and functionality. Also later he stayed an active part in the different phases of the project.[122] In the beginning, Pininfarina did not like the idea to take their most advanced car, the Enzo, and give it a retro design. But at the end, the result had been a modern and usable car, not only for the driver, but also relatively comfortable for the passenger aside. So far, it was no official Ferrari yet, as the company from Maranello had not been involved. When they gave their original blessing, the car received its official name: "Ferrari P4/5 by Pininfarina".

---

[122] Pininfarina (2006): "Three questions for James Glickenhaus"

Even if not designed by Pininfarina, the lines of Ferrari P4/5 by Pininfarina remind less to the Enzo, but in some aspects more to the later LaFerrari. The Enzo went 2002 into production and the LaFerrari in 2013. Therefore, the 2006 Ferrari P4/5 by Pininfarina was the ideal link. It can be assumed that Ferrari not directly copied the design, but that it was a natural development, especially as the original P3/4 was a processor not only for the Ferrari P4/5 by Pininfarina, but also the LaFerrari. A proof that the car was a real Ferrari, not only because of the official badges, but furthermore as it became part of the company's history, just as the 250 GT SWB "Breadvan" did in the sixties. Also for Pininfarina it became a longer business relationship, as Glickenhaus later bought two of their show-cars, the Dino 206 Competizione Prototipo and the Ferrari 512 Modulo.

2006: Ferrari P4/5 by Pininfarina, 6.0L, V12, 660hp @ 7800rpm, 375km/h, design by Jason Castriota. Photos with friendly permission from SCG Cars.

2006: Ferrari P4/5 by Pininfarina, 6.0L, V12, 660hp @ 7800rpm, 375km/h, design by Jason Castriota. Photos with friendly permission from SCG Cars.

For Jim Glickenhaus the car was like a virus, he not only wanted to use it on legal streets, but similar to the original P4, race it. In that sense he thought like a 1950's gentlemen driver.

Even if the Ferrari P4/5 by Pininfarina was promising, it had the disadvantage, that the regulations from the actual tournaments disfavor the strong, but thirsty V12-engines. With the goal to have a competitive race car, there was no other solution than to build a second car, similar in design, but based on a different technical platform. To decide how to create it, Jim reached out to the different race organizers and finally started a good discussion with the German Nürburgring. Their 24-hours-event is hosted once a year on big parts of the original race track, also known as the "Green Hell". They had been open to adapt the rules for a one-off competitor, so that Jim and his team could start building up a car based on the Ferrari 430 Scuderia. During the process nearly all parts had been changed, so that from the original car only got used the block and some further parts. The design had been similar to the street Ferrari P4/5 by Pininfarina, but in reality, the P4/5 Competizione was a complete different machine. As planned, the car not only started at the 24 hours of the Nürburgring, but finished the race on position 39, second in its class. A great result for the small team! For the next year's race the team included a hybrid-system and thanks to this, achieved position twelve and victory in its class.[123]

3.6 "If it goes badly, I'm not going to spend money on this kind of motorsport anymore."

The Scuderia Ferrari is a founding member of Formula 1. For Enzo it was clearly his passion, and even if there had been longer periods without success, the participation here was never seriously questioned. Other races and series had been handled more as a business model. Based on the concept that positive race results support the sales figures of the company and the other way around that sales finance the racing team, Ferrari tried several times to expand and have more activity in the important US market.

1952: Ferrari 375 Indianapolis, 4.5L, V12, 400hp, designed by Aurelio Lampredi

In '52 the Scuderia identified an opportunity to race at the famous Indianapolis 500. Because of new rules, the 1951 Formula 1 car could not participate anymore in the championship, but got used as base for an Indy car. With some technical changes as a longer wheelbase and chassis, including suspension strengthening, the 375 complied with the US rules. First tests in Italy brought promising results, but the race itself was a disappointment. From the four cars just the one driven by Alberto Ascari qualified and even he had to retire with technical problems after only 40 laps.

---

[123] Fast Lane Daily (2014): "James Glickenhaus Garage"

Thanks to the persistence of the US importer, Ferrari came back four years later. The same then, the mission was to get additional attention by potential clients. A six cylinder engine was included in a chassis by US manufacturer Kurtis Kraft. Driver should be Nino Farina, former Formula 1 champion with Alfa Romeo, but '56 being without a contract. But again the results had not been more positive, the car did not qualified for the race.

"Racing supporting Sales" is based on the AIDA-formula:

$$\text{attention} \rightarrow \text{interest} \rightarrow \text{desire} \rightarrow \text{action.}[124]$$

Car racing proved to generate attention, especially at the Ferrari relevant target group. In a second step it is up to the racing team to create attention inside the event. This starts with the red signal color, but must be supported by positive results. Of course the Ferrari myth plays a positive factor here, so that the team today always receives attention. But nevertheless, it is imperative to create favourable results, if not, the attention is on the negative side, what definitely is not boosting sales. As racing is a very emotional event, it should start and maintain the interest of the spectators on the tribunes and TVs. With this awakened interest, people start to inform their-selves about racing and car technology. Hopefully they would learn that the Ferrari street cars offer a race feeling for the private client. The myth is supporting the image transfer from race to production cars, we have now the desire to buy the car. This would lead to the final step, the action; meaning the potential client enters the Ferrari store and buys the car, or at least some of the merchandising. The AIDA-formula is one of the first attempts to explain the marketing impact on a person. In the meantime newer models came up, but all more or less are still are based on this early approach. One of critic points is the step from desire to action, as there are several hurdles, it would be more a jump. The most obvious one is the price of the product, but there are also other ones, as the opinion of one's peers or how socially accepted is the usage of this product. Besides, different types of products can compete with each other. Am I buying the boat, house or car. Further, the action is not the end. The new Ferrari client is

---

[124] Russel / C.P. (1921): "How to Write a Sales-Making Letter"

still highly involved in his new car and continues watching the races as the positive results would now confirm his buying decision. If the racing team could not produce them anymore, the client would feel an inner dissonance and could be tempted to sell his car and change to the competitor.

The third attempt to enter the Indy 500 and the CART series ended before the car even reached the US. In 1985 Enzo Ferrari was again in dispute with Formula 1 boss Bernie Ecclestone, regarding the distribution of F1's income to the participating racing teams and also technical specifications. Regarding the game theory (see the sustainability-chapter) he knew that he needed an additional "ace" in his hand. For this, one year later, the Scuderia began to design the Ferrari 637.[125] To prepare themselves for this task, they borrowed a March-Cosworth car, carried it together with Indycar car champion Bobby Rahal to the Ferrari own race-track of Fiorano and tried to learn as much as possible from this training sessions.

The 637 looked similar to the F1 87, not surprisingly as both cars had been designed by Gustav Brunner. But besides this similarities, both cars had been significantly different, the 637 bigger and directly built after the actual CART specifications. In summer 1986 the car got presented to the international press, but at the end never employed in a race. Thanks to threat that Ferrari could leave the Formula 1 circus, Bernie Ecclestone overworked his proposal so that Enzo Ferrari was satisfied with it. Due to limited internal resources and the task to create a car for next year's Formula 1 season, the Scuderia dropped the Indy project.

---

[125] Oreovicz, John (2013): "When Ferrari Almost Came to Indy"

1990: March Alfa Romeo 90 CA, 2.6L, V8, 720hp, design by March

Even if not the whole car, at least the engine found its way to the US. Relabeled as Alfa Romeo, it should support the company's presence on the this important market. But also here the results stayed quite mixed, the best result was a 4th place in 1991.

Bobby Rahal remembered later in his biography: *"In the end, Enzo was just pulling everybody's chain."*[126] As Enzo not believed in back luck, being in negotiations, he prepared himself for all possible moves of the counter side. This included also an analysis of the own situation in comparison of the opponent's one. If it was not enough to win the game, the own position had to be fostered. In this example Enzo knew that he needed a strong threat, so that Bernie would not disqualify Enzo's arguments to leave Formula 1 as a pure bluff. His weak point in the starting position was that he was known for his racing passion and that he could not live without it. For this it was clear to Bernie that the risk to lose Ferrari for his championship was not significant. But having a competitive car to participate in the US CART series had changed the situation. Still Enzo was perceived as being near to Formula 1, but for the first time ever, there was a theoretical possibility that he would leave it and search his luck in another series. The balance of power had changed from an advantage for Ecclestone to being now in favor of Ferrari and explained the improved offer.

---

[126] Kirby, Gordon (1999): "Bobby Rahal: The Graceful Champion"

Wanted Enzo really to leave Formula 1 or what would had been his reaction, if there not had been the concession? As we will never know it, it is a another piece fostering the myth. Just to complete the story, even if not with the monoposto racers, but with the long distance races, as the famous 12 Hours of Sebring, Ferrari had been successful also in the United States.

3.7 *"I believe most things can be said in a few lines"*

As engineer Enzo Ferrari was interested to have efficient communication, what from his point of view was to communicate as much as necessary to deliver the message, but not more to not stop others and himself from their primary tasks. This is today as relevant as it was for Enzo. Especially today as we have so many communication channels, it is nearly impossible to receive undivided attention by anyone. Even in business meetings, managers are listening, but the same time using their tablet or smart-phone. If not this, they are mentally often already in another meeting. This includes a high-risk that if content get presented too complicated or detailed, attention gets lost or even that the managers leave the room. Being short and precise is imperative! Also where in in the presentation you include your important message is relevant, as it should be in the beginning or end. According to the framing effect, if you present your core message right at the beginning, all other presented information will be perceived in the light of this first message. On the other hand, the last message, is normally the one which stays best in people's mind. So you may like to include it here or, if not, include a slide with key-takeaways at the end.

As it was his straight forwarded nature, Enzo Ferrari asked in 1958 the actual Maserati Formula 1 driver Phil Hill: *"How would you like to drive for me at Le Mans?"* As he was active for Ferrari's direct competitor, it was a very direct question, but Enzo had known about the importance and the prestige of Le Mans in that time and was sure to have a trigger to get the talented driver. Not just for the '58 Le Mans race, but also that Hill would change the year after from Maserati to the Ferrari F1 team, where he became champion in 1961. In Le Mans he was already successful in his first Ferrari race and should repeat his victories in '61 and '62.

Ferrari 250 Testa Rossa, 3.8L, V12, 360hp @ 7200rpm, design by Scaglietti

In opposite to the big car manufacturers, Ferrari not raced to sell cars, but sold cars to finance the racing team. Even though having the talented US driver Phil Hill in the team helped to develop the US market, which every year became more important for the company. It started in the late 1940s, when the driver Luigi Chinetti imported the first Ferraris to the US, including the 166 Inter.[127] In 2012 the US was the biggest market with a total share of 25%, before Germany with 11%, UK with 9,2% and China with 8,2%. The Italian home market only meant 3,4% of the annual sales.[128]

Edgar Schein presented in the 1970s his "career anchor-concept, where he explains five different career drivers, in two steps until 2008, he expanded his concept to 9:[129]

- Technical / Functional: Employees with this emphasis are interested to used their individual skills and also want to get perceived as an expert.

---

[127] Hall-Geisler (fetched 28.08.2014): "The Italian Stallion: A History of Ferrari"

[128] Felipe, Juan (2013): "Ferrari Sales 2012 Full Year Analysis"

[129] Danziger, Nira (2008): "The construct validity of Schein's career anchors orientation inventory"

- General Managerial: For these type of employees it is important to be responsible and accountable inside the organization, including to have a proper head-count.

- Autonomy / Independence: Such employees want to execute their task in a most possible independent way, but without losing the security of working inside a bigger company.

- Security / Stability: For these employees stability and the ability to plan into the future is most important.

- Entrepreneurship: Employees with a high level of entrepreneurship not want to limit their selves on the independent execution of company tasks, but want to go a step further and create their own enterprise.

- Creativity: These kind of employees want to solve their tasks their own way; understand the problem, and solve it based on their own ideas.

- Service / Dedication to a cause: For these employees a work or enterprise is not all about the money, but they want to have the opportunity to give something back to the society. This can be done in their leisure time or with the output of their work.

- Pure Challenge: These people look for the impossible challenge, the work place is a part of the total adventure of living.

- Life Style: For this class of employees, it is important to get an optimal life-work-balance between their work-place and family life.[130]

---

[130] Cardiff University: Edgar Schein's Career Anchors (Fetched 13.08.2014)

Edgar Schein's concept got published more than 10 years after Enzo Ferrari's question to Phil Hill, but following his instinct, Enzo acted accordingly to this concept. He wanted Hill to drive for his team and used the Le Mans race as bait, knowing that Hill's actual employer Maserati could not offer him a competitive car to win the 24h-race and as ambitious driver, of course he was keen on take on one of the hardest races. It was a clear question, directly aimed at Hill's motivator, so he had to say yes. Beside the Formula 1 Grand Prix of Monaco and the Indianapolis 500, the 24 Hours of Le Mans is one of the three most prestigious races.

With his idea that everything important can and should be said with just a few lines, Enzo was again in best tradition to another famous Italian. Nearly 500 years earlier the universal genius Leonardo da Vinci stated that simplicity would be the ultimate sophistication; a worthy behavior for the Commendatore.

2016: Leonardo da Vinci, Piazza della Scala, Milan

Besides the message itself, timing is an important factor. US race driver Mario Andretti came via the North American Racing Team already in the 1960s in contact with the Scuderia Ferrari. In the first time he participated in endurance racer. Later in '71 and '72 he drove also in the Formula 1 championship. This sporadically, as parallel he started in the USAC

Championship. Nevertheless he won already his first race with a Ferrari 312B.

1982 he came back to the Scuderia to replace Didier Pironi, who had to finish his Formula 1 career after he broke both legs in an accident. In an interview explained Andretti, why he accepted to return ten years later to Ferrari: *"What kind of guy can say no to Ferrari at Monza?"*

As the Ferrari team was without a driver before the prestigious Italian Grand Prix, Enzo called personally Mario to invite him to drive for Ferrari for the last three races of the season. Born and raised in Italy, Andretti had known Monza, not only as driver, but also as fan, where he cheered as little boy to his ideals, including Alberto Ascari. Coming the two legends together, Ferrari and the Monza Grand Prix, he could not do anything different than accept. Even if he was not familiar with turbo race cars, he achieved on Saturday the pole position and finish the race being third. With these results he himself became a legend for the Italian tifosi.[131]

1982: Ferrari 126 C2, 1.5L, V6, 650hp, design by Mauro Forghieri, Harvey Postlethwaite

Another important factor is "who" is asking. If it is done by a person who is respected for its integrity, knowledge & experience, the probability of a positive answer is higher than if it would be done by a person, for whom apply only one or two of these factors.

---

[131] Formula1.com (2015): "Do you remember... Mario Andretti's superb Monza comeback"

Thanks to his positive performances, the Argentinian driver José Froilán González got Enzo Ferrari's interest in 1951. The *Commendatore* wanted José Maria, also called Pepe, to join his racing team. For this he sent his sports director Nello Ugolini to make González an offer. Knowing who Ugolini was and who he represented, González not even let Ugolini explain:

Nello Ugolini: *"Mister Gonzalez, I have an offer for you."*
José Froilán González: *"I accept!"*
Nello Ugolini: *"Before you know what I want to propose you?"*
José Froilán González: *"Yes."*

The same happened later in the contract negotiations:
Enzo Ferrari: *"Gonzalez, this is your contract. Sign in on the last page."*
José Froilán González: *"Thanks a lot, Mister Ferrari".*
Enzo Ferrari: *"You do not want to read it?"*
José Froilán González: *"It is not necessary, I trust in you."*[132]

Nevertheless Enzo resumed the content of the contract including the base salary, what was defined with 150.000 Lira. But he was transparent about the fact that the young Ferrari company maybe would not be able to pay this sum. For this case José would receive a car at the end of season. The behavior to accept a contract without even knowing what is inside was not completely out of the ordinary, but based on Latin business culture, where the reputation (integrity, knowledge & experience) of the business partner in most of the cases is more important than a signed contract. Of course, the behavior is different, if you are lowly or highly involved in the decision. In average we would expect people to read a contract if it is about an important decision as the acquisition of a car or house, but if it is about a decision, which is perceived as a lower relevance, as the contract of the new mobile phone, people may like to skip reading the whole text, especially the whole terms & conditions, and just concentrate on the key information as price. Nevertheless reputation stays a key factor.

---

[132] F1 Al Dia (2011): "Silverstone 1951: Que hiciste, Pepe!"

José's first race for the Scuderia was the 1951 Grand Prix of England, taken place on the Silverstone circuit. Thanks to technical problems of the superior Alfa Romeos, but also to his talent, he won the race and this reached the first victory for the independent Ferrari team. A very emotional situation, which gave mixed emotions especially to Enzo Ferrari, on the one hand he has happy, as it was the desired result for what the whole team was working for, but on the other hand he felt sad for Alfa Romeo, as this company made him the person he was now, with everything he learnt there and all the experiences, no matter if they had been positive or negative. Perfectly resumed by his quote: *"It's just like I've killed my mother."*

1951: Ferrari 375 F1, 4.5L, V12, 850kg, design by Aurelo Lampredi

Also the event became the beginning of another tradition, as the Father of the catholic Maranello community was Ferrari fan, he let the church bells ring after the victory. A celebration, what we still find today after each Ferrari Formula 1 victory. The next weekend, Enzo presented a new contract to José:

Enzo Ferrari: *"Gonzalez, this is your new contract. Sign it on the last page."*
José Froilán González: *"Thanks a lot, Mister Ferrari."*
Enzo Ferrari: *"You are not thinking to read it?"*

José Froilán González: *"It is not necessary, I trust in you."*

Similar to the first contract negotiations, Enzo nevertheless resumed the content. The salary went up to 6 million Lira a year and included preferences for him in the technical materials of the car.[133]

Reputation is a precious factor for the company's success and must be handled with care, as it takes a lot to establish is, but can be easily destroyed. Later the US investor Warren Buffet brought it to the point: *"Somebody once said that in looking for people to hire, you look for three qualities: integrity, intelligence, and energy. And if you don't have the first, the other two will kill you. You think about it; it's true. If you hire somebody without, you really want them to be dumb and lazy."*[134]

---

[133] F1 Al Dia (2011): "Silverstone 1951: Que hiciste, Pepe!"

[134] good reads (fetched 20.09.2015): "Quotes / Warren Buffet"

4 SUSTAINABILITY

4.1) *"When I see a car which uses one liters or 1.2 liters of fuel for every kilometer it travels, I ask myself, 'Is this a racing car or is it a tank wagon?'"*
4.2) *"Bad luck does not exist"*
4.3) *"Equally valuable lessons are learnt in defeat and victory"*
4.4) Cars and drivers
4.5) The last Lap
4.6) *"I don't think that there's car in the world that hasn't yet been improved by competition, a car which hasn't been influenced by others."*
4.7) *"In Modena there is a psychosis for racing cars."*
4.8) *"The most important victory is the one which has to arrive"*
4.9) *"What has instructed all of the world's builders of safe, efficient cars? Auto racing."*
4.10) *"What's behind doesn't matter"*
4.11) The Value of the Myth
4.12) The Green Hell
4.13) *"The horse doesn't push the cart, it pulls it."*
4.14) White Elephants
4.15) Fiorano
4.16) Diversity as Key to Success
4.17) The diversified Portfolio

4.1 *"When I see a car which uses one liters or 1.2 liters of fuel for every kilometer it travels, I ask myself, 'Is this a racing car or is it a tank wagon?'"*

The "UN Brundtland Report" defines sustainability as *"meeting the needs of the present without compromising the ability of future generations to meet their one needs."*[135] Seen as this, sustainability was interpreted from an economic point of view by Erich Gutenberg and his "principle of profit", as corporations in a market-based system are striving for to maximize their profit, based on the used resources, on the long-run.[136]

Enzo Ferrari was aware of the sustainability-concept, what got reflected by several of his quotes. As director of the world's most famous sports car company, you normally would imagine that he also drove privately his own cars. Of course he did, but not always, for daily use he had for example a 1966 Peugeot 404 Saloon, '69 Peugeot 504 Saloon, '70 Peugeot 504 Coupe[137], '72 Fiat 128[138], and also he owned a Mini Cooper S.

Ferrari's latest super sports car included the philosophy to produce more fuel efficient cars. The LaFerrari has two additional electric motors, one to boost the traditional V12 and another one drive to electric accessories. The KERS (kinetic energy recovery system) uses therefor the energy, which in a traditional car would get lost, for example breaking energy.[139] This used hybrid technology comes directly from Formula 1, where it got implemented in the 2009 season, used by the teams of BMW, McLaren, Renault and Ferrari.

---

[135] Brundtland, Gro Harlem (1987): " Our common future", part of the Brundtlandreport

[136] Gutenberg, Erich (1979): "Grundlagen der Betriebswirtschaftslehre, Band 1: Die Produktion

[137] Nedelea, Andrei (2014): "Did You Know that Enzo Ferrari's Personal Cars Until the Early 70s Were Peugeots?"
[138] Lorio, Joe (2012): "Collectible Classic: 1971-1979 Fiat 128"

[139] Howard, Bill (2013): "Ferrari's new 'mild hybrid' LaFerrari supercar produced 963 hp"

BUSINESS PHILOSOPHY ACCORDING TO ENZO FERRARI

2013: LaFerrari, 6.3L, V12, 963hp @ 9000rpm, 350km/h, 1255kg, design by Flavio Manzoni; photo with friendly permission from David Lee

As the KERS is additional to the traditional engine, its efficiency effect is limited. For this the hybrid engine is an evolution. A revolution, as for example a fully electric car, is at the moment not to be expected from Ferrari. Here lays a problem for Ferrari, as the car gets esteemed by its complete appearance, which is including performance, design, but also the mechanical master work of its engine and the sound what it is creating. Due to Enzo his company only engineered once a twelve cylinder engine, this was in 1947 the famous 1.5 Colombo-engine, which got used the same year in the Ferrari 125. This was the revolution, after this the company never developed a complete new V12, but created different variations from this original engine. As an electric engine has no comparable sound, a Ferrari key-element would be missing, as Austrian conductor Hermann von Karajan compared once the unique sound of the Ferrari V12 with his orchestra.

Creating a pure electric car would be a clear challenge for the company, as the Ferrari key-elements "tradition" and "sound" would be missing. But as Enzo as person preferred looking into the future rather than back, it would follow the tradition, even if it meant breaking with parts of it. At least the company's long time competitor already announced a full electric car for 2020. Due to Porsche, all-wheel drive and two electric motors could power such a car equivalent to 600hp.[140]

Not done by the company itself, but the Californian company Electric GT, specialized in engineering, design, and conversions of existing road cards to electric ones, took an 80s Ferrari 308 GTS with an unrepairable engine and replaced it with an electric drive, comparable to 415HP. This new creation now is called 308 GTE. The car has a Ferrari like performance, but the typical engine sound is missing. Will the future have demand for electric Ferraris? This strongly depends on the technical infrastructure and, of course, how emotional positive electric race cars would get perceived by the target group.[141]

2016: Ferrari 308 GTE, 415HP, 1519kg, design by Pininfarina (Leonardo Fioravanti), photo with friendly permission from Electric GT

Of course Electric GT is not a competitor comparable to the seize of Tesla, but it is a way back to the roots, where clients bought a Ferrari car as base and modified it due to their requirements and preferences, examples are the '52 Ferrari 212 Ouvo Export Berlinetta or also the later '62 Ferrari 250 GT

---

[140] Thompson, Cadie (2016): "Here's the stunning electric car Porsche is making to take on Tesla"

[141] Autoblog.com (2016): "This electric Ferrari 308 GTE would do Magnum PI proud"

SWB "Breadvan". Even if in the past such rebuilds went the other way around, they kept the engine, but used their own car design. Mostly the Ferrari company not supported such projects, but nevertheless had an eye on them. So rejected Enzo for a long time the idea to put the engine in the middle of the car, and not in front of it. So it was up to the Scuderia Eugenio Castelloti to take the successful Cooper T51 chassis and implement a Ferrari engine to it. With this their T51 became the first mid-engine Ferrari formula racer.

The strategy not to be the pioneer in a market, but a "fast second" is in many occasions the preferable one. This because of the high failure-rate of an innovation, not only based on the product itself, but further the possibility to develop a sustainable market for it.[142] Mostly it is the technical knowledge, power and marketing experience what makes a new product successful. Ferrari not evented the twelve cylinder engine, the same as Apple not invited the MP3-player and TESLA not the electric car. In fact the last was introduced already back at the end of the 19th century. The fast second company is often in the better position, but there are also constellations, where it is better to be the pioneer. This if the market success does not depend on economics of scale or also, if the copy of the product could be avoided through robust patents or other market entry barriers. Being the fast second is not a sign of missing creativity, as taking on an existing product and make it successful may include as much ingenuity as the original implementation. For example having a portable MP3-player was a good idea, but the real commercial breakout was to have a portable MP3-player automatically linked to an online-store.

Time will tell, if Ferrari will change its strategy and include electric cars into its portfolio, but independent from this, Electric GT will be forever in the books as the creator of the first electric Ferrari car.

---

[142] Markides, Constantinos / Geroski, Paul A. (2004): "Fast Second: How Smart Companies Bypass Radical Innovation to Enter and Dominate New Markets"

4.2 "Bad luck does not exist."

As Enzo Ferrari was a firm believer that the only way to reach its own targets is by hard work, he excluded pure luck as possibility. With his statement *"Back luck does not exist."*, he demonstrated that he knew the history of his country, as this philosophy is based on a quote by the Roman philosopher and dramatist Seneca the Younger, who lived around the year 0: *"The best wrestler is not he who has learned thoroughly all the tricks and twists of the art, which are seldom met with in actual wrestling, but he who has well and carefully trained himself in one or two of them, and watches keenly for an opportunity of practicing them."* Later these lines should be shortened to: *"Luck is what happens when preparation meets opportunity."*

Ferrari driver Kimi Räikkönen started with a victory into the 2007 Formula 1 season, but it was a long way to win the championship. The third last race of the season was in Suzuka, Japan. Lewis Hamilton won this race and as result he had now a twelve points lead over his teammate Fernando Alonso and even 17 points over Kimi. As for every won race you received 10 points, the chance to still win the championship had been bad, but theoretically still given. The Finnish driver won the next race in Shanghai and benefited from the situation that Hamilton committed a driving error in the pit lane, what meant that he had to retire from the race. After this grand prix, Hamilton had 107 points, Alonso 103 and Räikkönen 100. With just one race to go, a nearly impossible position to win the title. The spectators at the season final in Brazil saw leader Hamilton again being beside the race track, at the end only the 7th position for him, with this outside the points. Kimi won before his team-mate Felipe Massa and Fernando Alonso. This meant for the final standings that he did the impossible, passed both, Hamilton and Alonso and won the championship for himself and Ferrari. Of course he benefited from the other driver's errors, but it was not pure luck (or bad-luck from the other point of view), but a sign that he was physically and mentally prepared and believed in his opportunity to win; his opponents not.

BUSINESS PHILOSOPHY ACCORDING TO ENZO FERRARI

2007: Ferrari F2007, 2.4L, V8, 800HP, designed by Aldo Costa, Nicholas Tombazis

Based on the philosophy that bad luck does not exists, employers see the output of the employee as result of his or her work input. Of course, in a single event, luck can be an important factor to win or lose a relevant project, but on the long run, statistically, good and bad luck will equal each other. Based on the principal-agent-theory, an employer cannot (and also does not want to) control its employees completely. For this a manager is not fully aware, if its sales employees are hard working or not. To overcome this problem, the salary is not fixed, but including a flexible part, based on the results of each employee. With this the manager ensures that the employees really give their best for the company. As he or she wants to reward the behavior and not a possible good luck, the manager has a new problem, as there is no guarantee, which of the two factors (hard work or good luck) let to the success. To reduce the luck factor, the success part can be divided into two parts, the results of the employee itself and a second one, based on the results of the whole team. As statistically, good and bad luck will equal each other, the luck of the team members will do so. As side effect the manager ensures with the flexible salary based on team results the required team-work, but of course has to pay attention that groups inside the team not try to get rid of perceived weakest parts, to receive a higher bonus.

In 2008 both Ferrari drivers had mixed results. Kimi Räikkönen could win 2 and Felipe Massa 6 grand prix. Not enough that one of them became champion that year, but both drivers complemented each other that the team won the constructors' championship.

2008: Ferrari F2008, 2.4L, V8, 19000rpm, 605kg, designed by Nicholas Tombazis

4.3 *"Equally valuable lessons are learned in defeat and victory."*

A logical consequence from the idea that there is nothing such as bad luck is the philosophy that you can lean from both, defeat and victory. As in motorsports you cannot win every race, also in business you do not win every possible project.

As usual, design-studios celebrate their anniversaries with a concept car. Due to good relation with Ferrari, Pininfarina decided to create a four door-sedan for its 50th company anniversary in 1980, called the Ferrari Pinin. The car received positive feedback, while it got unveiled at the Turin Auto Show and later also presented at other expositions. Even Enzo Ferrari liked the car and discussed with Sergio Pininfarina the possibility to bring the car into production.[143] But after the talks he dropped the idea. It was never made public why, but it can be speculated that Enzo was well aware of his company's possibilities, and being honest to himself, he knew that Ferrari could not produce the car with the same finishing quality as its German competition from BMW and Mercedes-Benz. This was not of because of missing mechanic skills of the Ferrari employees, but plain and simple based on the situation that these two companies are working with high quantities and automation and Ferrari in opposite, manufactures highly

---

[143] Carscoop (2011): 1980 Ferrari Pinin Four-Door Sedan Concept up for Grabs

specialized and exclusive cars, which includes a more artisanal process. A fact what is not that relevant for sports cars, but a sedan would attract a different target-group.

For this the Ferrari Pinin stayed an unique show car, but even if Ferrari not wanted to include the sedan in its portfolio, the car got important for Pininfarina's business, as the concept set the basics for the lines and designs of later mid-range to luxury sedans, as the Peugeot 405 and the Alfa Romeo 164. Both cars hit 1987 the roads, not only looked similar to the Ferrari Pinin, but also should meant a big commercial success for their companies. Even if not designed anymore by Pininfaria, but the Centro Stile Alfa Romeo, the lines of the Pinin still could be found in the Alfa 166, which got produced until 2007, 27 years later after the original concept.

1998: Alfa Romeo 166, 3.0L, V6, 226hp @ 6200rpm, design by Centro Estilo Alfa Romeo (Walter de Silva)

A similar story share the 1981 Audi Quartz and the later '94 Alfa Romeo GTV. The prestigious Swiss automobile magazine "Automobil Revue" was going to celebrate its 75th Anniversary. An ideal opportunity for Sergio Pininfarina to dedicate a show car to the publication. As it should not be limited to a design study, he was searching for a fitting technical base and had been successful at the German car manufacturer Audi. In 1980 they introduced the Quattro Coupe, the start of their successful four wheel drive series. Sergio contacted Audi and convinced them of the project, so that they contributed with a body-less Quattro. Pininfarina created an edgy futuristic design, what was shorter, lighter and more aerodynamic than the original Quattro. The functional design had been presented at the '81 Geneva Auto Show. Beside the technical base, Audi had little input for the concept, but appreciated the ideas. They bought the concept and included the Quartz into the collection of their museum.[144] They used several technical ideas, but the design line had not been used further for Audi street cars. Exactly ten years later Alfa Romeo presented the Proteo at the '91 Geneva Motor Show. Not directly done by Pininfarina, buy similar to the 166, Alfa's internal designer Walter de Silva took on the idea and used it for its own creation. Technically based on the 164 sedan, there had been a small production of 2000 units planned. Unfortunately the Alfa Romeo management stopped the project in the last moment.[145]

But finally three years later two similar looking cars hit the markets, the '94 Alfa Romeo GTV and Spider. Adapted to technical progress and actual fashion, both had a much rounder design, but the original 80's design still was obvious to recognize, especially between the Quartz and the GTV.

---

[144] Banovsky, Michael (2014): "Audi Quartz by Pininfarina"

[145] Diseno-Art.com (fetched 17.9.2016): "Alfa Romeo Proteo"

1981: Audi Quartz, 2.1L, Straight 5, 218km/h, design by Pininfarina, photo with friendly permission by the Unternehmensarchiv der AUDI AG

1996: Alfa Romeo GTV 2.0L, Straight 4, 150hp, design by Pininfarina (Enrico Fumia) & Centro Stile Alfa Romeo (Walter de Silva)

For another example we are going further back in time, until the year 1934. The racing season went not well for Alfa Romeo and its Scuderia Ferrari, as the German competitors of Mercedes and Auto Union dominated the races. For Enzo the power of the engine was the key to success, that is why he came to the solution that more is better. He decided to develop a race car with two engines, one in the front of the driver and one behind him. Luigi Bazzi let the project as the head designer and the Scuderia developed the "Bimotore" based on the P3-chassis. Although its revolutionary concept, beside a second place in the '35 Avus-race, the car only had limited success. Due to its weight and power, it used too much fuel and tires, so that in most of the races it was not competitive. For this the Scuderia dropped the project soon after.[146] Nevertheless the Bimotore can be seen as the first Ferrari car. Much later the idea of having two or more engines should return in the form of the hybrid cars, where an electric motor is supporting the traditional combustion engine. Especially the development of efficient electric motors could make it interesting again to have several engines divided in the car, instead of just one big one. An example for this is the experimental Peugeot BB1 from 2009, what featured two electric wheel bub motors. 73 years after the legendary Alfa Romeo Bimotore, Formula 1 and Ferrari came back to idea this idea in 2009, when the KERS (kinetic energy recovery system) could give additional power to the race car. According the Ferrari philosophy to offer racing technology also for its productions cars, the LaFerrari combines a 800hp combustion engine with a 163hp electric motor, so that for short bursts the car has the overall capability of 963hp. Back in '35, Enzo was never ashamed of the Bimotore, as through the realization of this project they learned that two engines at that time was no solution to the task of getting faster cars. An important lesson.

---

[146] Gran Prix History (fetched 24.10.2014): "Alfa Romeo Bimotore"

In front, photo with friendly permission by the Alfa Romeo Historic Museum:
- 1935: Alfa Bimotore, 2x V8, 6.3L, 540hp @ 5400rpm, 321km/h, design by Luigi Bazzi

4.4 Cars & Drivers

The relation between Enzo Ferrari and his drivers had been complex. On the one hand he had been driver himself, so had empathy for them and even stylized them as classic heroes: *"The greatest drivers were distinguished by their supreme ability to handle any kind of situation, and car, and driving condition, any kind of race.".* Similar to classic Greek or Roman tragedies: *"He flirted with death in every race."*[147]

On the other hand, he underlined the importance of the car, and as engineer he described his relation to his creations as this: *"...then he goes to races and see his machines, this part of himself, being maltreated, ..."* Such honest statements often got interpreted as he just cared for his cars, but not for the drivers, especially if they suffered accidents. As Enzo not liked being in public or contact with the media, he never did much to counter this image. As a reporter asked him, if he suffered for the car, but not the driver, he

---

[147] Botsford, Keith (1977): "The pride and passion of Enzo Ferrari"

just replied: *"The driver too, of course."*

There is no reason to discuss that the first priority of every company has to be a "0 harm culture" *("There is no triumph or glory in the world that's worth an inch of human skin.")* and that every leader has to take care of their employees. Later he explained in an interview that he tried to have no personal relations with his race drivers as a result of his friendships with Alberto Ascari and the later suffering after his accident. Based on this experience he tried to have a pure business relation with his drivers, knowing they are flirting with death every time they sit in the car and to protect himself not to suffer again. A philosophy what in reality was not that easy to follow, as especially Gilles Villeneuve's deadly accident impacted him. Not only that he was maybe the most talented driver at that moment, but he also reminded Enzo due to his character and driving style to his old times friend: *"I see a little of Nuvolari in you."*

A lesson what is not only true for motorsports, but also for office life, as it may be easy to build up friendships, but difficult to keep, as careers may move into different directions. No doubts that networking is most important in business life, as it helps you, when you start in a new company or site, as you do not just have to know the official policies and processes, but understand how are the "real life"-processes and whom can help you and whom may be conflictive. It helped Enzo as he moved to Turin and start here his engineer- and racing career, and does the same for everybody. Ideally, such connections can help over the years, but sometimes careers will develop into different directions and even against each other, especially if a promotion is open and there is only one, who can get into this new position. Or personnel has to be reduced and management has to decide, whom to stay and whom to go. Mostly employees first think of their personal career and only second of their office friendships. A logic reality as most of them are here because of the paid salary. Not that they are egoistic, but have to finance their own life-style plus other family members. Enzo identified a similar trend: *"A driver today is an athlete out for hire, his mind is on profit."*

Apart from the human factor not to suffer, Enzo's decision to reduce his relation with the drivers to a pure management, is also based on sustainability and includes a basic truth, the lifecycle of an employee is different from the one of the company, what can lead to conflicts of interest.

- Self actualization
- Ego
- Social
- Safety
- Physiological

needs

To understand this better we have to go back in time; until the 40s of the last century. "The Hierarchy of Needs" by the Abraham Maslow. In this original model, also known as his pyramid, he is defining 5 different levels of needs. First the physiological, then safety, social and ego needs; at last the wish for self-actualization.[148] We have the general idea that an individual first has to satisfy the needs from a lower level, before it feels the needs from the higher ones, for example first you must have something to eat today, before you want to ensure that you have enough to eat for the whole month.

But there are exceptions, a racing driver is on the third level of the pyramid and now in the process to satisfy his ego needs of the fourth level, but at the same time this means to give up the primary needs for security.

Especially in the earlier days heavy accidents, including fatal ones, had been a part of each year's season. The drivers had an outstanding position inside the team, but if necessary, they had to be replaced from one day to another. In opposite to his philosophy, it was difficult for Enzo to keep his distance to the race drivers. Even if he always underlined the importance of the car and team, as he started himself as a driver, he knew about their importance and especially the death of Gilles Villeneuve hit him deeply and due to the legend he always kept a photo of him in his office.[149]

---

[148] Maslow, Abraham (1943): "A Theory of Human Motivation", published in Psychological Review

[149] Miller, Aaron / Gushue Ted (2014): "20 things you did not know about Enzo Ferrari"

Coming back to our company, we can have a theft out of the pure need for money, based on the basic needs of the first or second level, but it can be based also on the third following level and beyond. Maslow introduced in a later model of his pyramid an even higher level, which he just describes as "transcendence". An incompatibility between the personal values of an employee and the perceived values of the company is leading to an inner dissonance. As the individual feels the need for a positive self-perception on the higher levels, it tries to get its life back into harmony; it can be with a simple leaving of the company or the leaving with a "big bang", like a fraud.

The motivational risk is known, but what can a company do to reduce it? Human resources together with the management must understand which the different needs of the employees are, and what would make them happier. As we have learnt this is not automatically a higher loan, but also beeing part of a community, receiving recognition or living out its personal creativity. Of course each character is different, someone is happy if told what to do, another one wants to have more space to make its own decisions. One employee, might like an office with a window, another one prefers a smaller laptop. Important is that HR and management know and understand their people. Only if we know what our employees need and drive, we can really integrate them into our company.

Based on H. Bundtland we understand sustainability (as medium level of Maslow's hierarchy of needs): *"Sustainable development is the development that meets the needs of the present without compromising the ability of future generations to their own needs."*[150]

Hereby the compliance strategy plays an important part of sustainability. This is easy to explain. If you leave any ethical thoughts aside for a moment, the task of the Compliance department is simple to avoid that the company gets engaged in any unlawful business, which can lead to high fines combined with black-listing. This can pose a relevant risk for the prosper future of the company. For this compliance and sustainability are part of the company's middle and long range strategy. The problem hereby, a human being and a company think in other time dimensions. 5 years for a 70 years (as in the case of Ferrari S.p.A.) old company is nothing, but for

---

[150] Brundtland, Gro Harlem (1987): " Our common future", part of the Brundtlandreport

the employee in 5 years you can be in a complete new situation of life: marriage, new-born baby, house sale, child in high-school or university, etc.

Clean business is important for the company to be successful today, but also in future, even if the main part of employees are not planning that far on the long run. For them the question how to pay the summer holidays can be already strategic. That is why we have to be aware that a (very) small part of our employees might be motivated to take an ethical short-cut.

Needs are nothing fixed and nothing objective. For example the marketing business spends lots of money not just inform us which new products are out there, but also on the emotional level, to make us wanting them, making us aware of needs we maybe not perceived before. Emotions and the creation of needs are both, an opportunity and also risk for corporate compliance.

An employee may not always be fully aware of what is motivating her or him. Group pressure, for example can be a subconsciously motivational factor. This as a risk factor, but you can use this also for the good. If you are living a positive ethics culture in the company, the correct work of the numerous employees not just puts a good example for new people, but also creates a positive pressure (conscious or sub-conscious) on doubting employees. Just as Solomon Asch predicted it in his famous conformity experiment.[151]

4.5 The last Lap

Nigel Mansell was the last driver, who got personally selected by Enzo Ferrari. Nevertheless he should have two years with mixed results in 1989 and '90. The season after he changed back to the Williams Renault team, where he reached the second position in the World Championship, but not without teaching us and himself a relevant lesson. One he nearly had won the race and used his big advantage to the second to slow down in the last

---

[151] Asch, Solomon (1940): "Studies in the principles of judgments and attitudes: II. Determination of judgments by group and by ego-standards."

lap and already started to wave to the spectators at the tribunes. Unfortunately by doing this, he stalled his engine and never reached the finish-line. Instead of winning the grand-prix, he only gained one point for the 6th position.

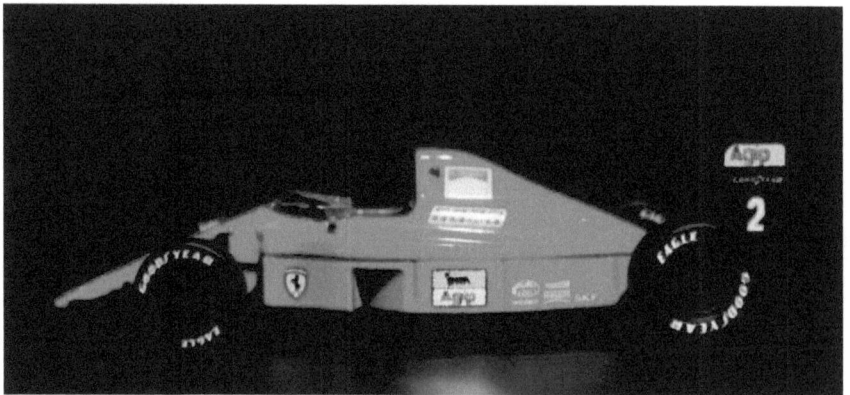

1990: Ferrari 64, 3.5L, V12, 680hp, design by Enrique Scalabroni & Steve Nichols

The same can happen in business. A project is not won, before the signature is on the contract.

4.6 *"I don't think there's a car in the world that hasn't yet been improved by competition, a car which hasn't been influenced by others."*

The 1950s have seen five times a Jaguar as the winner of the prestigious 24 Hours of Le Mans, the last victory had been in '57 with the D-Type. Of course, the company wanted to continue with this successful tradition and developed the E-Type, a sports car, which was available as coupe and convertible.

BUSINESS PHILOSOPHY ACCORDING TO ENZO FERRARI

1961: Jaguar E-Type, 3.8L, Straight 6, 256hp, design by Malcom Sayer

The car was presented in '61 and Enzo Ferrari called it: *"The most beautiful car ever made."*[152] As he was an engineer and not a designer, his quote was not only based on the car's aesthetics, but also on its concept and potential possibilities to win races. The E-Type not only received Enzo's attention, further Ferrari's sales manager Girolamo Gardini saw its presentation at the Geneva Motor Show and came to the same conclusions. Back in the Ferrari plant he convinced Enzo to develop a car, which would be able to compete with the new Jaguar and beat it on the track. The 250 GTO project was born. It did not start under a favorable star, as due to internal disagreements not only Gardini, but also the responsible engineers Giotto Bizzarrini and Carlo Chiti left the Ferrari Company. Luckily, Enzo had talented and well-prepared younger engineers in the company which he promoted to lead the GTO to its later success.

Without the Jaguar E-Type, the Ferrari GTO maybe never existed. Enzo Ferrari was clear about his philosophy: *"I don't think there's a car in the world that hasn't yet been improved by competition, a car which hasn't been influenced by others."* Even if he was never a political person, he supported the freedom of the market, as this guaranteed the competition between the companies. Due

---

[152] Curtis, Sean: "Jaguar E-Type"

to this philosophy, he never asked for governmental protection for his company. He understood well the idea of markets and the participants, as even if the market is free, the participants are not. Competition follows the rules of the "game theory". Similar to a game of chess, every move a partner makes, provokes a counter-move by the other side. Evolution vs. Revolution:

- Evolution: The free market is like a race, only that the winner is not receiving a medal, but a client for its product or project. If there is no monopoly or near-monopoly, the distance between the cars can be quite small. You can accelerate with better products and / or cheaper prices. So when the car comes in for a pit-stop, the crew installs some updates on the car and the driver accelerates to get back into the race. The crew develops the ideas for updates to receive, based on their own knowledge and by observing the race, including the competitors. Getting secrets from other pit-crews is of course forbidden! The problem of the situation is that if you need too much time in the box, you lose also too much time against the other racers. This is the reason why in a free market, most developments are only evolutions, better versions of the already existing, independent if these are products from the same company or adaptions of the competitor's solutions.

- Revolution: As the established companies are often busy in the race, in several cases the real revolutionary products came from companies, which not had been active players in the market so far. Some examples are Apple, who re-invented the market for downloadable music or Tesla, which introduced a successful electric car. Less known is Count Marco Risotti, who understood the importance of aerodynamics, as this was still a complete unknown topic for most car producers. To prove his idea, he bought an Alfa Romeo 40-60HP and contacted Carrozzeria Castagna to build a torpedo-like chassis for this car, looking just as coming directly out of a Jules Verne-book. The result was the Alfa Romeo 40-60HP Aerodinamica. The 1914 car proved his theory, as it could reach a maximum speed of 139km/h, 19km/h more than the normal 40-60HP. Nevertheless the car unfortunately stayed unique and even got lost over the time, so that today stands only a replica in the official Alfa Romeo museum.¹⁵³

1914: Alfa Romeo 40-60 HP Aerodinamica, 6.0L, Straight 4, 70hp @ 2400rpm, 139km/h, design by Carrozzeria Castagna (Giuseppe Merosi)

The examples makes it clear that it is most important not just to ensure perfect competition inside a market, but also have it open, so that new players can enter the game.

"The world is a jail and we all are prisoners. The bars on the windows are called egoism." With this quote Enzo described perfectly a situation what should become known as the "Prisoner's Dilemma": The individuals A and B had been members of a criminal gang and got caught by the police. In the cell they swore not to say anything, as this would present the best combined result for the two of them. There is not enough evidence to accuse them for their complete crimes, so if no one of them would start confessing, they just could be jailed for 1 year. The police offered them separately each of them a deal that if they would start talking and blaming their partner, they will be set free, but on the other hand their partners had to stay 3 years in prison. Ideally the police would need both of them confessing, so that they would have enough evidence to send them for 2 years to prison.¹⁵⁴

The prisoners have two possibilities: confess or not to confess. Important in this situation is, how much the individuals trust each other. They know that the police talk to both of them with the same proposal. In a climate of

---

¹⁵³ Chierici, Sergio (2007): "Speciale Virtual Car: A.L.F.A. 40/60 HP Aerodinamico (carr. Castagna), 1914"

¹⁵⁴ Tucker, Albert William (1950): "A Two-Person Dilemma – The Prisoner's Dilemma"

distrust, they assume that the other individual cooperates with the police, for this start to confess and with this, reduce their personal penalty. Or they trust that the other one refuses to speak and then confess to get an advantage against the other prisoner. Either way, in most of the situations, both confess to receive an advantage, but with the result that they together achieve the least positive possible solution.

In the example, even if they had sworn something different, both gangsters first of all thought of their personal benefit and decided to start blaming each other. The result was that instead they maximized the overall result, through their try to get the best personal result, at the end they both ended up sent for 2 years to jail, what is the worst overall result.

		B	
		confessing	not confessing
A	confessing	2 / 2	0 / 3
	not confessing	3 / 0	1 / 1

		B	
		confessing	not confessing
A	confessing	4	3
	not confessing	3	2

This model often gets used in team-buildings to explain the benefit of good and trustful collaboration. But beside this, it can also explain competition in mature or saturated markets. Here A and B represent independent companies. In a growing marketing the companies show a friendly and respectful behavior with each other, as both can turn non-clients into clients. This treatment changes in the later mature or saturated markets. There are only a non-significant number of non-clients, so at the moment both companies try to keep their status quo. Even without participating in a legal or illegal cartel, both players have a good idea of each other's prices, capacities, quality, etc. With "1/1" they achieve the best possible combined result for them. On the other hand the total of "2" represents the clients' benefit.

A healthy company requires regular growth, this to satisfy its stakeholders, but further to motivate its employees. Due to this, it is only a question of time, until one of the companies will start to violate the non-spoken agreement and try to win market-shares. Both are locked up in their cells and only can assume what the other will do next, we have a situation of distrust.

If diversification is not possible, winning market shares means lowering prices. With "0/3" or "3/0" the company, what lowered its prices gained a temporal benefit. Also it is for the clients' benefit, what shows the total of "3".

As every action provokes a counter-action, the other company will follow and lower its prices. The second company gains market shares again, but the total earning of the market lowered 2 points since the beginning. These two points earned the clients thanks to the companies' competition. Their benefit grew to "4".

As A and B are inside the prison and do not see a possibility to escape, they may be tempted to secretly meet inside closed walls and agree on prices and strategies. Or maybe the prison management allows them to move into a double-cell. Here they can work officially together or in other words, both companies can merge into a joint-venture. Both steps would limit the market and could lead to higher prices again. A more favorable solution would be that the clients' use their savings to buy more, which would be also to the benefit of the companies. But, of course, they could also take the money and spend it on another market.

We can take the prison-model further, as it not only explains competition and antitrust-risks, but also illustrates Compliance risks. For management, mature until shrinking markets may get perceived as being inside a prison, as no new non-clients mean no places to step out the given territory of the market. With the pressure to gain grow, the environment gets perceived as hostile and the competitor as enemy, similar as the atmosphere inside many jails. As the companies feel as in a war-like situation, the tone from the top gets aggressive and may be interpreted by middle management or other employees, as this is an approval to by-pass certain guidelines and laws. Continuing with the analogy, the Compliance Officer will be seen more as the prison guard instead of the trusted colleague. Overall, it is an important task for the company to overcome this situation, if not; it will lead, similar to the "prisoner's dilemma", to the least positive output. A key to open the door is a possible competitive advantage, which can be new products or production processes, but also a focus on the client, ethics and integrity.

Rome: The Colosseum

Even if the prisoner's dilemma is a theoretical model, it is based on the US police, which used similar methods to solve important Mafia cases. And again, similar ideas we already can find in the Roman Empire, where part of the gladiators had been criminals, slaves and prisoners of war. But only a few of them had been forced to fight in the Colosseum or other arenas. Most of them had been volunteers, as being a famous gladiator also meant freedom and wealth, even if this meant to kill the other prisoner or gladiator.[155]

"The world is a jail and we all are prisoners. The bars on the windows are called egoism." An example that long-term business success requires the overcoming of personal vanity is the Maserati MC12. Based on a

---

[155] Colosseum.net (fetched 25.08.2015): "Who were the Gladiators?"

restructuring of the Fiat company, Ferrari received a 50% ownership of Maserati. The other half stayed directly with Fiat. As part of the concept, Ferrari took the technical leadership. A direct result of this had been the MC12. The car had been developed for one task: after 37 years of absence, Maserati should successfully return to motorsports and with this, support the marketing for the company's important regions US and Asia. For this, the MC12 used the chassis of the Ferrari Enzo. Further the project received the experience and input of several Ferrari key-employees, including Formula 1 world champion Michael Schumacher became one of the test drivers. In the FIA GT Series, the car achieved victories already in its first season 2004 and one year later, it won the FIA GT Manufacturers Cup. Until 2009 Maserati teams won the team championships.

It was a business decision to develop a successful race car out of the Maserati, which meant that Ferrari had to step back putting their own products first, as the Enzo sister-model gave the platform for the MC12, but besides this never received the opportunity to enter in motorsports itself.

2010: Maserati MC12 GT 1, 6.0L, V12, 660hp, design by Frank Stephenson

Another example of Enzo's competitive spirit leads us back to 1969 and the European Hill Climb Championship. After the Scuderia won the sports car category of this tournament in '62 with the Dino 196SP and in '65 with the Dino 206P, they wanted to try their luck now with the complete new 212 E Montagna. This championship was in fact one of the few examples where Ferrari directly challenged their German counterpart Porsche, as most of the times both had been in different series or categories active, and also their street cars normally not had been direct competitors. Now it should be direct comparison of two different concepts: the 375kg Porsche 909

Bergspyder against the around 125kg more heavy Ferrari 212 E Montagna. As Ferrari not had Porsche's expertise in building ultralight cars, they concentrated on their core knowledge, powerful twelve cylinder engines. Unfortunately it never came to this duel, as Porsche wanted to concentrate on other tournaments, they pulled their car back. As result, the 212 E won the tournament without a serious competitor. It should be the last season for the sports car category, as without competitor, also Ferrari pulled out the championship.[156]

1969: Ferrari 212 E Montagna, 2.0L, V12, 290hp @ 11800rpm, 240km/h, 500kg

As it was not in the European Hill Climb Championship, the Ferrari-Porsche Duel took place in the FIA World Sportscar Championship, especially at Le Mans.

From 1963 to '65 the Ferraris had been unbeatable at Le Mans, but after this period came the time for Ford. The company used the experience of the AC Cobra and developed the GT40, which won the famous race from '66 to '69. Enzo had to accept that his company was too small to finance alone the development of its future race cars. After he declined earlier Henry Ford's offer to overtake the company, finally in '69 he agreed to sell half of the company to Fiat, what allowed him to stay in charge of the racing team and further to develop the new endurance car 512 S, including its mandatory production of 25 cars, so that he was able to start at Le Mans.

---

[156] Rossbach, Rainer (2011): "Ferrari 212 E Montagna: Ueberflieger"

1970: Porsche 917, 4.5L, V12, 730kg

With Porsche entered a third powerful competitor. Already in '68 and '69 they reached the second position, for this they had been the favorite for the 1970 Le Mans event, also as Ford stepped out the race. But this was no automatic development, as Porsche wanted more than the reached second positions; they developed already in '69 the iconic 917, including the needed small production of 25 cars. The company used their experience from the last two years and developed based on this the new car with the direct task to win the famous 24 hours-race. The preparation paid out, and as expected the experienced Porsche team had no problem to beat the complete new Ferrari. The race itself was also used to film scenes for Steve McQueen's movie about Le Mans, still today seen as the best Hollywood racing movie.

1970: Ferrari 512 S, 5.0L, V12, 550hp @ 8000rpm, 340/km/h, 840kg

Due to changes of FIA rules in the next year, Ferrari decided to start only with the semi-official N.A.R.T team in Le Mans. The US team did a good job and finished on third position behind two 917s, both strongly supported by the Porsche Company. In the meantime Ferrari started the development of the 312PB. Thanks to acquisition by Fiat, the Scuderia had the financial possibilities to reach something, what was seen to be impossible at that day. The Ferrari engineers and mechanics created an endurance engine out of the actual Formula 1 unit. For this drivers as Mario Andretti liked it, as its handling was very similar to the lighter monoposto car.[157] The first appearance of the car at the 1000kms of Buenos Aires had a tragic end, as its driver Ignazio Giunti died in a race accident. But the next year, the 312PB dominated the FIA World Sportscar Championship and its Porsche competitors, wining all races except Le Mans, as the Scuderia skipped it due to missing 24 hours testing.

---

[157] MotorSport (2006): "Great racing cars: 1971-73 Ferrari 312PB"

BUSINESS PHILOSOPHY ACCORDING TO ENZO FERRARI

1971: Ferrari 312 PB, 3.0L, V12, 460hp @ 10800rpm, 665kg, design by Mauro Forghieri

The next year, Ferrari came back to Le Mans with a special 312PB long-tail version. But the race luck was not with the Scuderia, as the leading Ferrari with Jacky Ickx and Brian Redman had a defect engine only 30 minutes before the end of the race. As result, the victory went to the Matra Simca 670B driven by French driver combination Henri Pescarolo and Gerald Larousse. It was also the last time the Scuderia Ferrari participated in Le Mans, as even with the Fiat support, Formula One and Sports Cars became too different, as one team could be successful in both events. Ferrari concentrated on Formula One. In 1973 this was urgently needed as the 312 with its last B3-version was hopelessly outdated, so that the Scuderia even had to skip some race weekends. The sole focus on F1 brought first positive results already in the next year, as Clay Ragazzoni and the young Nike Lauda reached the second and fourth position of the championship.

Competition not only leads to technical progress, but also centralization, as in a mature market, further progress is difficult to reach, and requires, in opposite to young markets, high investments. Costs, which single companies alone often, cannot finance anymore. Joint-ventures and acquisitions are the results. Ferrari is since 1969 part of Fiat, in the same year Porsche collaborated a first time with Volkswagen to develop the 914 street car. Since 2013 it became a part of the VW Corporation. So theoretically competition leads at the end to an oligopoly or monopoly. Anti-monopoly laws have to limit this trend and ensure a fair race. On the other hand, new competitors can enter the market. Such companies may come from a completely different background, such as iPhone, Uber or Tesla, and due to this, may accelerate thanks to their fresh ideas. For this it is the governmental task not only to limit market-concentration, but also to keep the market entry-borders as low as possible.

That racing means competition and leads to technical progress confirms also Dallara Automobili, founded in 1972 in Varano de' Melegari, near Parma, Italy. The company started designing race cars, including Formula Three, 3000, Indy and Formula One. In the 1992 F1 season the BMS Scuderia Italia team used a previous year Ferrari V12-engine and a Dallara chassis. With a similar red as the Scuderia Ferrari, the car looked as their junior team and could reach a tenth position in the that year's Constructors' Championship. Thanks to their leadership position in designing the chassis for the US Indy Car-championship, Dallara came in contact with Haas F1 and built their 2016 chassis.[158] But the premium class of motorsports was not the end of Dallara's ambitions. Thanks to their experience to manufacture products for extreme conditions, the company designed the drill for the 2004 Rosetta space probe, which landed in 2014 on the comet 67P.

4.7 *"In Modena there is a psychosis for racing cars."*

Not just that Turin, Milan and Genoa built the "economic triangle", Northern Italy was further a center for car manufacturing and motor sports, with a high concentration of regarding companies. In January 1957 this led to the unique situation that at the Grand Prix of Argentina all starting cars had been manufactured in Modena, eight by Maserati and six by Ferrari.[159]

---

[158] Formula1.com (2015): "Gene Haas Q&A: We're no Ferrari junior team"

[159] Racing.Reference.info (fetched 8.7.2016): "1957 Grand of Argentina"

1957: Ferrari 801, 2.5L, V8, 285hp, 280km/h, 650kg, design by Vittorio Jano

No surprise that the city became a place for networking, changing key-players, support and, of course, also confrontations. Modena, and around, in the 50s and 60s was determined by different small independent car manufacturers and racing teams. It was a time before automatization arrived at the small companies. Works had to be done by hand and nearly no car was identical to another one, as they had been individually produced for the client. This gave the companies the possibility to implement technical updates and new ideas directly in the next car, they had not wait until a new product year to include all the required changes into one big update. So it is no surprise that Enzo understood his team and himself as craftsmen, the way he learnt his profession and further, how he liked it. If you see the results, you can go even one step further, they had been artists. Modena could be compared to the Renaissance Florence, when the city had been the home of such extraordinary artists as Leonardo da Vinci (1452 -1519), Raphael Sanzio da Urbino (1483 – 1520) and Michelangelo di Lodovico Buonarroti Simoni (1475-1564). Even if they had been part of the same epoch, Leonardo was the oldest of the three and for this, already an established artist and scientist when Raphael and Michelangelo started with arts. Raphael admired Leonardo and used his works as inspiration, especially in the time from 1500 to '06, when Leonardo returned to Florence. Raphael's paintings became notable more dynamic and complex. Different was the relation between Michelangelo and Leonardo. Once both surprisingly met passing by the Santa Trinita Church, where a crowd of people discussed a passage from Dante's book. Seeing such famous and knowable people, they turned first to the elder Leonardo to explain the text. He just replied that Michelangelo can do this: *"Explain this passage from Dante for us, Michelangelo. They say you know so much."* Based on the conflict regarding the interpretation of art, the last countered: *"No, explain it yourself, horse-modeler that that you are, who, unable to cast a statue in bronze, were forced to give up the attempt in shame."* Knowing that he touched Leonard's most bitter defeat (he never finished the horse statue), he walked away from the scene.[160]

Both artists had been complete opposite characters, Michelangelo coming from a rich family, concentrating on art and not his outer appearance. On the other side Leonardo, coming from a modest family, interested in all aspects of life, including to allow himself a certain vanity.[161] The rivalry became a direct competition, as in the beginning of the 16th Century both artists had been commissioned to redecorate Florence's Council Hall of the Palazzio Vecchio. Leonardo painted the "Battle of Anghiari", while Michelangelo did the "Battle of Cascina".[162] It was not only a comparison of different painters, but also technics, as Leonardo experimented with a new technology avoiding to paint fresco. This as he saw himself more as universal scientist than a pure artist. In this case the invention not worked out, the colors began to run. Michelangelo, who most of his life concentrated on painting, used a classic painting method and succeeded.[163]

For both men, Raphael and Michelangelo, Leonardo was an engine of motivation. A lesson that a geographic concentration of artists leads to competition and progress. One used it as source of inspiration, the other one declined it and found his own way. Competition triggers automatically emotions, it is up to the involved players to decide if these should be positive or negative. Of course, competition brings up our best efforts and results, but on the other hand, personal life-balance is important, too. If competition brings up hate and other negative findings, it is time to decide, if the task is worth it, or if it is not better to leave the scene and look for other ones. Raphael's and Michelangelo's opinion towards Leonardo avoided that the two could became friends. Further, it affected the complete local art community.

---

[160] Da Vinci, Leonardo / Richter, Irma A. (1999): "The Notebooks of Leonardo da Vinci"

[161] The Best Artists (2011): "Why Michelangelo Disliked Leonardo da Vinci"

[162] Jones, Jonathan (2002): "And the winner is…"

[163] The Best Artists (2011): "Why Michelangelo Disliked Leonardo da Vinci"

In motorsports being near, related to a geographic concentration or being inside the same team, meant competition; competition meant emotions. The involved people not only went up to their limits, but passed them. Decisions on the limits led on the one hand to violations of technical rules, non-logical decisions and tragic accidents, but on the other hand to progress and triumphs. Similar to Florence, Modena had been a modern place for automobilist artists:

- Abarth (founded in 1949, since '71 part of Fiat; Bologna, 50 km driving distance from Maranello): Already four years after its founding, Abarth constructed the Ferrari 166 MM/53 Abarth Spyder. The car was used in several South American races, but after a season got send back to Italy, where its owners exchanged for unknown reasons the body for a Scaglietti design.[164] In the following time Abarth stayed successful in racing, using their own cars, before they got the official Fiat racing department.

- Alfa Romeo (founded in 1910, since '86 part of Fiat; Milan, 188 km driving distance from Maranello): The original production site had been in Portello, Milan; in 1961 Alfa added Arese as its second factory. Both sites are not active any more. Today the former Portello facility houses the city's biggest commercial center and Arese is still used by the company as test track, archive, showroom (due to actual FCA-strategy, there are two separated showrooms, one for Alfa Romeo and another one for the company's other global brand, Jeep). Most important in Arese today is the Alfa Romeo Historic Museum "La Machina del Tempo" (Italian for "The Time Machine"). It is not only since '76 the company museum, but since 2011 protected by the Minestry for Cultura Heritage[165], what underlines not only the importance of the Alfa Romeo for the region, but car manufacturing in general. The museum includes 69 cars, starting from the first A.L.F.A. 24HP and further including many models, which are described in this

---

[164] Vaughan, Daniel (2007): Ferrari 166/250 MM Abarth

[165] Alfa Romeo Press Release

book, as the 1914 A.L.F.A. 40-60 HP Aerodinamica, the '50 159 Alfetta, the green '68 Carabo, the Tipo 33 prototype race cars or the '93 155 ti. Beside preserving the heritage, the museum not only wants to present history, but to let the visitor experience it. Thanks to its architecture, the usage of modern multimedia and a 4D Cinema, a reached goal.

1961: Arese, Photo with friendly permission of The Alfa Romeo Historic Museum.

Enzo's career began at Alfa Romeo and later he took several employees with him to form his own company, the best known was Vittorio Jano. But it went also the other way around, as the technical director Carlo Chiti went back to Alfa and became a key employee to develop the successful Tipo 33 racing cars. Enzo often related the development of his racing team to Alfa Romeo, as on the one hand he saw himself taking on Alfa's history, as the company left Formula 1, but also nevertheless his relation to his former employer stayed difficult and for this the first victory on track stayed a remarkable moment in his memory: *"It's just like I've killed my mother."*

1972: Alfa Romeo 33.3 TT, 3.0L, V8, 440hp @ 9800rpm, 650kg

- Autodelta (founded in 1963, closed in '77; Tavagnacco, 315km driving distance from Maranello, later located in Milan, 188km driving distance from Maranello): Former Alfa Romeo and Ferrari employee Carlo Chiti founded together with the Alfa Romeo dealer Lodovico Chizzola Autodelta S.p.A. in Tavagnacco in the Province of Udine, not far from the border with Slovenia. Since the beginning, Autodelta had close relations to Alfa Romeo and their president Giuseppe Luraghi. Originally in '62 he had invited Carlo to establisn an Alfa competition department, but at that time Carlo was still responsible for ATS. After this company had to close, he had been free to join the Autodelta project.

First task for Autodelta had been the production of the Giulia TZ1. Alfa Romeo had already developed the car, but not wanted to disturb the busy assembly line of the original Giulias, the sedan, coupe and cabriolet. For this, Autodelta with its technological experience and knowledge was an ideal solution to outsource the assembly and maintenance of the Giulia TZ1.[166] Later they developed also the TZ2.

Due to this business relation, Alfa required Autodelta to move closer, so in 1964 the company changed to Settimo Milanese, Milan. Two years later Alfa acquired the company. As governmental company, they perceived public responsibility and

---

[166] Chizzola, Gianni (2004): "AUTODELTA and surroundings"

liability; for this Alfa not wanted to be directly involved in motorsports, but instead kept Autodelta as legally independent company, let by Carlos Chiti, as his partner preferred staying in Udine. Thanks to his good reputation as leader and expert, he enjoyed maximum independence and continued perceiving Autodelta has his company.[167]

1965: Alfa Romeo Giulia TZ2, 1.6L, Straight 4, 170hp @ 7000rpm, 245km/h, 620kg, design by Zargato (Ercolo Spada)

Thanks to being economic and geographic close to its main customer, Autodelta had its golden age, developing the successful Tipo 33 prototype race cars. Later they used the engine to let Alfa Romeo re-entering Formula One, but with limited success.[168]

---

[167] Vack, Pete (2013): "Carlo Chiti: An Appreciation in English and Italian"

[168] Italiancar (fetched 07.06.2016): "Autodelta – a history"

From left to right: 1963: Alfa Romeo Romeo 2, 1.3L Straight 4; 1965: Alfa Romeo Giulia Sprint GTA, 1.6L, Straight 4, 170hp @ 7500 rpm, 220km/h, 700kg, design by Bertone

- Bugatti Automobili (founded in 1987, closed in '95; Modena, 23 km driving distance from Maranello): Mauro Forghieri, long time technical director of the Ferrari Formula 1 team served from 1992 to '94 as technical director for the resurrected Bugatti company. After this, he founded "Oral Engineering" and some of the company's projects brought him back in contact with Ferrari, as they worked on the "Pinin"-study and updated in 2005 the existing concept-car into a working automobile, 25 years after its original presentation. Bugatti Automobili's most famous client had been Michael Schumacher, who owned his EB110 from 1994 to 2003. He purchased the car as he was still part of the Benetton F1-team, before he joined Ferrari two years later. This EB 110 was not only special because of its bright yellow color, a tribute to the Modena region, in opposite of the traditional French Bugatti blue, but also as it was the only factory build Super Sport version featuring the luxury interior.[169]

---

[169] DeMeza, Todd (2010): "Michael Schumacher's Bugatti EB110 Super Sport For Sale"

1991: Bugatti EB 110, 3.5L, V12, 611HP @ 8250rpm, 335 km/h, 1735kg, design by Marcello Gandini

- De Tomaso (founded in 1959; closed in 2004; Modena, 23 km driving distance from Maranello): Both companies shared the same home town and further its founder Alejandro de Tomaso admired Enzo Ferrari's persistent to create the world's best sports car. But nevertheless there had been never a stronger relation between the two companies. This also based on De Tomaso's strategy not to create the best, but a good car, including the decision not to use a self-developed V12, but a Ford V8. This made it not an attractive choice for a skilled engineer. Alejandro nevertheless understood to have the company profitable for the time-being as he was able to close a deal with Ford to export his cars to the US and let them sold there via its red of dealers. In so doing, he profited from Enzo's decision not to sell the Ferrari company and so to have Ford looking for another possibility to include European sports cars in its portfolio. On the long run this was not a sustainable solution as the company went out of business in 2004, only one year after Alejandro de Tomaso's dead.[170]

- Fiat (founded in 1899, since 2014 part of Fiat Chrysler Automobile; Turin, 304 km driving distance from Maranello). Before entering in Alfa Romeo, Enzo spent some time in Turin to try get a position inside Fiat, which already in that time, was the biggest Italian car manufacturer. Due to missing official education,

---

[170] Wan, Mark (2009): "De Tomaso"

he not received such an opportunity, but at least could use the time in the city to make contacts with actual and potential Fiat engineers. Thanks to this network he convinced later several Fiat employees to join his company, the most important one was Luigi Bazzi. In '34 he worked on the Alfa Romeo "bimotore", a fascinating concept, as the car really featured two engines. On the track the car could not fulfill its promises, as it was too heavy for the competition. But even more important was Bazzi's role to convince his former colleague Vittorio Jano to change from Fiat to Alfa Romeo.[171]

- Lamborghini (founded in 1963, since '98 part of Volkswagen; Bologna, 50 km driving distance from Maranello): The relation between the two men Enzo Ferrari and Ferruccio Lamborghini never became very friendly. *"You stick to building tractors and I will stick to building sports cars."* Nevertheless Lamborghini became an important rival and motivator for Ferrari to always improve and create the best possible sports cars. Also employees switched from one company to the other, what should play a key-role in the development of the Lamborghini Miura. A group of employees developed in their leisure time the concept, as it originally meant to be a pure racing car. This was against Ferruccio's strategy, as he saw motorsports as too expensive for his relative small company and wanted to concentrate on street models. Two top engineers of this group had been Gian Paolo Dallara and Bob Wallace, both former Ferrari employees and racing enthusiasts. Later Ferruccio explained that his absence from motorsports (he himself participated in the 1947 Mille Miglia with a Fiat 750 Testa d'Oro) was based that he was father of a son. Understanding the danger of the sports, Ferruccio not wanted to bring him into contact with it.[172] Nevertheless its origins, the Miura stayed his favorite creation.

---

[171] Grandprix.com (fetched 02.09.2014): "People: Luigi Bazzi"

[172] Thoroughbred & Classic Cars (1991): "Interview with Ferruccio Lamborghini"

- Lancia (founded in 1906, since '69 part of Fiat; Turin, 304 km driving distance from Maranello): Ferrari acquired in '55 the Lancia Formula 1 team, including their cars, knowledge and key employees, as Vittorio Jano. Later in the '86 both companies, now part of the Fiat corporation, worked together again to create the Lancia Thema 8.32, a traditional Lancia sedan, but featuring a 3.0L Ferrari V8. A similar engine, which worked also inside the Ferrari 308 and Mondial.

- Maserati (founded in 1914, since '93 part of Fiat; Modena, 23 km driving distance from Maranello): Both companies had been based in the same city, what made them, of course, to healthy rivals, especially on the race track. Juan-Manual Fangio joined Ferrari, coming from Maserati and engineers as Alberto Massimino went from Ferrari to its inner-city rival. As today both companies are part of the Fiat corporation Maserati came under Ferrari lead from 1997 to 2010, Ferrari concentrating on the extreme sports cars and Maserati including a touch of luxury. A visible result of the partnership became the Maserati MC12, which was based on the Ferrari Enzo. Since 2010 Maserati formed a group with Alfa Romeo and Abarth.

- Modena Team: A young Mexican businessman called Fernando Gonzalez Luna had the vision to establish an all Mexican Formula One team, owned by Mexicans and employee local drivers. Similar to the 1974 Brazilian Copersucar team, founded by Wilson and F1 Champion Emerson Fittipalidi and the earlier North American Racing Team. The last founded in '58 by the Italo-American businessman and driver Luigi Chinetti and the main goal to promote the Ferrari brand inside the USA.

  At the end of '89, Gonzalez founded Gonzalez Luna Associates (GLAS) and began to search for local sponsors and investors. This beginning of the project went well, so the second step was to find an adequate engine. Thanks to his good connections and persuading skills, he could convince the Italian Lamborghini Engineering, at that time part of the Chrysler group, as potential provider; not just for the motor, but also to develop and produce the chassis. To do so, GLAS promised to invest 20 Million USD.

Out of nothing, in June 1990 Gonzalez disappeared into the nothing, without any trace and still today is searched by international police. Without him the money flow dried up. But instead of giving up, the employees of GLAS Formula 1 believed in the project and could establish an alternative financing plan and keep Lamborghini on board, the name changed to "Modena Team Spa", also known as "Lambo" due to their close relation with their main supplier and now mother company. Lamborghini had been highly interested to enter Formula 1 and for this former Ferrari lead engineer Mauro Forghieri (responsible for the successful 312) received the task to develop a competitive V12-engine. Further he was responsible to organize the Modena Team as independent department from Lamborghini, which had to find its own financial sources.

Despite all obstacles the team reached its goal and started in the 1991 F1 season with later Ferrari and Alfa Romeo driver Nicola Larini and his Belgian colleague Eric van de Poele. Race success had been limited, as expected for a small and new team; for most of the races the cars not even qualified. The best result stayed their first race, Larini's 7th position at the US Grand Prix. For a second year it was not possible anymore for the team to win new sponsors, so that the end of the season meant also the end of the Modena Team.[173] The employees left to new teams and companies, as Nicola Larina joined Alfa Romeo to win the 92' Italian Touring Car Championship and the next year the German one. Mauro Forghieri stayed in the Modena region to join Bugatti Automobili S.p.A. and become their technical director. Their car, the 603hp EB110 of course also featured a V12-engine.

---

[173] Saward, Joe (1999): "Stranger than fiction: Strange Formula One team owners."

- Pagani (founded in 1992; San Cesario sul Panaro, 14 km driving distance from Maranello): The company was founded by the former Lamborghini manager Horacio Pagani. Based on his Argentinian heritage, the company's first prototype was called "Fangio". Similar to him as driver, this car was powered by a Mercedes V12-engine. Later the final cars was renamed to "Zonda C12". Then in 2011 Pagani introduced the Huayra. Up to today, the company stayed independent and is a good example that the Modena cluster is not only historically based, but stayed attractive for startup-companies.

As Enzo Ferrari understood the forces of the free market, he was always a supporter of competition and avoided stronger arrangements with other local companies. With this setting his company had climbed up to the top of motor sports. But on the other hand it could not prevent crisis in the team. 1983 the Scuderia won with Rene Arnoux and Patrick Tambay the constructor's title, but after this the team stayed over a decade without any title, until 1999 when the constructor's title got won again, this time with the driver combination Michael Schumacher, Eddie Irvine and Mika Salo.

1999: Ferrari F399, 3.0L, V10, design Rory Byrne

Big parts of the 1980s and 90s got dominated by British teams, as the new center of Formula 1 was now on the island.

Constructer's title / driver's title

- 1983: Ferrari / Nelson Piquet (Brabham - BMW)
- 1984: McLaren-TAG / Niki Lauda (McLaren-TAG)
- 1985: McLaren-TAG / Alain Prost (McLaren-TAG)
- 1986: McLaren-TAG / Alain Prost (McLaren-TAG)
- 1987: Williams-Honda / Nelson Piquet (Williams-Honda)
- 1988: McLaren-Honda / Ayrton Senna (McLaren-Honda)
- 1989: McLaren-Honda / Alain Prost (McLaren-Honda)
- 1990: McLaren-Honda / Ayrton Senna (McLaren-Honda)
- 1991: McLaren-Honda / Ayrton Senna (McLaren-Honda)
- 1992: Williams-Renault / Nigel Mansell (Williams-Renault)
- 1993: Williams-Renault / Alain Prost (Williams-Renault)
- 1994: Williams-Renault / Michael Schumacher (Benetton-Ford)
- 1995: Benetton-Renault / Michael Schumacher (Benetton-Renault)
- 1996: Williams-Renault / Damon Hill (Williams-Renault)
- 1997: Williams-Renault / Jacques Villeneuve (Williams-Renault)
- 1998: McLaren-Mercedes / Mika Häkkinen (McLaren-Mercedes)
- 1999: Ferrari / Mika Häkkinen (McLaren-Mercedes)

Since the beginning of Formula 1, most of the teams came from Great Britain and in the decades of the 80s and 90s they definitely used better the opportunities, which offered the high concentration of teams and knowledge, as the Italian ones did (a part from its owner, Benetton was a British team). They had been in a better position as Ferrari, as the Scuderia was the only Italian top team, as Alfa Romeo, Lancia and Maserati left the F1 a long time ago. In the UK they reached not only to have a competitive atmosphere, but also a continuous evolution, from year to year one team introduced a real revolution, which brought the regarding team into a unique position. As hard work and experience attracted talent and luck, they also received the most talented drivers as Alain Prost, Ayrton Senna and Michael Schumacher.

4.8 *"The most important victory is the one which has to arrive"*

One thing in business and sports is for sure, no success lasts forever. Winning is always a temptation, as you are getting regularly confirmed that you are the best. This situation is difficult to make big steps to progress. As you already have a proven successful solution, you will avoid the revolution and start all over again, but instead try to improve with evolutional steps. For a period, this is the most successful strategy, but it has the risk that you waiting too long to develop something completely new.

In 1996 the Ferrari Formula 1 Team was far-away from winning, in fact they had been now 17 years without a driver's championship and 13 years without the constructor's one. Traditionally the Scuderia always had the focus on the car and the engineers, but due to missing success, they tried out something completely new, working with a dominant driver. Not only that Schumacher was the fastest at this time, we was also known to be a perfectionist and to demand the same from all other team-members. As he came from the actual champion, the Benetton team, he was quite aware that the chances to defend his title the first year with Ferrari were quite low, but nevertheless, he took not any holidays after the last season's race and used the summer to test his new car. Due to contract provisions, still in a complete white overall.

1995: Ferrari 412 T2, 3.0L, V12, 600hp, 595kg, design by John Barnard.

Schumacher became a strong part of the team and thanks to his demands and connections, Ross Brawn (technical director) and Rory Byrne (designer) changed in 1997 from Benetton to Ferrari, as talent attracts talent.

1998: Ferrari F300, 3.0L, V10, design by Rory Byrne

It was a revolution for the Scuderia and it brought up a complete new Formula car, the F300. The countable results had been five driver's championships for Schumacher. But also this dominant time ended. Rules changed in the 2005 season, especially regarding tires. Ferrari was not able to adapt to them as good as the Renault team, for what that year's championship went to Fernando Alonso. As it was Enzo's objective: "*always improve*",[174] Ferrari worked hard and won the championship again with Kimi Räikkönen in 2007.

4.9 *"What has instructed all of the world's builders of safe, efficient cars? Auto racing."*

The competitive surrounding of car racing was for Enzo the ideal atmosphere to create innovations. Something which was not limited to the engineers. The drivers changed over the time. In the beginning he was working with the so called "gentlemen drivers", men coming from rich families, interested in motorsports and bought their selves their first race car. The complete opposite to the professional athletes which we find today in the highest racing events. To get back from his horrible fire accident,

---

[174] Ferrari.com (fetched 28.04.2014): "Enzo Ferrari – an example for the future"

Niki Lauda worked with a special diet and a for a racing driver aligned fitness program, which should later be perfected by Michael Schumacher. "The professor" Alain Prost studied rules and politics and also understood the importance of having good relations with the Formula 1 officials, doing lobbying for his own interest. Gilles Villeneuve understood the importance of the grip, especially at the start. With spinning wheels he put rubber on his starting position, so that he could accelerate faster at the start.[175]

But, of course, especially the engineers came up with new ideas, and these found later their ways to get implemented into the normal production cars. Some examples are rear view-mirrors, multi-function steering wheels and the evolution of tires and disc brakes.[176]

As Enzo was both, racing driver and engineer, a race for him was the final challenge for the driver, but also car. It was the ultimate laboratory, not just that the car, including all its parts, had to survive the extreme usage on the track, but also the always unpredictable human factor, by its own driver or the other ones.

Ferrari 250 LM Pininfarina Berlinetta Speciale, 3.3L, V12, 310hp @ 7500rpm, design by Pininfarina

---

[175] Holiday (fetched 07.09.2014): Erfindungen in der F1

[176] Bevis, Daniel (2013): "Eight Driving Innovations which came from F1"

Not just limited on safety, but a list of further inventions, which made it from motor-sports to daily life:
- Automatic and semi-automatic transmission
- Engine start-stop button
- Carbone fiber materials
- Rear-mirror[177]

A race is not just an ordinary test-drive, it has the full public attention, including the emotions of the fans and spectators. It is more than just sports, but a week-end long commercial, for the manufacturers. *"The racing cars are our most effective way of making the Ferrari way known, and selling what we produce."* As many of the Ferrari cars also had been available as street cars, the company had it easy to create the image-transfer from race- to street-cars.

4.10 "What's behind you doesn't matter"

Quite in the beginning of the 1992 season it was clear that new concept of the F92A with its double-flat bottom was not leading anywhere.

1992: Ferrari F92A, 3.5L, V12 700hp @ 13500rpm, 505kg

So instead of investing more money to save the concept, Ferrari gave up the task of winning the championship that year, and used car and season to test other new technologies (like an active suspension), which should bring the

---

[177] Deaton, Jamie Page (Fetched 10.08.2014): Top 10 Everyday Car Technologies That Came From Racing

team the next year back on track.

1993: F93A, 3.5L, V12, 740hp, design by John Barnard, Jean-Claude Migeot

Ignoring the costs you already invested into a project, and just analyzing the status-quo is important to decide in which direction the company should go in the future. This process is often difficult for the involved employees, as they have invested time and passion. With this, they lost their objectivity to see just the pure facts, but somehow have personalized "their project". Nevertheless, invested time and money is gone ("sunken"). The project status has to be analyzed, including with its linked resources, to ensure if it is really in the best interest of the company to continue using them here, or maybe, close the project. The now free resources can be used for other purposes. Enzo is right that what is behind you does not matter anymore.

1955: Lancia D50, 2.5L, V8, 265hp @ 9000rpm, 300km/h, 620kg, design by Vittorio Jano

A similar decision was already taken decades earlier. In 1954 Enzo's friends and former employees, engineer Vittorio Jano and driver Alberto Ascari worked for the newly formed Lancia Formula One team. Vittorio created the D50 with a revolutionary design, including two fuel cells on the side of the car to achieve a better weight distribution. As the testing time was short, the team could not liberate its potentials. Due to its missing reliability it only debuted in October at the end of the season. The next year started promising and Alberto could win the non-championship races in Valentino Park, Turin and Posillipo, Napoli. After he survived crashing into the harbor at the Monaco Grand Prix, soon after he got killed while testing a Ferrari 750 at Monza.[178]

1954: Ferrari 750 Monza, 3.0L Straight 4, 250hp @ 6000rpm, 260km/h, 760kg, design by Scaglietti.

Enzo was originally friend with Antonio Ascari, Alberto's father. Based on this, he convinced young Alberto to switch from motor-cycle races to automobile sports. First to drive the AAC 815 at the Mille Miglia, later also Formula One cars, where he became World Champion in '53 on Ferrari 553.

---

[178] Dal Monte, Luca (2018): "Enzo Ferrari"

1953: Ferrari 553 F2, 2.0L, Straight 4, 180hp @ 7200rpm, 260km/h, 600kg

Alberto Ascari's death deeply hit Enzo and influenced him for the rest of his life. Nevertheless his mourning, he understood the technical and economic opportunity to take over the complete equipment of the Lancia, as it was offered to him for free in July '55, and so to abandon the further development of Ferrari's existing Formula One car, the 555 F1. On top, he received a relevant finance investment from Fiat, behind the scene partner of the Lancia Formula 1 program.

1955: Ferrari 555 F1, 4.0L, Straight 4, 260hp @ 7200rpm, 280km/h, 590kg

The same year Ferrari and Pininfarina delivered a one-off to the Head of Fiat Gianni Agnelli, the 375 America Couple Speciale. For the special client the car included not only the most modern technology, two-paint design and sunglass, but even included an untypical horizontal grill.

The car inspired press and visitors at the '55 Turin Motor Show, before it was handed over to Agnelli, who drove this car for 5 years, before he sold it to the next owner. Due to this, the 375 America Coupe Speciale became also known as the "375 Agnelli".

This positive contact with Fiat owner Gianni Agnelli should latter support the respectful negotiations to sell the Ferrari Corporation. One year later, Fiat president Vittorio Valletta reinsured that Enzo could always count on his company. Without doubts Gianni and Enzo had been born into different social realities and kept on living different life-styles. Nevertheless, the developed a mutual respect for each other.[179]

1955: Ferrari 375 America Coupe Speciale, 5.0L V12, 330hp @ 6500rpm, 240km/h, 1341kg, design by Pininfarina

But what is right for resources and projects, is also valid for you career? The same as for projects is also important for discussions, which are inevitable in business: keep it focused on the topic, not switch to a personal level! If you follow this rule of thumb, you prevent that the emotions from the past have an influence on today's decisions and discussions.

---

[179] Dal Monte, Luca (2018): "Enzo Ferrari"

1951: Alfa Romeo 159 Alfetta, 1.5L, Straight 8, 425hp @ 9300rpm, design by Alfa Corse (Gioacchino Colombo)

"What's behind you doesn't matter": true as personal attitude and valid for companies. After his separation from Alfa Romeo and officially having installed his own company, 1951 became an import year for the still young Ferrari racing-team. July should bring the first ever Formula One victory, reached by the Argentinian driver Froilán Gonzalez on a 375 F1 at the Silverstone circuit. Even if this positive result was not enough to win the championship, which went to Juan Manual Fangio and Alfa Romeo (159 Alfetta), but it was the a first view on what Ferrari should become later for Formula 1: Already one year later, Alberto Ascari won the first driver's championship for the Scuderia.

This first victory by Froilán was a very emotional moment for Enzo as he expressed with the famous quote: *"It's just like I've killed my mother."* An acknowledgement that this achievement was because of his time at Alfa Romeo. The team manager Enzo Ferrari was born in and by Alfa, but now he was independent from the company and not resisted to compete against them. Even stronger than today, in that time the Italian culture was based on strong family structures, where the mother played an important role. Based on this, you can understand the importance and mixed emotions Enzo Ferrari felt in the moment of victory. Also it underlined the deep respect he felt for his competitor. A circumstance which was not only relevant in sports, the same philosophy he applied for management. He not only respected his employees and partners, but also his competitors. His goal was to beat them because of the quality of his products and fair sportsmanship.

The duel between Alfa Romeo and Ferrari continued in Formula 1, but also in Le Mans, until both companies became a part of Fiat and avoided the direct competition. Besides Enzo's emotional separation from Alfa Romeo, both companies normalized their relationship over the time. A first sign was their shared work for the Alfa Romeo Indycar (chapter 3.5). Later in 2015, 64 years after the first Ferrari victory against his mother, Alfa Romeo became a main sponsor for the Scuderia's F1 team, visible on the Ferrari ST15 Formula 1 car.

Looking forward does not exclude respecting the past. Every decision an individual or company did before let to the actual position. Difficult situations in the past may strengthen the individual or organization and may turn later into a benefit and / or opportunity.

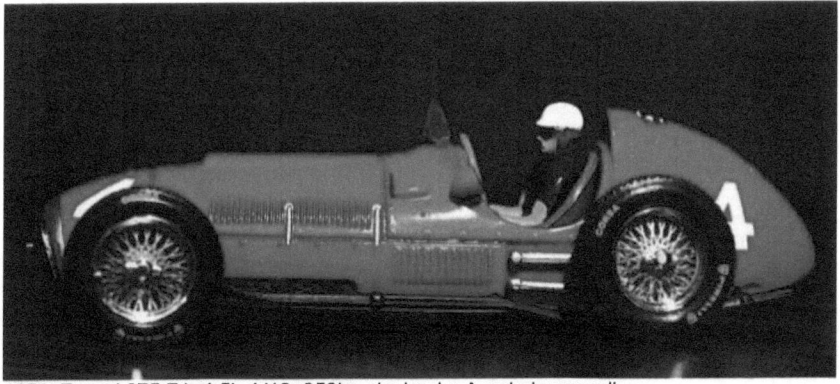

1951: Ferrari 375 F1, 4.5L, V12, 850kg, design by Aurelo Lampredi

Enzo's attitude about the past and always to look forward also influenced the company's handling of last season's race cars. Especially in the earlier years the Scuderia recycled the old cars, or took off the old bodywork and put a new one on the chassis. With this, we lost many unique cars, which luckily got reconstructed later. For example, from the Ferrari 156 F1 exists today only a replica, exhibited in the "Galleria Ferrari" Maranello. The original got scrapped at the end of the '63 F1 season.

1961: Ferrari 156 F1, 1.5L, V6, 190hp @ 9500rpm, 1256kg

"I am bitter at my stupidity in not keeping at least one example of all the models we have built since 1940!" Today Ferrari could use these lost models perfectly in the numerous museums, shops and amusement park around the world.

Ferrari store in Munich, Germany

4.11 The Value of the Myth

In different parts of the book we have spoken about the Ferrari myth, something what Enzo (sub-) consciously fostered right from the beginning. Every product can be divided into a tangible and a non-tangible part. For a typical Ferrari car it can be like this:

- Tangible: Fast sports car
- Non-tangible: Exclusivity, status, part of myth & history

Both, the tangible, but also the non-tangible part are satisfying a potential need and the target-group is willing to pay for the combination. For this a manufacturer with reputation can ask for a higher price than its competitor, who has a similar product, but no similar image.

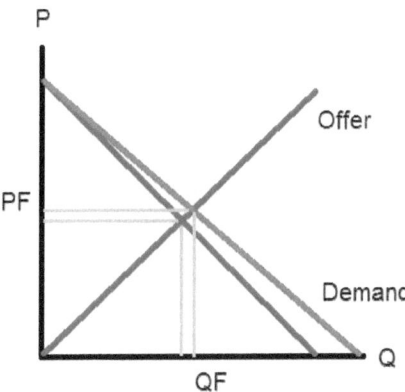

Thanks to the strong myth and tradition, Ferrari can change his "demand"-line to right, as it is attractive for a customer and a sales-argument. Besides, it is difficult until impossible to build up a similar strong brand-image, it stays an advantage for Ferrari. Of course, it is imperative for the corporation to maintain and fuel this myth, for example by delivering positive race results and keep the product limited. As the cars bear the name of the founder, the boundaries between the myths of man and machine vanished. Enzo as the person who built up the company to follow his dream to create the world's fastest race cars and the machine what offers these possibilities. As up to today the production stayed limited, there is not one Ferrari completely identical to another one. This supports the perception that each car is more than a machine, but nearly a living being, including a part of Enzo's soul and vision. Each year there are less contemporary witnesses, who remember the person Enzo Ferrari, so more and more the myth overtakes, just as he planned it. Similar to companies as Apple, Ferrari is related to his founder. The corporation celebrates this with the Museum Enzo Ferrari and sufficient interactive possibilities, where fans can read about Enzo and describe him in their own words,[180] but also included his thoughts in the corporate code of conduct, vision and values.[181]

A study by the consumer intelligence firm Motista came to the conclusion *"that the most effective way to maximize customer value is to move beyond mere customer satisfaction and connect with customers at an emotional level."*[182] In numbers, a client, who is emotionally connected to the product and / or the company has more than the double value with a one, who is "only" highly satisfied.

The myth is not a non-logical feeling, but indeed can be interpreted as trust. Even if there is the possibility of a test-drive, the potential client cannot be sure if he or she will be satisfied with owing the car, so is searching for clues to see if the car can be trusted. The myth is one of clues, as people believed in it for a long time, it gets perceived as it has to be good.

But this confirmation is not only important before buying the car, also after the sale. Before you are signing the contract, you spend more or less time to find out, what you want. Is the Ferrari really the best solution, or maybe you prefer a Porsche or Lamborghini? Or not why better use the money for a house? You are now in a position where you have many options. Unfortunately there is seldom an option which is the best in all details. If you make an important decision, with high possibility, you will get later a slight feeling of regret. This due to Festinger's theory of cognitive dissonance. After taking the decision which car to buy and signing the regarding contract, new customers continue seeking information about the topic. Before the decision about all available solutions, then after he or she signed the contract, in particular about this one selected product, as there is a need to confirm that it was really the best option. If this gets achieved, the person feels relieved and is satisfied with the acquired product. For this the myth is an additional factor, which supports the potential arguments to buy

---

[180] Ferrari.com (2015): "Enzo Ferrari in your own words"

[181] Ferrari (fetched 11.6.2017): "Values"

[182] Zorfas, Alan / Leemon, Daniel (2016): "An Emotional Connection Matters More than Customer Satisfaction"

a Ferrari car, so that the reasons are not just limited to the pure technical aspects, but furthermore include it's emotional universe. This gives the new customer a big possibility to confirm the buying decision and get out the after-buy depression.

The myth fosters the unique selling proposition of the car, as in opposition to a temporal fashion, it is difficult for a competitor to copy this. It is quite common in the automobile industry to buy competitor cars. The engineers use them for extended test-drives and sometimes also dismantle them to get a better understanding of the used technologies. A process which was used also by Honda, as they acquired a Ferrari 458 to compare it to its own NSX. Especially impressed they that had been by the aluminum construction, so that several details should have influenced later versions of NSX.[183] Similar did Honda also with a Porsche GT3.[184]

2010: Ferrari 458 Challenge, 4.5L, V8, design by Pininfarina

With this they understood the technical components of the car. But with the technical comparison they left out the psychological effect that people in general are attracted by authenticity. A concept what professor Glenn R. Carroll identified as a trend, starting in eighties, where individuals began to preference products from smaller manufactures against mass production.[185] Due to this consumers not only value the product itself, but further, how

---

[183] Autocar (2016): "Autocar confidential: Aston Martin, Honda NSX, Renault, Nissan Nismo"

[184] Perkins, Chris (2016): "Porsche Left a Cheeky Message on the 911 GT3 Acura Bought to Develop the NSX"

[185] Hawk, Steve (2016): "Authenticity's Paradox: If You Flaunt It, You Lose It"

much the product is still based on the original company's founder's values and ideas. Carroll underlined the importance for marketing: *"When people are attracted to your moral authenticity, it gives them a unique attachment to your product, because your identity is inalienable. Nobody else has your story. That's the ultimate strategic position a firm can have."* Still today, each of today's produced Ferrari cars include Enzo's philosophy. This heritage is important for the company's success and has to be taken care off. Production can be raised and even the portfolio diversified, but management has to ensure that additional products still are compatible with the person of Enzo Ferrari. This includes two tasks, first to present the company founder and underline his or her relevance for today; second how today's production and products are based on the founder's ideas and philosophy. To ensure this, Ferrari has not one, but two official museums in Maranello. The Museo Enzo Ferrari Modena is dedicated directly to person and like two expositions in one. The modern futuristic part presents Enzo through the different parts of his live and career. Starting from how he discovered motorsports as a child, continuing with the period as race driver and later as leader of the company. The museum is built around his father's original workshop, where visitors can discover today some of the company's famous creations, including the 1947 Ferrari 125, the company's first car development.

Maranello: Museo Enzo Ferrari E Dei Motori, photo with friendly permission by the Museo Enzo Ferrari

Maranello: Museo Enzo Ferrari E Dei Motori, photo with friendly permission by the Museo Enzo Ferrari

Already the architecture is message, as the classic workshop stands directly together with the modern organic wing of the museum. The visitor experiences the grounds where little Enzo started to work on his dream and perceives step by step how today's cars still include this spirit. With the shuttle service people can continue the tour with other official Ferrari Museum, the Museo Ferrari Maranello. Here the focus is directly on the race- and street-cars. Interaction is given, as visitors can try the simulators or even practice a tire-change under race conditions.

Beside the long-term "myth", new cars can have the luck to meet the zeitgeist or the fashion of the moment.

1984: Ferrari Testarossa, 4.9L, V12, 390hp @ 6300rpm, 290km/h, 1506kg, design by Pininfarina

The Ferrari Testarossa was no technical revolution, as the car was quite similar to its predecessor, the BB 512i, but is design clearly stood out. Its unique side and back design got copied by several tuners, which offered kits, to put similar parts on all kind of other cars. Also special was the high position of left side mirror on the first Testarossa generation. Even if we already had been in 1984, the car not featured a right side rear-mirror, Ferrari only offered this as additional option. Rear-mirrors came originally from the motor-sports and according Enzo, the '84 Testarossa was a luxury sports car, in opposite to the same year's GTO, what was a more radical car, designed for the racing ambitious driver. Even if quite similar to the BB512i, the complete different design hit perfectly mid 80's zeitgeist, as especially young and successful bankers and managers wanted to enjoy their short leisure time with the most exclusive and striking toys. And clearly Pininfarina's design was anything but reluctant. The car even became a part of the actual pop-culture as it played a main role in the US hit-series Miami Vice. The car stayed in production from 1984 to '92 and became a mayor success for the company. The high demand had been based because of the product itself, the long-term Ferrari myth and the short-term fashion.

Even if in the 80s most of the Ferrari production went to the export, the Italian culture of the same decade played an important role for the creation of an automobile as the Testarossa. Similar to most western countries, the time was characterized by fun and optimism, what led to the situation that people spend money and also liked to show their status symbols. The fashion became extravagant, what included the car designs. More than in earlier decades, "Made in Italy" became a globally recognized branding for style.[186] Especially in the US, the YUPPI (young urban professional)-generation, who became extremely rich in a short time period, looked for possibilities to spend their money. Doing so, they had their focus on fun and provoking designs. No surprise that the 80's Testarossa became a success, even if the car had only little connection to the traditional race cars.

Another way to foster the myth of a brand is the regular presentation of new show cars. Manufacturers use them to try out new technical solutions, but also to just let their designers play without that the form always have to follow the function. Results are objects which are the highlights of the actual expositions and so catch the interest of the visitors. Simultaneously they present the company's vision of the future.

The 60s brought a revolution to racing cars, the engine changed from the front to the middle, where it sat now right behind the driver. With this development engineers could improve the handling of the car. As super sports cars wanted to offer the real race feeling to the ambitious client, several companies adapted this concept. Alfa Romeo presented 1967 the "33 Stradale", a direct street version of its 33 racing cars. Only one year later Ferrari launched the Dino 206 GT to the market and later in '73 the 365 GT4 Berlineta Boxer, then featuring the typical Ferrari V12-engine. In '72 Lancia presented the Stratos, which with its Dino V6-engine (like the earlier Dino 206 GT) secured mayor success in the rally sport. Even if not active in any motorsports, in '73 also Lamborghini presented a mid-engine street car, the famous Countach. Having the engine behind the driver, the cars could had been lower than front-engine ones. A circumstance, which invited designers to play around with this new concept and started a non-official competition to build the lowest car. Designers as Bertone, Italdesign and Pininfarina used the new platforms and designed their visions of the future. The highest numbers of show cars at that time had Alfa Romeo with the Carabo, P33, Iguana, 33.2, Cuneo and Navajo; all based on the Tipo 33. One of them, the 33.2 had a direct relation to Ferrari. One year earlier in 1968 Pininfarina created the futuristic 250 P5, built on a 330 P4 chassis. Keeping a line similar to the successful P4, Ferrari's mission for Pininfarina

---

[186] Life in Italy (fetched 12.12.2015: "Life in Italy 1970s to 1980s"

was to explore further aerodynamic possibilities. Despite its positive critical acclaims, Enzo was not found of the P5, so it became clear the 250 prototypes would not continue and the P5 not presented the company's future. At this time Dr. Giuseppe Luraghi, Chairman of Alfa Romeo, called. He had an unusual request for his old friend Enzo, Alfa had been interested in the concept and asked if they could develop it further. Both companies had been direct competitors, but nevertheless Enzo agreed. A sign of respect for the P5 and his competitor. Pininfarina created a new design, and this time it was built on the chassis of the Alfa Romeo 33 Stradale. Beside this, the 33/2 looked like the P5's twin. Nevertheless, also with Alfa the concept had no bright future, as another 33 concept car should determine the company's future lines: the Carabo implemented the typical Italian wedge design.

From left to right, photo with friendly permission by the Alfa Romeo Historic Museum:
- 1969: Alfa Romeo 33/2 Coupe Speciale, design by Pininfarina (Leonardo Fioravanti)
- 1969: Alfa Romeo 33 Iguana, 2.0L, V8, 230hp @ 8000rpm, 260km/h, 700kg, design by Italdesign (Franco Scaglione, Giorgetto Giugiaro)
- 1996: Alfa Romeo Nuvola, 2.5L, V6, 300hp @ 6000rpm, 280km/h, design by Alfa Romeo Centro Stile

BUSINESS PHILOSOPHY ACCORDING TO ENZO FERRARI

From left to right, photo with friendly permission by the Alfa Romeo Historic Museum:
- 1968: Alfa Romeo Carabo, 2.0L, V8, 230hp @ 8800rpm, 1000kg, design by Bertone (Marcello Gandini)
- 1969: Alfa Romeo 33 Iguana, 2.0L, V8, 230hp @ 8000rpm, 260km/h, 700kg, design by Italdesign (Franco Scaglione, Giorgetto Giugiaro)
- 1969: Alfa Romeo 33/2 Coupe Speciale, design by Pininfarina (Leonardo Fioravanti)
- 1914: A.L.F.A. 40-60 HP Aerodinamica, 6.0L, Straight 4, 70hp @ 2400rpm, 139km/h, design by Carrozzeria Castagna (Giuseppe Merosi)

Another one of the spectacular Ferrari prototypes was the 512 S Pininfarina from 1969. As it had been typical for the end of the 60s and the beginning of the 70s in Italy, the design is practically a wedge. Its futuristic design not included any doors, instead the whole cockpit opened. Technically it was more conservative, as it based on the 512 racing car. One year later Pininfarina still went a step further and presented the Modulo, a futuristic and geometric interpretation of the 512. As in its earlier study, also this time Pininfarina gave its creation no traditional doors, but an opening roof, what is clearly the best solution for a car, which is only 93,5 cm high. The Modulo was completely different from everything that people had seen on the streets before, looking less than car and more than a spaceship.[187] Exactly this was designer Paolo Martin's vision as he first thought of this

---

[187] Schleuning, Sarah / Gross, Ken (2014): "Dream Cars"

concept, it had to be *"violent, unique, inimitable and conceptually different."* [188] It would had fitted perfectly in Stanley Kubrick's movie "2001: A Space Odyssey"[189], which its shape and white color (Even if the car was originally painted in black, it got better known in its later white version). Nevertheless Paolo stated that he did not saw a science fiction movie the night before he drafted the Modulo. As such show cars, even more than the production models, represented actual fashion and further were not bounded to functionality, the results sometimes were a fascinating mixture between modern design and art. Especially several decades later they turned into pure art, so that was is not surprising that the Ferrari Modulo was presented 2014 in Atlanta's High Museum of Art, standing right beside the not less artistic Lancia Stratos Zero.

1970: Ferrari 512 Modulo, 5.0, V12, 557hp, 900kg, design by Pininfarina (Paolo Martin). Photo with friendly permission from Paolo Martin.

Design critic Paolo Tumminelli resumed this inside his report on the 512 M: *"Paolo Martin has not made a car for Pininfarina but made a monument!"* Very true, as vision and concept had been by the designer, who later approached his employer Pininfarina, with the request to realize it. His direct manager Franco Martiengo on the one hand loved the first sketches, but on the other hand had been afraid to use resources for such a futuristic concept. Pininfarina did show cars, but none of them had been so far away from

---

[188] Martin, Paolo (2017): "Pensieri in tre dimensioni – Martin's cars"

[189] Kubrik, Stanley / Clarke, Arthur C. (1968): "2001: A Space Odyssey"

actual street or race cars as the this one. Despite his doubts, Franco approved to continue with this project. In the next year Paolo had a relapse, as Pininfarina decided against the realization of the Modulo, but instead the less radical 512 S should be presented at the '69 Geneva Motor Show.

1969: Ferrari 512 S Pininfarina, 4.9L, V8, design by Pininfarina (Filippo Sapino)

Luckily for Paolo, the company was lacking an adequate show car for the '70's show, so finally Pininfarina took the risk to receive mixed critics by the press and decided to present the 512 M to the world. A good decision, as the feedback was enthusiastic so that the company presented the car later the same year also in other expositions. Sergio Pininfarina himself complimented Paolo to his successful creation and at the same time excused for delaying the approvals.

Similar to Enzo Ferrari's philosophy that racing drivers should stand in competition, including with their team-mates, also inside the Pininfarina corporation the different designers had to compete with their colleagues to achieve that their projects get approved and budgeted. Nevertheless this happened in an open and positive work atmosphere, comparable to today's creative agencies.

As Paolo Martin was working on the Modulo, Ferrari was already planning to replace the 365 GTB. An opportunity to bring at least parts of the Modulo on public streets. So Paolo did a sketch for the Ferrari BB, which was less radical than the 512 M, but nevertheless its clear lines showed the show car's strong influences. With this, he was ahead of its time and Pininfarina selected again a more conservative approach, which was realized later as the Ferrari 365 GT/4 BB.[190] Nonetheless this setback, Paolo kept the Modulo alive and even designed with the Enzo Modulo II a potential actual version of the original proposal. This fictive car from 2010 based on alternative design for the original '67 Modulo and been rendered to fit on the platform of Ferrari Enzo.

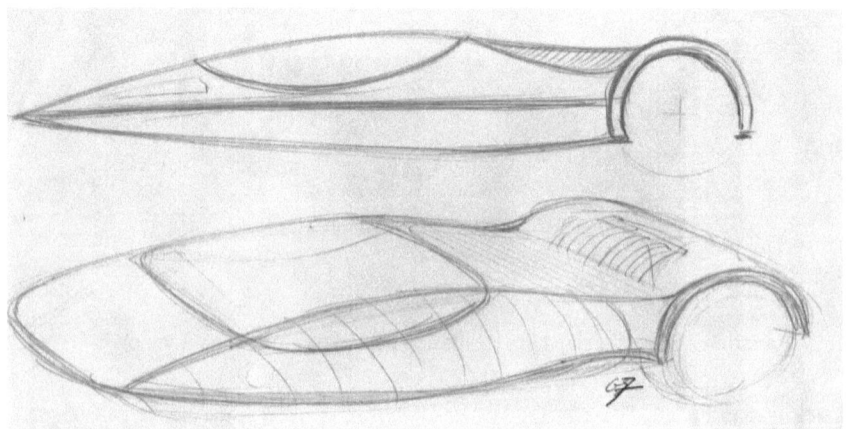

1967: alternative design for the Ferrari 512 Modulo. Drawing with friendly permission from Paolo Martin.

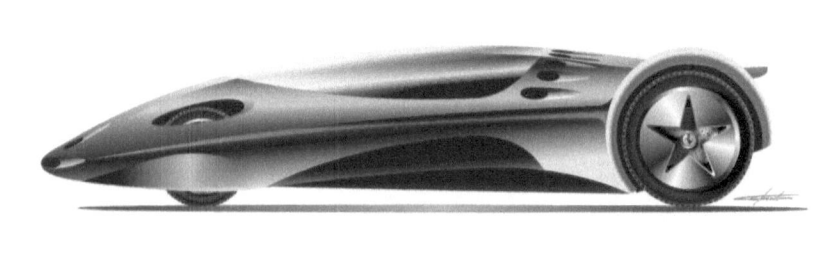

2010: Ferrari 512 Modulo II, design by Paolo Martin, with his friendly permission.

---

[190] Martin, Paolo (2017): "Pensieri in tre dimensioni – Martin's cars"

Even if the Modulo's line not had been used by Ferrari's designs in the 1970s, it influenced later company creations. In opposite to Paolo Martin, Ferrari design director Flavio Manzoni mentioned on different occasions that he likes science fiction, including comic books, 1950's designs of gliding cars, but also arthouse movies as "2001: A Space Odyssey" As a private sideline project he designed a futuristic flying car, inspired by typical UFO creations. Flavio convinced the company's 3D modeler Guillermo Vasseur, who elaborated a 3D model out of his sketches.[191] Even if it started as a hobby, this UFOs directly influenced Flavio's work at Ferrari. As he explained at London's Design Museum to celebrate the special exposition "Ferrari: Under the Skin", the silhouettes of his creations, such as the LaFerrari, the J50 and 488, are shaped based on his UFO-idea, especially the middle-parts.

2016: Ferrari 488 GTB, 3.9L, V8, 670hp @ 8000rpm, 330km/h, 1370kg, design by Ferrari Styling Centre (Flavio Mazoni)

Fostering STEM (science, technology, engineering and mathematics) is the new buzzword to discuss raising competitiveness in science and technology. The idea is to present these topics more vividly at school to motivate more pupils to choose related topics later at university. The Talking Heads became famous for progressive pop music, which they combined with artistic videos. For this, it is no surprise that their former front-man David Byrne argued that *"in order to really succeed in whatever… math and the sciences and engineering and things like that, you have to be able to think outside the box, and do*

---

[191] Phillips, Tom (2015): "Flavio Manzoni designs Ferrari UFO"

creative problem solving... the creative thinking is in the arts."[192] Arts has be included into the concept (now STEAM) and the schools' timetables. With a further step, educators underline the importance of reading. This as books not only transport information, but furthermore inspire the readers. STREAM explains why business leaders should not only read regarding books and articles, but furthermore science fiction. Many of today's developments had been described a long time before, and tomorrow's risks and opportunities also already had been addressed.[193] Flavio's creations are based on his background as an industrial designer, but inspired by books and art. As homage to the 512 Modulo, the original Ferrari UFO, Flavio's virtual model features a red horizontal line, just like the white version of Pablo's creation.

Having these different inspirations available was a big help for Flavio, as he headed the relative young internal Ferrari Styling Centre. Until the LaFerrari the cars had been styled by externals like Pininfarina. After more than 60 years, it was a strategic decision to insource these tasks. Due to Flavio, Pininfarina submitted a design for the LaFerrari, but for the Ferrari company it was no adventurous enough. They wanted to change the general line of their cars; less classic beauty, but more emphasis on the function. Having a holistic approach with all aspects of development in one hand allowed Ferrari more freedom to implement the required technical innovations. The whole group has been under one roof and they had not to consider the artistic views of an outside partner. This was the best decision for the moment. Both companies share a high respect for each other, and changing economic and technical environments will see again Ferrari's designed by Pininfarina.

The Ferrari UFO may look as pure art, but even if not on the short-run, on the long it may become reality. Today, the first companies already started to sell passenger drones. So far, the form followed the function, a situation which the Italian designer Pierpaolo Lazzarini wanted to change. His Hover Coupè concept combined classic Italian design with the actual drone technology.

---

[192] StarTalk Radio (2017): "The Science of Creativity, with David Byrne"

[193] Henz, Patrick (2017): "Access Granted Vol.2 – Tomorrow's Business Ethics"

2017: Hover Coupè, 4 turbo engines, design by Lazzarini Design (Pierpaolo Lazzarini), with friendly permission from Pierpaolo Lazzarini.

The drone is inspired by the Isotta Fraschini Tipo 8, originally introduced in 1919. Isotta Fraschini was founded 1900 in Milan by Cesare Isotta and the brothers Antonio & Oreste Fraschini. Similar to other companies, including Alfa Romeo, Isotta Fraschini also developed aircraft engines, so the potential development of a flying car would be a natural evolution, especially as the turbo engines planned for the Hover Coupè are similar to ones used in commercial planes, only smaller in diameter.

Vincenzo Trucco won 1908 the third Targa Florio with an Isotta Fraschini Type I, 15 years before Alfa Romeo and 40 years before Ferrari. There is one connection between Ferrari and Isotta Fraschini: Aurelio Lampredi. The talented engineer started his career at the Vespa-manufacturer Piaggio to join later Isotta Fraschini. As World War II started, he joined Reggiane to design aircraft engines. After the war, he went in '46 to the Scuderia Ferrari to work on their V12-engines. Shortly after the in '47 he went back to Isotta Fraschini, but already in the next year joined Ferrari again. First to continue developing the V12 "Colombo"-engine and later in '51 to create the four-cylinder "Aurelio"-engine,[194] which had been used in the Ferrari 500 F2 from 1951 to '52.

---

[194] Shippingnet (2016): "JUNE 1 in history, Lampredi the myth of Ferrari, died

1952: Ferrari 500 F2, 2.0L, 165hp @ 7000rpm, 240 km/h, 560kg.

Flying cars look like a complete disruption of the car industry, but if we analyze the long-term relation, it is a continuous process. As Lazzarini Design's claim: *"Think about the future, never forget the past."*[195] Tradition does not mean to stay in the past, but a tradition of progress is based on the company values and fosters a continuous evolution. A focus on transportation includes different disruptive situations, such as the electric or even flying car, but at the end, they are part of the overall vision.

That history & myth are required to sell premium cars also got discovered by the 21th century company Tesla. Officially founded in 2003, it launched its first car, the Tesla Roadster, 2008 to the market, followed 2012 by the luxury sedan Tesla S. The company took its name from the charismatic electricity pioneer Nikola Tesla, who lived from 1856 to 1943. One of his inventions was an AC induction motor. Even if the Tesla Company has no participation of any Tesla-family member, it can appeal to this long tradition of electrical motors and further use the positive image of

---

[195] Lazzarini Design (fetched 30.12.2017)

invention, which Nikola personified. There had been many technical and financial reasons involved, but it can be stated that Tesla had been much more successful than its 2007 founded rival Fisker Automotive (named after its founder Henrik Fisker), what went into bankruptcy in late November 2013.

4.12 The Green Hell

The 1920s had been a decade of economic growth in Germany. The recovery began in the cities and from their spread out over the country, but it took time until it got perceived everywhere. One of the most remote places had been the mountain region of the Eifel. With small farmers, the region was one of the country's poorest. To support the local infrastructure, the German government decided to build a race track in the middle of the mountains. In 1925 began the construction, and around 2 years later, one of the most modern race tracks was ready. A closed circuit, nearly 21 km long and with its countless curves similar to the Italian street race Targa Florio.

The "Green Hell", as the race-track got called by racing-fans, is not just a circuit, it is our today's business reality. To develop new clients and markets, companies send their employees to far-away countries and new cultures; and if they do not do this, the unknown could come to them, for example in the form of a cyber-attack.

Austrian Ferrari driver Niki Lauda won sovereign the '75 Formula One championship with nearly 20 points advantage to Emerson Fittipaldi. On the German Nordschleife track he started that year from the pole position and also let for a long time the race, before a problem with the tire forced him to an additional pit-stop. Even with this lost time, he still could get on the podium for the third position.[196] In the qualification training he was able to set with 6:58,6 and an average speed of 196.4 km/h a record lap.[197]

---

[196] Wikipedia (2014): 1975 Formula One Season

[197] Wikipedia (2014): List of Nordschleife lap times (racing)

1975: Ferrari 312 T, 3.0L, V12, 485hp @ 12520rpm, 575kg, design by Mauro Forghieri

In opposite to 1935 and Nuvolari's famous "impossible victory", 41 years later the track was not one of the most modern constructions anymore, right the opposite, the long track was seen as a relic from another era. Especially the safety standards not developed with the progress of modern Formula One cars. Niki Lauda's nickname was "The Computer"[198], this as he was known for his emotionless ability to analyze a given situation and find the perfect set-up for the car. Besides, he had simple philosophy: *"I accept every time I get in my car there's 20% chance I could die."* Later he clarified that this was not meant as a statistical calculation, but as a general statement.[199] For this, it was no surprise that in a drivers meeting Lauda was the biggest supporter to cancel the rainy '76 Nürburgring race. But at the end the proposal got declined, too strong had been the pressures from organizers & sponsors, and the temptations to win points, money and glory. Even Lauda ignored his own philosophy and accepted a risk which was subjectively higher than 20%. The result was his well-known tragic fire accident, which nearly ended deadly and should mark him for the rest of his life. Even if he returned in record time to the '76 race season, he lost the championship against his rival James Hunt.

---

[198] Fearnley, Paul (2016): "Lauda's comeback"

[199] Barnes, Hannah (2013): Lauda, Hunt and Rush: How deadly was 1970s Formula 1?

The 1976 Formula 1 season (Lauda vs. Hunt)
1) January, 25: Brazil (Lauda 9 points / Hunt 0 points)
2) March, 6: South Africa (Lauda 9 points / Hunt 6 points)
3) March, 38: United States West (Regazzoni 9 points / Lauda 6 points / Hunt 0 points)
4) May, 2: Spain (Hunt 9 points / Lauda 6 points)
5) May, 16: Belgium (Lauda 9 points / Hunt 0 points)
6) May, 30: Monaco (Lauda 9 points / Hunt 0 points)
7) June, 13: Sweden (Scheckter 9 points / Lauda 4 points / Hunt 2 points)
8) July, 4: France (Hunt 9 points / Lauda 0 points)
9) July, 18: Great Britain (Lauda 9 points / Hunt 0 points)
10) August, 1: Germany (Hunt 9 points / Lauda 0 points)
11) August, 15: Austria (Watson 9 points / Hunt 3 points / Lauda 0 points)
12) August, 29: Netherlands (Hunt 9 points / Lauda 0 points)

Getting to know that the Argentinian driver Carlos Reutemann had been hired to replace him and further seeing Hunt winning in the Netherlands, had been a strong motivation for Lauda to return into the cockpit only six weeks after his accident. Even if he was perceived as a computer that particular week-end he was not. The first time back in his Ferrari he was nervous, as he later remembered: *"I had felt insecure and overreacted."* Thanks to his strong character he identified the inner problem and came to the conclusion: *"Don't push yourself under so much pressure, take it easy, drive more slowly. And that's what I did."* He started the Sunday race from the fifth position, but then fell back to the midfield as he could not go keep up with the speed. Only around half time he found back to his normal capabilities and with two fastest lap times still could reach the fourth position. His team mate Clay Regazzoni made the second. From Lauda's point of view, the team should had called him to slow down, so that Lauda would ended up on the third position. This would have decided the championship in favor of the Austrian.[200]

---

[200] Fearnley, Paul (2016): "Lauda's comeback"

13) September, 12: Italy (Peterson 9 points / Lauda 3 points / Hunt 0 points)
14) October, 3: Canada (Hunt 9 points / Lauda 0 points)
15) October, 10: United States East (Hunt 9 points / Lauda 4 points)
16) October, 24: Japan (Andretti 9 points / Hunt 4 points / Lauda 0 points)

The last race in Fuji, Japan started under pouring rain. Also this race weekend saw a lively discussion in the drivers meeting, if under the given weather conditions the race should take place the Sunday or not. At the end the result was the same as earlier that year at the Nürburgring, the race started as scheduled. Lauda again started, but just for a few laps, then he went back to his box and stepped out of the car, as based on his personal philosophy the heavy rain made it too dangerous to drive. He watched the race until the end and saw his rival becoming third, with this overtaking him in the overall ranking and winning the '76 world championship: Hunt 69 points / Lauda 68 points. Just one point stopped him to defend his title. If you take the '76 race results you can easily assume that a healthy Lauda would have won at least 2 points in the Austrian and / or Dutch Grand Prix. The conclusion is that if Lauda would have followed his personal 20%-risk philosophy and skipped the Nürburgring race, most probably he would have won the '76 championship and even more important, avoided his terrible accident.

This example explains the key responsibility for a Compliance department: protection, for the company, but also for each employee. First to conduct a risk assessment together with the internal stakeholders. Here the relevant risks get analyzed and decided how management wants to handle them, including which risk levels the organizations wants to accept. More or less than Lauda's famous 20%?

Different risk strategies are to avoid, reduce or accept them. Doing business always means taking on risks, all participants have to be clear about this. It is management's decision, how much risks you want to take on. You have to be aware of them, to be able to manage them. Of course each stakeholder is responsible to reduce them as low as possible. Compliance is responsible to manage its own risks, this includes protection against renegade employees, who are planning a fraud for personal enrichment, but also to protect employees against themselves, who want the best for the company and get trapped by ethical blindness or at least a regarding limited tunnel vision. Guidelines and tools should support that that the company only takes on the agreed risks. Bypassing such policies means that the company takes on higher risks, as originally agreed.

We have two given variables: "values" and "behavior". Normally the behavior should be motivated and based on one's own values. But this does not automatically have to be the case. The strength of the values (and derived attitudes) determinates how easy or difficult behavior can be distracted from the values, for example through temptations or urgent needs. Values and attitudes are learnt in the different stages of socialization.

As values and attitudes normally are a part of the actual culture, these values get regularly fostered by surrounding. As the person understands his or her own culture, values and attitudes are aligned with the culture. This changes if the company sends the employee to a different culture, like a foreign country. Due to missing cultural understanding, the employee is not receiving anymore the positive signals, or worse can interpret the new signals as that his attitudes are not wanted in the new surroundings. Now it depends on the strength of the person's values and attitudes, if the he or she changes behavior or not.

Niki Lauda had the idea not to take on a risk-level higher than 20%. We can assume that this attitude got fostered by his family and friends. In the race weekend he was taken out of this circle of trust, but surrounded by his competitors. In this atmosphere he was not able anymore to behave according his own values and ignored his own rule. For a company ignoring its own rules of conduct can mean deviations against health & safety and compliance, accepting to high financial risks or ignoring the needs of the employees. As Lauda's accident, such a deviation can jeopardize the health of the company until its failure, as bankruptcy.

After his accident Niki Lauda worked through an intense and personalized physical training program to come back to the races.[201] He not only used this to get back into his sports, he kept it up to have equilibrium between mental and physical strengths. With this he established a new prototype of racing driver; a fit sportsman in opposite to the earlier gentlemen-driver or party-king.

If we compare this to business, we can say that the natural speed of a racing driver is similar to the employee's values & attitudes and the physical training to business trainings & workshops. Values & trainings together are the best protection if we send our employees on the business race-track! We can take Lauda's approach and implement regular trainings for our employees.

The company has two opportunities to reduce the possible wrong-doing and with this, protect the employee against him- or her-self:

- Foster values: Training can be explaining what is the desired behavior, but it can go further than that and try to foster the values. For this it is imperative to take the employee serious and switch from a one way communication to two day discussions. This way the communication not limits it-self of what is to do and what is forbidden, but trainees understand the why behind the rules. The individual can make the connection how the desired behavior is not just a benefit for the company, but also for the society ("cost of corruption") and him- or her-self.

- Strengthens intercultural-knowledge. Each race-track is different and includes new risks and temptations. The same with business sectors and geographic regions, it is required to get experience. Learning-by-doing is the easiest way to understand action and result, but as the output maybe be significant for the company, the costs for try-and-error are in most situations too high. For this a company can create special workshops, where employees get prepared for new situations. This is similar to a racing driver, who

---

[201] United Press International (1985): "Niki Lauda Closes In on Formula One Mark"

prepares himself with a simulator or videogame for the next race.[202] As a the player can start again if he crashed the car in the game, employees can try out different behaviors in a role-play or discuss different cases with the colleagues.

The usage of computers today go even further, "Virtual Heritage" not only wants to virtually preserve ancient sites, but also to resurrect lost archeological treasures. This idea is applicable for historic cars and race-tracks. "Gran Turismo 6" not only features actual Ferrari cars, as the 485 Italia or the California, but also let the player drive historic automobiles as the 1967 330 P4 or the '71 Dino 246 GT. Cars, which in many cases do not exist anymore in the complete original versions or got completely lost over the time. The same is possible for race-tracks, as it is virtual possible to recreate the original tracks, which based on safety requirements had to be changed over the decades. A fascinating possibility for today's drivers to understand how yesterday's cars handled and how different the tracks had been.

As Nicola Larini came 1993 to the Nürburgring Nordschleife, he was in the complete opposite situation as Tazio Nuvolari 58 years earlier. Alfa Romeo built the 155 V6 TI tailor-made to the rules and regulations of the German Touring Car-Championship (in German DTM for Deutsche Tourenwagen Meisterschaft) and had the technically best and fastest car in the field. They professionally prepared their entrance into the championship, testing their cars already one year earlier on the different German race-tracks and deployed international experienced drivers as Larini, who was the same year also a test-driver for the Ferrari Formula 1-team.

---

[202] Dutton, Fred (2012): "F1 driver uses videogame for practice"

1993: Alfa Romeo 155 V6 TI, 2.5L, V6, 420hp @ 11500rpm, 1100kg, design by I.DE.A Institute (Ercole Spada)

In opposite to its competitor from Mercedes Benz, the 190E 2.5-16 Evo2, the 155 had all wheel drive, as the car's street version as front-wheel-drive was not-efficient for the race usage. Thanks to this the Alfa team was dominating the first two races on the Belgian Zolder-track, as the whole day saw heavy rains. But already the second race week-end on the dry Hockenheimring made it clear that the Alfa 155 was the car to beat that year. In June Larini came with a comfortable lead in the championship to the Nürburgring Nordschleife. As the technical superiority was obvious, he wanted to demonstrate that he is not just leading because of the car, but also his personal driving skills. Clearly he wanted to repeat the success of his idol Nuvolari. Also thanks to his preparation he won both races in the "green hell", including a fastest lap of 8.47,71 minutes, nearly 2 minutes faster than Nuvolari at his famous victory.

DTM Season 1993[203]

- April 4: Zolder (winner first race: Larini / winner second race: Larini)
- April 18: Hockenheimring (winner first race: Schneider, 9th: Larini / winner second race: Schneider, 2nd: Larini)
- May 5: Nürburgring (winner first race: Larini / winner second race: Ludwig, 16th: Larini)
- May 16: Wunstorf (winner first race: Larini / winner second race:

---

[203] DTM.com (fetched 06.01.2015): "Die DTM-Saison 1993"

Thiim, 15th: Larini)
- June 10: Nürburgring Nordschleife (winner first race: Larini / winner second race: Larini)
- June 27: Norisring (winner first race: Larini / winner second race: Larini)
- July 18: Donington (winner first race: Danner, 3th Larini / winner second race: Larini)
- August 8: Diepholz (winner first race: Asch, 10th: Larini / winner second race: Larini)
- August 29: Singen (winner first race: Larini / winner second race: Schneider, 2nd: Larini)
- September 12: Avus (winner first race: Asch, 6th: Larini / winner second race: Asch, 3th: Larini)
- September 19: Hockenheimring (winner first race: Nannini, 4th: Larini / winner second race: Nannini, 19th: Larini)

In opposite to Lauda in the 70s, Larini had one electronically helper, as '93 DTM cars featured detailed telemetry. In all training sessions and races the cars had been wireless connected with the computers of their teams. Mechanics and managers got real-time information regarding engine, brakes, accelerations, torque, temperatures, times, etc. In that year the track was clearly out of date and shifted modern race drivers out of their comfort-zone into a complete unknown environment. If they should get any problem, they could be like 10 minutes or 20 kilometers away from their colleagues in the pits, a real nightmare in green. A comparable situation for some company employees, as in our globalized work we send them to far-away countries and unknown cultures. As the individual has no experience in this new environment, there is a risk of a "loss of control"-effect (chapter 2.3) and with this danger that the employee does something what he or she would never do in the known home environment. Telemetry helps the team to understand how the car behaves on the track, gives this important information back to the driver and eventually to change the setup at the next pit stop. It supports the driver to stay on track with these two effects:[204]

---

[204] PM Magazin (fetched 06.01.2014): "Telemetrie: Der 'gläserne Rennfahrer' verstrickt in 3.700 Meter Kabel"

- With the permanent contact the distance is perceived smaller and the driver stays inside the team, in opposite of being completely alone on his lap.

- The information makes his actions transparent. As he would be physically with his colleagues, all behaviors are visible. There is no opportunity to ignore unidentified the guidelines from his manager and crew.

Wireless computing and virtual networks (including Internet of Things) have the same effect as telemetry. The employee can work from the hotel or the local cafe, as WiFi is not limited to Starbuck's anymore; this ensures the connection with the colleagues back in office, but also any other location. On the other hand, the employee has to comply with the same obligations, regarding the usage of company laptop, smartphone or tablet, as the colleagues inside the physical office. A combination of these devices ensure that the individual is always connected, even if sent to a completely unknown place as the "green hell". As 24 hour connection is still not possible in all regions, companies may like to create special travel documents, cards and hotlines. Equipped like that the employee feels less far-away and less tempted to give up the learnt value-based behavior. If something is not working out as planned, there always can be contacted the specialists at home and it is not necessary to take own decisions based on limited information. For this, training, documentation and devices are supporting the employee's values & attitudes, or in other words: natural speed has to be supported by trainings, simulations and telemetry!

With this preparation, the racing driver should be able to avoid getting a penalty communicated through the radio or even see the black flag, which indicates his or her disqualification. In-between the trainings sessions, the drivers get informed about the possible consequences; for the case an employee overstepped a limit, the company has to ensure that the required flags get shown and consequences applied. If not, employees learn that there are rules in places, but also that they could get riskless breached.

Employees often justified their deviations to guidelines and policies with that it was in the best interest of the company. But if you analyze the cases, it was in their personal interest. If they had no financial gain, at least they had the benefit to avoid internal bureaucracy or the need to for superior's approval. That way they made their own life easier, what they perceived as increase of efficiency, but ignoring that this meant that the company is taking on higher internal and external risks. Risk levels which Company management not wanted to take, and especially to limit such, implemented the regarding guidelines. As this relation is not always transparent to the employee, it explains why a company has to protect the employee against him- or her-self.

Lauda's accident in 1976 was the beginning of the end of his good relationship with Enzo Ferrari, as according to his opinion, Lauda returned too early into the cockpit and with this jeopardized the winning of the team championship. Even with Lauda's accident, the championship for the team got won and the next season should see Lauda's second world championship title, including again the constructor's title for the team. Nevertheless he left the Scuderia at the end of '77 to start in the next season for Brabham Alfa Romeo. In today's business reality an employee who deviated knowingly internal guidelines or external laws would most probably face a similar situation, as for general management the sustainability of the company is more relevant than one single employee or even a small group. Even if they perceived to have done this for the company's best interesting, on the other hand, the company would turn against these renegade employees. A required behavior by an organization to protect itself.

Larini's constant positive results kept him the seat in the Alfa 155 TI for the complete 4 years the team started in the DTM and beyond, as Alfa Romeo deployed later the 156 in different European touring car championships. In parallel he continued his work as Ferrari Formula 1 test driver and had '94 the opportunity to substitute the injured Jean Alesi in two of the championship races. Later, he used his connections to start for the Sauber F1 Team in the '97-season. This as the Swiss team started to use Ferrari client engines.

1994: Ferrari 412 T1, 3.5L, V12, 750hp @ 15,300rpm, design by John Barnard, Gustav Brunner

4.13 *"The horse doesn't push the cart, it pulls it."*

The 1976 and '77 Formula One seasons saw an extra-ordinary car, the Tyrell B34. The first and last six-wheels car that should win a Formula One grand-prix. The car had three axles, two in the front with relative small wheels and one at the back with normal sized wheels. Apart from the victory at the '76 Swedish Grand Prix, overall success stayed quite limited. Nevertheless, different teams experimented with the idea to have more than just four wheels. One of them Ferrari. In opposite to the Tyrell, the Scuderia not used three axles, but stayed with the normal two, just putting four wheels on the back axle.

1977: Ferrari 312 T6, 3.0L, Flat 12, 500hp @ 12,200rpm, design by Mauro Forghieri

In fact not a complete new idea, as Ferrari used this already in 1933 and the following years for hill climb races, where the Ferrari-team put four wheels on the back-axle of the Alfa Romeo P3.

1935: Alfa Romeo P3, 3.2L (German Grand Prix), Straight 8, 330hp, design by Jano Vittorio

In 1977 the idea stayed limited to testing. With the four tires at the back, the car was wider than the regulations allowed. Besides, the results had not been that astonishing that the team requested a change of regulations. The Ferrari 312 T6 got tested by both pilots, Niki Lauda and Carlos Reutemann.[205]

Getting to learning from competitors, Enzo Ferrari was always quite stubborn and tried to go his own way as long as possible. *"The horse doesn't push the cart, it pulls it."* With this quote Enzo wanted to explain that the engine had to be in the front of car and not in the middle as many of the competitor's cars at the end of the 50's.

---

[205] Stefan_ (fetched 10.01.2015): "Built but unraced Formula 1 cars"

1958: Ferrari Dino 246, 2.4L, V6, 280hp @ 8500rpm, design by Vittorio Jano, Carlo Chiti

Nevertheless in 1958, Ferrari driver Mike Hawthorn still could decide the Formula One World Championship for himself, but the constructor's title already went to the British Vanwall team. One year later the front-engine the Scuderia was out of chances. The best Ferrari driver became Phil Hill with a fourth position in the overall standings and in the constructor's championship it became again a second place. 1960 became worse, Hill as best Ferrari driver on the fifth position and the team on the third one. Now Enzo understood the requirements to get successful again, so the end of the season already saw a mid-engine car, the 246 P F1. The gained experience got included in the '61 Ferrari 156 F1, which should bring the driver's and constructor's title back to Maranello.

Enzo's stubbornness was against his normal tendency to follow the Italian philosopher Machiavelli, as he advised: *"A prudent man should always follow in the path trodden by great men and imitate those who are most excellent, so that if he does not attain to their greatness, at any rate he will get some tinge of it."*[206]

In 1978, with his change from the Scuderia to the Brabham Alfa Romeo team, Lauda got involved with another car that was constructed on the limit of Formula One rules, the BT46, also known as the "fan car".

---

[206] Machiavelli, Niccolo (ca. 1543): "The Prince"

1978: Brabham Alfa Romeo BT46, 3.0L, Flat 12, 520hp @ 12000rpm, design by Gordon Murray

1978: Brabham Alfa Romeo BT46, 3.0L, Flat 12, 520hp @ 12000rpm, design by Gordon Murray

With a second place in Argentina and a third in Brazil, the Brabham Alfa Romeo team had a good start into the 1978 Formula One Championship. But unfortunately suffered technical problems in the next two races. The team had been aware that their car in general is competitive, but still with a small gap to the fastest, including a problem with its reliability. A challenging situation, as they had to focus on two problems on the same time. Then in the middle of season, at the Swedish Grand Prix, the car featured a fan at the back of the engine, officially to increase the cooling, but with the favorable side effect to generate relevant levels of downforce to create superior ground effects and acceleration. Thanks to this, Lauda could win the first Grand Prix of the season. Already before the Sunday race, the officials received the first protests by the competitors. To avoid later disqualifications, the team decided not to use this technology beyond that week-end. Due to the withdrawal, it never came to an official investigation and decision if the technology was indeed against the rules or not.[207]

Engineers, as all employees, are creative people if it comes to the need to discover the limits of laws and guidelines. Regarding complying with technical specifications, this is a desired behavior, as even small technical changes can have a big impact on costs and performance. This is in opposite to company values and codes of conducts. As even in the best phrased documents you can find a potential loophole, it is imperative that management makes it clear that the company expects complying in words and spirit of the guideline. If such clear guidance is missing, employees have to assume what is expected from them. In doing so, they are exposed to different business and social pressures and may repeat successful behavior regarding technical specifications and mirror that for ethical and legal topics. The result is that identified loopholes and grey areas get exploited. With this, the employees start to work against the company's vision and jeopardizes it's sustainability strategy, as with going to the limits and beyond, legal safety gets lost.

4.14 White Elephants

The North American Racing Team (NART) was more than just a private Ferrari racing team, as it was owned by Luigi Chinetti. An Italo-American race driver and later owner of the first Ferrari dealership in the US. Due to this status, NART could be seen as the official US racing team, participating in Daytona and the Panamericana, but also in the traditional European races.

---

[207] Orosz, Peter (2010): "Brabham BT46B Fan Car: Making Lemonade from Lemons"

In 1965 NART received the 330 P2. With this prototype race car they could win the 1000 km of Monza and the Nürburgring, as also the Targa Florio. One year later they still used these cars, including one with an updated engine and a new bodywork by Piero Drogo. The 365 P2, a white long-tail race car, nicknamed "White Elephant".[208]

1966: Ferrari 365 P2 "White Elephant", 4.4L, V12, design by Piero Drogo

In business life, a "white elephant" is defined as a project, which most likely will create a negative profit. This based on potential high costs and / or risks.[209]

Most companies define "sustainability" to use natural resources with care, so that they continue to exist for tomorrow's generations. Further its neighbors are important, as good citizens it is imperative to support the community. This is not limited to found schools or plant trees, but includes that the company is not just today working efficiently, but does the same tomorrow and beyond. With this it can continue to support the community, be a reliable source for taxes and stay available to offer jobs for local people.

---

[208] Supercars.net (fetched 17.03.2015): "1966 Ferrari 365 P2 Spyder"

[209] Investiopedia (fetched 16.03.2015): "White Elephant"

A long-term strategy based on the company's vision and values is required! But this alone is not sufficient to ensure the future results. Guidelines and processes have to be implemented, if not it would be a pure accident to reach the company's targets. Surely it is possible to find short-cuts and win projects with ignoring laws and regulations. But most of the times, there are just victories on the short run. Maybe not at once, but years later such deviations get discovered. The results are high fines, loss of reputation and can even include black-listing. Not to talk that the cost of corruption are paid by all. Corruption not only brings the company down, but with it the local community.

A company needs the will to accomplish its vision, just as Vincent van Gogh said it once: *"Great things are not something accidental, but must be certainly be willed."* For this all employees have to walk in the same direction to not reach this goal. Compliance ensures that the company's vision is lived and respected; it is the will to create great things together.

This leads to a formula:

$$\text{Values} + \text{Strategy} + \text{Compliance} = \text{Sustainability}$$

This is valid in a theoretical environment, where we have complete transparency. In reality our information is incomplete, in private and business life surprises are always to be expected. For this we need to be prepared for the unprepared. Our strategy must be able to handle unforeseen opportunities. The same is valid for an ethics & compliance program, as processes, guidelines and IT tools have to give the employee flexibility to answer the sudden opportunities of the market. This to avoid the temptation that employees try to bypass such internal processes. Further it is an important task of the company to prepare its employees to such situations. Several pressures are working together:

- Most employees (as sales department) have ambitious annual targets. A surprisingly appearing opportunity often seems to be the only possibility to reach them.

- People assume that such opportunities could disappear as fast as they appeared. For this, sudden opportunities tend people to act fast and bypass their normal decision making process.

- Depending on a person's character, employees overestimate their possibility to control a scenario. This is especially true for "success seekers", they tend to overestimate their own abilities and underestimate the risks of the situation. For the "failure avoiders" it is the other way around. Thanks to self-selection the first group of people will try to get more risky tasks with the goal that they can prove them-selves and advance faster in their career. It is them which apply to positions in sales or become a race driver. In sudden and new projects they see the opportunity, but not the risk.

Compliance has to be aware of such psychological effects, as they can lead to ethical blindness. Vincent van Gogh himself was aware of this risk: *"I put my heart and soul into my work, and have lost my mind in the process."*

But Counter measures can be implemented, as training & workshops, but also a strong position of the Compliance Officer is required, who has to be a trusted business adviser. White elephants are a relevant risk factor. A company may wrongly calculate the business risks, as costs are higher than expected, the company's experience and products are not adequate or also the potential attractive project got won with bribery. This leads us to an updated formula:

Values (fixed) + Strategy (flexibly) + Compliance (flexible) = Sustainability

To offer the required flexibility and with this value for the business, Compliance cannot limit itself to approve or not. Instead, if something is not possible, it has to be analyzed, if the same result can be reached via a different route. Most employees do not want to do something forbidden, but maybe not had been aware of the risks and specific regulations. Here the Compliance tasks are to adapt the planned actions, so that they comply with all laws and regulations. A good example is the mixture between GPS and social network: "Waze". This App, available for Android and iPhone, tells the user the quickest way from point A to B, this is not always the shortest way, but also traffic and even police controls, construction sites or accidents play a role. Just as the app, the Compliance Officer guides the way through the unknown territory and keeping the employee on the legal paths; educating about legal realities on the map.

Back to the Ferrari 365 P2. Was it a white elephant for the company? From 1960 to '65 the Scuderia won each year the 24 Hours of Le Mans. In this last year, even the whole podium was reserved for the Ferrari drivers. This result was also based on the fact the Ferrari's strongest competitor the Ford GT 40 still lacked reliability. But race-luck changed in '66. The GT 40 finally lasted the 24 hours and the Ferraris had to give up with accident (as the cars of the Scuderia) or technical problems, as the as NART's "White Elephant". One year later, the car came back to Le Mans, but this time featuring a rear wing. Already in the '66 version the car was innovative, as Drogo designed a long tail race car especially for Le Mans and its long straights. Later to be copied by Alfa Romeo, Ferrari, Porsche and others. The same for '67, as the car introduced the rear wing to endurance races. The race-luck was still not with the car, as it had to retire after 30 laps. Just on the results this 365 P2 was a real white elephant. But on the long run, it was an important step of the evolution, and influenced later successful designs.

1970: Ferrari 512S, 5.0L, V12, 550hp @ 8000rpm, 340km/h, 840kg

4.15 Fiorano

Ferrari constructed in 1972 a private 3km race-track in Maranello, not far away from its plant, and directly besides Enzo's private home. With this they gained the possibility to test their street and race cars, potential new race drivers and further, to give their clients a place to use their products under race conditions.

An important step as a race not starts with the main event or the qualifications, but with the original development of the car and continuous improvement, meaning that before and after the race week-ends, the cars are running on the Fiorano test-track. Imperative for cars and also relevant for business processes. As these processes are based on the company's core values and its founder's vision, it is mandatory that they work on the highest levels. Internal controls have to test if the processes are effective, but on top of this, it has to be regularly confirmed that these controls are really testing the parts, where they are aimed on. As the business environment is changing, so are processes and controls.

In Carlo Carlei 2003's TV-series "Enzo Ferrari", a biography, we can see Il Commendatore standing at the Fiorano track with his son Piero. In his hand is a stop watch, controlling the lap times of new race drivers. If he decided that some of them had potential to join the Scuderia, he told his son to give this candidate as information the lap-time. Not the correct one, but a version with one second on top.[210] This to ensure that the driver keeps the respect for car and track, but also to keep him motivated to push himself faster to the limit.

This can be transferred again to business controls. Such constructs are designed for the normal business use, but if necessary, have to identify potential criminal power. As such cases are luckily not part of the daily reality, it is advisable to push the implemented controls from time to time. One person, or also a group, can take the role of the "renegade employee". An intelligent person, who wants to commit a fraud, to bypass internal processes and related controls. Such a successful stress test reduces the risk of potential frauds, which could jeopardize the sustainability of the business. If the test results deliver the insight that the company's controls are vulnerable, the company can learn from this and create processes controls.

---

[210] Carlei, Carlo (2003): "Enzo Ferrari"

As test track Fiorano is relevant thanks to its curves. To connect two points, a straight is the fastest option, but this does not mean that it is also always the best idea. As all Ferrari drivers can confirm, the most attractive connection between A and B is the curve. Here driver and car both get challenged and due to this, both collect experiences. The human directly and the machine via the data. In opposite to this, drivers, as for example Michael Schumacher, stated that the high speed straights are often boring. Even if the car goes faster than 300 km/h, the driver does not have to concentrate 100%, but may take seconds to look at the spectators or think about complete other topics. Curves require full concentration, and these are the areas where drivers can grow. For this, famous curves get named after legendary drivers, as the "Ascari Variante" (Monza) or the "Senna S" (Interlagos).

Companies can take this idea and apply it for their employees. Job-enlargement pushes the individual outside its monotone tasks and create a more challenging work-life. The boundaries between work-and leisure-time are blurring, so for a person are not only the number of working hours relevant, but also to include them into the employee's quality time. Companies are interested that their employees not always execute their tasks as fast as possible, but sometime go an extra mile, leaving the highway and take the curvy road through the mountains.

4.16 Diversity as Key to Success

Most people associate "Testa Rossa" with the 1958 models or the later '84 street car. Both have in common that they are powered by a twelve cylinder engine. As we know, Enzo Ferrari's favorite solution: *"I married the 12 cylinder engine and I never divorced it."* Less known is that the famous '58 car was not the one, which started the tradition of the red painted valve covers, but it's forefather from 1956, the Ferrari 500 TR. Interesting about this vehicle, it only featured a four cylinder engine.

Even if Enzo had a preference for the classic twelve cylinder engine, he was also let by objectives, which meant winning races. As smaller engines meant less weight, they became interesting for motorsports, especially Formula 2 what replaced temporary Formula 1 racing from '52 to '54. The four cylinder engine debuted in 1952 and Alberto Ascari took it to win the F2 World Championship. Nevertheless the motor never reached the fame of the traditional twelve cylinder engine, nor had its full orchestral sound, it played an important part of the company's success story, as it started the legend of the Testa Rossa vehicles and with this supported to create the company's myth.

1956: Ferrari 500 TR, 2.0L Straight 4, 180 HP @ 7000rpm, design by Scaglietti

As it was a capable race car, drivers took it to races all around the world. One of them was Anna Maria Peduzzi, one of Ferrari's first female factory drivers. Earlier in 1934 she had her first mayor race, the Mille Miglia together with her husband, Gianfranco Comotti, with an Alfa Romeo 6C of the newly formed Scuderia Ferrari. The outbreak of the Second World War and her Polio infection stopped her race appearances until she returned in '52. Four years later she went back to the Scuderia Ferrari and raced that year with the 500 TR. Together with her team-mate Gilberte Thirion they won the 2.0L class of the Paris 1000km, but mostly she stayed inside her home country Italy to participate at the different local events, like the Mille Miglia or the Targa Florio. As most of the Ferrari factory drivers, she owned the car and used it until '59. All her post-war career had been affected by the consequences of her Polio infection, so she not only had to fight her competitors on the track, but also her limitations, as missing muscle power, but nonetheless she was talented and reached several favorable results.

Anna Maria, or "Marocchina" (Italian for "Little Moroccan Girl", due to her dark skin), was not the only woman important for Ferrari. Enzo's first wife Laura Dominica Garello Ferrari, was strongly involved into the administrative part of the company. This was not appreciated by the all, so that it came in 1961 to the situation that leading employees, including sales director Cirolamo Gardini and chief engineer Carlo Chiti gave an ultimatum to Enzo that if Laura would not leave, they would do. This was not acceptable for Enzo, so he separated the rebellious employees from the company.[211]

At the end of the 1950's Enzo recognized that his cars mostly got bought by male clients and that their wives' often started to get envy, as their husband spent so much time with the elegant vehicles. Even if the husband at the end signed the sales contract, there had been an earlier phase inside the decision making process, where the wife, family and friends played a relevant role. The car had to compete against other possible investments, as the cars from other companies, or also summer houses, yachts, luxury holidays, etc.

For this it would be beneficial for Ferrari, if products and marketing are not only attractive for the buyer itself (husband), but also the other participants of the decision making process (wife). To achieve this, the Ferrari cars should get more attractive for the female target-group. Fiamma Breschi received the task to ensure this. She suggested the engineers to implement small changes to the vehicles so that they get more appealing to women. As Fiamma was part of his "circle of trust", Enzo began to send her to different races, as he in person preferred to stay in Maranello. Her mission was to report him later about the race week-end and the different incidents. Many times, he received different points of view, from her and the team manager.[212]

---

[211] H-G, Rachel (2010): "Anna Maria Peduzzi"

[212] Williams, Richard (2004): "Mistress of the maestro of Maranello"

Since the beginning of the 50's there had been two types of Ferrari street cars; the ones, which could be used in races and the ones, which are only meant to be driven and enjoyed. Women became more and more a relevant part of the target group, not only that they allowed their husbands to spend so much time and money on the car. Some of them drove the cars herselves, some few as race drivers, but most others only to enjoy the luxury vehicle and to be seen with it.

After the Danish driver Christina Nielson and her co-driver Alessandro Balzan won in 2016 and '17 the GTD class of the US American IMSA championship, Ferrari's partner Lego used the opportunity to market in early 2018 a 179 pieces set of their Ferrari 488 GT3, including a figure of the female driver. After Lego already published successfully the "Women of NASA" set the year before, another product aiming mainly at girls to fascinate them for former "boy topics".

4.17 The diversified Portfolio

Today Ferrari seems to be indissoluble connected to Formula One. More than 60 years ago in 1950 this was completely different. With the 196 Inter the still young company won the prestigious Mille Miglia. The 375 F1 reached a first victory against the "unbeatable" Alfa Romeo 159 Alfetta and further the 166 participated in the Formula Two Championship.

Started in 1948, in opposite to the F1 Championship, the F2 tournament was limited to the European continent, what combined racing tradition with controllable costs. For this the F2 was often a necessary step for young drivers to present their selves in front of the responsible F1 teams. One of these young Ferrari 166 drivers had been in 1948 the Argentinian talent Juan Manual Fangio.[213]

---

[213] Acerbi, Leonardo (2015): "Ferrari – all the cars"

1950: Ferrari 166 F2, 2.0L, V12, 155hp @ 7000rpm, 235km/h, 550kg.

Having a diversified portfolio can reduce the company risk, as even if one product line is struggling for the moment, others may be going strong. Success factors for such a strategy are:

- Economics of Scope: The products are different, but they have technical similarity; the products themselves, the production or logistics. Thanks to this, development and production costs get reduced. The company has an advantage against competitors, which just can offer one product. For example the Ferrari 166 F2 used as based the engine of 166 sister-models, just with an increased output thanks to different details.

- Compatibility with Core Strengths: At end of the 1960's, Ferrari wanted to enter another racing series, the popular Canadian-American Challenge Cup, or short "Can-Am". The series existed from 1966 to '74 and based on the FIA Group 7-rules, meant the engineers had very few restrictions. Over the time this let to spectacular light race cars with big wings and 1000HP engines. Thanks to the show, the series became popular with the North American fans. It was Luigi Chinetti, who convinced Ferrari to enter.[214] The company identified synergies with the Ferrari P4 and used this base to develop the 350 Can-Am. The biggest problem

---

[214] Lehbrink, Harmut / Schlegelmilch, Rainer (1995): "Ferrari"

had been the guidelines, which preferred big engines. Ferrari changed the motor from 4.0 to 4.2L, but this resulted still as a too small step to ensure competiveness.[215] The third and last try to successfully participate in the series had been the 715 Can-Am. Again not a complete new development, but this time based on the 512M. Especially for this prototype, Ferrari developed a 6,9L engine with 680HP. The result had been a promising victory in Imola at the European Inter series. Even if the car was now more competitive than its predecessors, more than a fourth position in the Can-Am series was not possible for Michael Andretti as driver. After the '72 season, Ferrari left the series. Only two years later, rising costs and the oil-crises caused an early end for the series. The main obstacle why Ferrari never had a 100% competitive car for the series had been that the company identified the Can-Am as attractive to participate and get positive attention on the important North American market, but even with the existing synergy effects never dedicated enough resources for the development and maintenance of car and team. One reason for this behavior was the company's core vision to sell street car versions on their successful race cars.[216] In '71 the company had several models in its portfolio, as the Dino 246 GT, 365 GT 2+2, 365 GTC/3 and 365 GTB/4 Daytona. None of these products had a 6.9L engine, nor the company planned to produce such a car. This explained why the first Can-Am cars used a smaller engine than their competitors and even the 712 never received the required internal attention. An important lesson for company strategists to always keep the company's core vision in mind, as violating it with additional portfolios in most cases will not lead to a positive result. This does, of course, not mean that a company can never change, but if this is planned, a change of culture must ensure that all levels of employees understand and support the new company vision.

---

[215] Nick D (2016): "1967 Ferrari 350 Can-Am"

[216] Melissen, Wouter (2005): "Ferrari 712 Can-Am"

1971: Ferrari 712 Can-Am: 6.9L, V12, 680HP @ 7000rpm

- Image Transfer: The potential customer perceives a relation between the different products. Due to this, a positive image of a known product can be transferred to a still unknown one. Since the beginning Ferrari marketed their success in motor sports to sell their street cars. This was necessary as these sales had to finance, on the other hand, the racing team again.

With the time products typically get more advanced and complex. The same parts cannot get used anymore in different products, so that the advantage of the economics of scope gets lost and the company gets a problem that they have to finance the development of different solutions. Due to this, after an economic trend to diversify the portfolio, the 90s saw the counter trend to focus on the company's core competency.

BUSINESS PHILOSOPHY ACCORDING TO ENZO FERRARI

5 PARTNERSHIPS

5.1) *"I don't sell cars; I sell engines. The cars I throw in for free since something has to hold the engines in."*
5.2) *"My cars have to be beautiful"*
5.3) A Joint-Venture
5.4) *"My loyalty to Shell springs from my experience with automobiles."*
5.5) *"I don't smoke and neither do my cars."*
5.6) *"A man has no need for entertainment. Entertainment only distracts from his duty."*
5.7) Donations & Gifts
5.8) Middlemen
5.9) *"La Ferrarina"*
5.10) *"Racing amuses me"*
5.11) Project Sigma

BUSINESS PHILOSOPHY ACCORDING TO ENZO FERRARI

5.1 *"I don't sell cars; I sell engines. The cars I throw in for free since something has to hold the engines in."*

This quote may sound surprising to the reader, but Enzo's heart always had been with the racing team. In opposite to this, he saw his street cars as requirement to finance racing. This confirms also his negotiation strategy in 1963, as first Ford tried to acquire the Ferrari Company, but Enzo declined this offer, and instead accepted later in '69 the offer from Fiat to acquire 50%. This deal included the Formula 1 racing team and infused fresh money to finance the development of new racing cars, as the 312 PB, but still kept Enzo in control of the racing activities.

1971: Ferrari 312 PB, 3.0L, V12, 460hp @ 10800rpm, 665kg, design by Mauro Forghieri

"My rights, my integrity, my very being as a manufacturer, as an entrepreneur, as the leader of the Ferrari works, cannot work under the enormous machine, the suffocating bureaucracy of the Ford Motor Company!"

In opposite to its end, the start of the negotiations between Ford and Ferrari started quite promising. In '63 Henry Ford II and his manager Lee Iacocca had the idea to acquire the Ferrari company. This to include European sports cars in the portfolio and so to complete the existing Ford line. Furthermore, Ferrari would bring racing experience and knowledge to the company. Being aware of the cultural differences, Ford chose their head of the Italian business, Phil Paradise, to start the contact with Ferrari. Similar to the existing setup, Ford wanted split up Ferrari in two companies:
- Ford-Ferrari: The actual Ferrari road car company.
- Ferrari-Ford: The Ferrari racing team, continued to be led by Enzo Ferrari. Ford would have the option to acquire the rest of the company after Enzo's death.

This concept was perceived positively by Enzo, as it considered his preferences and vision that the road car company financed the racing activities. Furthermore, he started to recognize that for a small company it would be impossible in the future to sustainable finance the participating in the different racing series. Enzo admired Henry Ford I's attitude, reputation and his ability to implement mass production. A strategy which he respected, but declined for his highly specialized production. At the end the negotiations failed because of two main reasons:

- Ford-Ferrari: For Enzo it was important the manufacture stayed hand-crafted, what ensured the possibility to create individual cars. Based on this, he perceived his employees not only as specialists, but being inside a circle of trust, similar to family members. He was proud of the production cars and his employees. A potential acquisition had to ensure that there would be no change of this setup and philosophy.

- Ferrari-Ford: Both companies had different ideas where to put the focus. For Ferrari it was clearly Formula One, but Ford saw this the focus on the GT series, also to ensure a more direct image transfer from racing to its mass production.

Both sides understood that it was impossible to find an agreement and stopped the negotiations.[217] As result of Ferrari's cancellation, Ford started its own project, the GT40, and wrote its own part of Le Mans history. Nevertheless, on the long run it was the right decision for Ferrari, as only the later deal with Fiat ensured that the company could continue to exist based on Enzo's vision; as small, but highly specialized auto manufacturer, together with a successful racing department. As history showed, both companies had a positive development after the termination of the negotiations. For this, the cancelation of discussions can be seen as a positive result, both companies had serious talks together to analyze the possibilities to work together and as a result it was decided that both companies are better off to stay independent.

---

[217] Sportscars.tv (fetched 24.11.2015): "For Negotiations to Buy Ferrari"

Ferrari Formula 1 champion Niki Lauda resumed in a book and interview his seven rules about financial negotiations. [218] As one of his partners had been Enzo Ferrari, these rules are a good base to discuss what happens, if a Latin and Northern European negotiation style come together.

- Prices: According to Lauda, preparation is an important starting point for all negotiations. In the case of salaries, you can investigate, what comparable colleagues are earning. Depending on the culture, you receive more or less valid answers. In the US people are used to talk openly about money and salary, in Germany this is a "no go". No need to say that in today's time you can find relevant information also online. What is valid for the negotiation of personal salaries, is strictly prohibited for corporate negotiations, as the interchange of non-public price and cost (including salaries) information between companies is forbidden by local antitrust-laws.

1976: Ferrari 312 T, 3.0L, V12, 485hp @ 12520rpm, 575kg, design by Mauro Forghieri

---

[218] Hoffmann, Maren (2015): "Gut, dann fahre ich eben woanders" – Niki Laudas sieben Verhandlungs-Regeln

- Emotions: Lauda's advice is to keep emotions out off negotiations. As example he mentioned his experience with Enzo Ferrari from 1976. He won the Drivers' Championship the season before, and not just because of this, at this time he was perceived as the most talented driver on the market. Not only being fast on the track, but also with technical understanding to support the development of the car. With this, it was clear to him that he was in a strong position and demanded a raise of salary. If Ferrari would not had agreed to this, he already had attractive alternatives to drive in other teams. At the moment this strategy worked out fine. But on the other hand, this is a double-edged sword. If there are no emotions when you start a relation, there are also no emotional connections, which could prevent the ending of this. Before the '76 season, Enzo Ferrari saw Niki Lauda as the best available driver. A perception which changed in the same year. After his heavy accident on the Nürburgring, Lauda returned to Formula 1 already three races later. A decision that surprised everyone, even his own team. As result, the Scuderia had to go with three cars into the Italian Grand Prix. Through Enzo's eyes, this was a selfish decision and risked Ferrari's chances to win the Manufacturer's Championship. At the end, Lauda lost his Championship Title, but nevertheless Ferrari won the team one. The next year, Lauda won again the championship, but nevertheless the relation between Enzo and him lost the base for further cooperation. Accordingly, Lauda changed in '78 to the Brabham Alfa Romeo-team. The same strategy as Lauda was used in '95 by Michael Schumacher, as he negotiated with the Scuderia. As result, he became Formula One's highest paid driver. At the beginning Schumacher got criticized by the Tifosi, as they perceived him as too cold and emotionless. An attitude what changed over the time, as Schumacher started to enjoy the Italian work atmosphere. Sebastian Vettel negotiated in 2015 his contract with the Scuderia. In opposite to Lauda and Schumacher, he had been emotionally involved at the time of the negotiations. Since right from the beginning, he stated that for all his life he had been a Tifosi, what included also a deep admiration of Enzo Ferrari. The different examples show another important factor, how to behave in negotiations: the person's character. If you are able to play with a "poker face", an emotionless strategy leads to success. If you cannot hold back your feelings, honest emotions, as admiration, can also develop into a successful strategy. As it honors the counterpart, it tempts them to lose their emotionless attitude and that way not "play too hard". Lauda's strategy to keep the poker face in the negotiations with Ferrari included to not use the Italian language, even if he would had been able to, instead he used a translator in such meetings.[219]

Even if the negation itself should be free of emotion, there is a ritual that before you are able to discuss business, it is recommended to conduct small-talk. This to set a positive atmosphere and avoid "critical rationalism", this means that people tend to elaborate a more extended decision making process, when they are in a neutral or slightly negative mood. If you are in slightly positive mood, you are tempted to use a short decision making process and act more spontaneously. This is the reason for the music in shopping malls. Not only before, also after the negotiations it is advisable to change back to emotional topics. Most people tend to get regrets after an important decision. After they took one decision, they not have the possibility anymore to go with another option. The missing possibilities are perceived as restriction. For this, emotional support is needed.

- Disinterest: If you are not really interested in an offer, it is on the other person to make it better. But attention, in a Latin culture disinterest in an offer or products can be taken personally. If the interest is only on the money, on a later point the other side may look for cheaper alternatives.

- Space: In negotiations is always space, if not, there would be no negotiations. Lauda remembered that in his talks with Ferrari he calculated with 5%, and used a two-step-strategy. In a first step he went 1% down and in second bigger step he offered to go 4% down, but at the same time he made it clear that this is final offer.

---

[219] Lauda, Niki / Voelker, Herbert (1986): „To hell and back"

Due to Lauda, this strategy always worked for him. He stayed in his original calculations and the other side, Ferrari, could present the success of negotiation. To open spaces, the negotiation should not be limited on only one topic, but, if possible, include several ones. Lauda's contract negotiations had been a focus on salary, but at the same time he demanded Clay Regazzoni as his team-mate. An strategic move, as he knew him for years and also was sure to be continuously faster than him.[220]

1976: Ferrari 312 T2, 3.0L, V12, 500hp @ 12200rpm, 320km/h, 575kg, design by Mauro Forghieri

- Being tough: *"Characters as Ecclestone or Ferrari respect you more, when you not come as a yes-man, but really hard negotiate."*[221] Business founders and leaders see their organizations not only as a source for income, but as a realization of their vision. Based on this idea, they demand respect, but also are able to give respect to successful competitors and tough negotiation partners. Negotiation skills are appreciated and are perceived as the person's value. As business is not only about money, but lifestyle, characters as Bernie Ecclestone and Enzo Ferrari enjoyed good negotiations. Based to their own work, they had been able to discuss with such talented drivers as Lauda.

---

[220] Lauda, Niki / Voelker, Herbert (1986): „To hell and back"

[221] Hoffmann, Maren (2015): "Gut, dann fahre ich eben woanders" – Niki Laudas sieben Verhandlungs-Regeln

- Do not renegotiate! On the other hand, being tough should not be confounded with exploiting of the other side. Only if both sides are satisfied, a sustainable relation can be established. If this is the task, renegotiations are not necessary. This includes not to negotiate if there is nothing to discuss. At the end of the '77 season Lauda felt the requirement for a change after winning twice the championship with Ferrari. For this, he avoided discussing a future contract with the management; instead negotiated and signed with the Brabham Alfa Romeo team.

- No scorched earth! As you always meet at least twice, not only in business life, negotiations have to stay always fair; hard, but played by the rules. An important lesson, as there may arise new situations, where you have to negotiate with the same people, but under other circumstances. After Niki Lauda and Enzo Ferrari had an open talk about their separation, both held a press conference to communicate that both sides agreed on this step. To finish, they thanked each other for the successful time, shook hands and went into different directions. Lauda was relieved, even if only hours later he had to experience that the VIP treatment of Ferrari drivers in Italy came to an end for him. This as similar to other passengers he had to wait at the airport because of a two hours delay of his plane.[222]

1960: Cooper Ferrari T51

---

[222] Lauda, Niki / Voelker Herbert (1986): „To hell and back"

As Ferrari understood the engine as focus and competitive advantage, the company not always engineered complete cars, but also sold just the engine. In the 2015 Formula 1 season, besides the Scuderia, which started with Ferrari engines, also the teams of Manor Marussia and Sauber used them. This business is not new for the company. Already in 1960 the Scuderia Eugenio Castellotti started with a Cooper, powered by a modified Ferrari engine. The Cooper T51 was originally developed for the Formula 2 championship, but then also used in Formula 1. Jack Brabham became F1 champion in 1959 on a Cooper T51. Important for the technical development: The T51 was the first mid-engine race car to win a F1 championship. Ironically, in 1960 the Scuderia Eugenio Castelloti competed with this Cooper Ferrari T51 at the Italian Grand Prix against the Ferrari team, who still deployed the front-engine 246. For this, the T51 can be seen as the first mid-engine Ferrari monoposto car. It is recorded that Enzo Ferrari himself had a positive attitude related this project. Even as not publically announced by then, he understood that the future of Formula One would be mid-engine cars. For this, the T51 brought important insights about the actual British constructions without own investments and even more important, without losing the face and having to buy such a car from a competitor.[223] Even if Enzo was a pragmatic manager, he was nevertheless Italian and based on his culture, a proud business man. If possible, he tried to avoid admitting that he had a wrong or outdated opinion.

---

[223] Nye, Doug (1993): "The Autocourse History of the Grand Prix Car 1945-65"

1948: Ferrari 125 F1, 1.5L, V12, 230hp @ 7000rpm, 710kg, design by Giocchino Colombo, Valerio Colotti

Ferrari also sold, and still sells, complete race cars. This is consequent as also their street cars started originally with the philosophy to offer cars, which could be used on the street, but also offer its ambitious drivers the base to compete in races. The British Industrial Tony Vandervell bought already in 1949 a couple of Ferrari 125s and later in '52 a Ferrari 375. The last one got nearly completely redesigned, including a new built body, to ensure that the Vandervell racing team would not run into the problem of missing Ferrari spare parts. Over the time the car received several updates, as disc brakes to replace the original Ferrari drum brakes. A technical innovation by Vandervell Products Ltd. Another good example how racing and competition supported the technical development. This way the car got used until 1954, and the racing team collected precious experience, what helped them to win the Formula 1 constructor's championship in '58.[224]

---

[224] MotorSport (1982): "Thin Wall Special 1952"

1952: Ferrari Thin Wall Special, V12

5.2 *"My cars have to be beautiful"*

In the second half of the 1980s it was the actual doctrine to diverse business, and based on this to reduce the business risk. The following decade of the 90s should inverse the message. Now business leaders learn to concentrate on the core business and outsource the rest of the activities. Since the beginning it was clear to Enzo what had been his strengths and where we wanted to lay the emphasis of his business: *"I build engines and attach wheels to them."* On one hand he knew that even the best engines must be part of a beautiful car. He acted here as a modern manager, not tried to build up this skill inside the own company, but left this task to external companies, which already had proven their capability. Enzo's first creation, the Auto Avio Costruzioni 815 got developed by former Alfa Romeo engineers, but the car received a bodywork from Carrozzeria Touring, which at that time was already 14 years in the business and famous for its beautiful car designs.

1940: Auto Avio Costruzioni 815, 1.5L, Straight 8, 75hp @ 5500rpm, 625kg, design by Carrozzeria Touring

Understanding the importance of the design, Enzo acted conform the "gestalt psychology", with its main statement *"The whole is greater than the sum of the parts"* (Kurt Koffka)[225]. Surely a Ferrari car is a high-end product, but it is always the fastest, the most reliable or the most efficient one? If Enzo Ferrari really just had sold his engine with some boring car design around, the company would never had reached the status, what it has today. A car, is really more than just the maximum speed or its accelerating time from 1 to 100km/h; it is the complete emotional universe, what it is creating for its drivers and people around; including the emotional connection between races on Sunday and the usage of the own car. So it is not enough for the car to be fast, but it also has to look fast. Even further than that, to make it easy for the customer to connect the productions cars with myth, a Ferrari car has to distinguished by its design.

Enzo added to his famous quote that his cars had to be beautiful, but also they had to be fast and reliable. People like to simplify problems. As speed and reliability are not decidable by a first view, we take our experiences from the past and think what looks fast and what looks reliable. Often we suffer here by a halo-effect. For example if we have one positive information, in this case the beauty of the car, and try to assume other positive characteristics as speed and reliability. Our view on beauty is shaped by the evolution, as our survival was depended that we find attractive what is good for us.[226] Thinking of cars, our view on beauty

---

[225] Tuck, Michael (2010): "Gestalt Principles Applied in design"

[226] Modern Issues: Psychology (2013): The Halo Effect of Beautiful People

includes in a subconscious way also our technical knowledge. As Kimi Räikkönen stated during the presentation of the 2015 Formula One car, the SF15-T: *"It looks nice, and when it looks good it should be a pretty good car."*[227]

Besides temporary fashions, it explains why car designs changed over the time ("Form follows function") and why we see today other designs as beautiful than people in the past did. Paul Frère was not only driver, but also had background knowledge about modern aerodynamics. For this he not perceived the 250 TR as a beautiful car (as we do generally today), but for his esthetic sense it was disturbing that the windshield as designed so steep (chapter 2.6).

1959: Ferrari 250 59 TR, 3.0L, V12, 308hp @ 7400rpm, 725kg, design by Pininfarina (Madardo Fantuzzi)

Even if Enzo did not designed the looks of the cars inside the company, it was a clear order to his partner that the new design had to have a "Ferrari face". Carlo Bianchi from Carrozzeria Touring remembered in a later interview that this was already in 1948 the case,[228] as it was Enzo's concern that his actual cars had been fast and beautiful, but still they looked too similar to the products from the competition, as for example the Auto Avio 815 had obvious similarity to the Alfa Romeo 6C 2500 Touring Spider of the same year.

---

[227] ESPN (2015): "'When it looks good it should be a pretty good car' – Kimi"

[228] Motor Trend (2007): "The Secret History of Ferrari: Outtakes"

1940: Alfa Romeo 6C 2500 Touring Spider, 2.5L, Straight 6

Carlo interpreted this with the Ferrari 125. Already an elegant design, even if still looked similar to a British roadster. He used this first Ferrari as a an inspiration and developed it further. The result became the 166MM, which its design a clear evolution and the first Ferrari, what looked typically Ferrari.

1950: Ferrari 166MM Touring Berlinetta Le Mans, 2.0L, V12, 140hp @ 6600rpm, design by Carozzerria Touring

As Enzo was a local patriot, he not just included the traditional yellow from his home-town Modena into the Ferrari logo, but also let a lot of cars painted in this same color. But if you think of the cars today, you normally associate a Ferrari with red, something they have in common with Alfa

Romeo. This preferred color was not an invitation of the companies, but was based on the international racing colors. Originally these codes had been introduced in 1900 by the Gordon Bennett Cup, an annual race organized the first time in France, but later also in other countries as Ireland and Germany. Here the participants agreed that blue had been for the French participants, yellow for Belgium, white for Germany and red for the USA. Italy received the red seven years later as Prince Scipione Borghese and Ettore Guizzardi won the "Peking to Paris" race with an Itala 35/45hp.

Today we associate Ferrari with a shining red, but over the time the racing team had changed the tone. In the beginning, as Enzo took over the Alfa Romeo racing department, he used a darker, nearly brownish red in opposite to the tone that Alfa used before.

1932: Alfa Romeo P3, 2.7L, Straight 8, 215hp @ 5600rpm, 232km/h, 703kg, design by Vittorio Jano

As it is beneficially to keep up a myth, it is not known, why the Scuderia changed the tone over the time. Even if we can assume that in the later time it was mainly for practical reasons, for example as part of the marketing, to have it more similar to the main sponsor Marlboro or just to have the cars look better on modern LCD flat screens. Latter in 2019 the Scuderia changes for a first time from a shiny color to a matt tone. The new team principal Mattia Binotto explained: *"The opaque color is due to technical reasons as the car is lighter and even if it's hundreds of grams, it can affect."*[229] In Formula One this was not the first case where weight influenced color. Back in 1934 at the Nürburgring the brand new Mercedes Benz W25 was slightly overweight, and not complied with the strict limit of 750 kilograms. Team manager Alfred Neubauer had the simple but effective idea to strip down the car's white paint and let it race with its pure aluminum body. The legend of "silver arrow" had been born.[230]

Even if the red not started with Italy or Ferrari, it stayed there as both fit perfectly together. Red is a signal color, people who chose this tone for their car want to be seen and recognized. The normal Ferrari driver is highly involved in cars, racing and technology. This is necessary as Ferrari has much less dealerships than, for example, its German competitor Porsche. Higher prices, longer waiting lines and more difficult to drive. If you invest that much in the choice of your automobile, you want to be recognized. Over the time red cars automatically got perceived as fast, here psychology turned around, as many fast cars had been painted in this color, people learnt that red meant fast.

Ferrari's traditional yellow received even more attention based on the fact that there had been only a small number of yellow cars on the street. But on the other hand there had been also much less yellow race cars on the tracks, so people less associated the color in relation with speed.

That products are more than just the tangible part, but have also an emotional universe, is today not only relevant for industrial designers, but especially for the developers of digital content. Most music, videos and software are not bought anymore in a physical store, but directly downloaded to computer, MP3-player, mobile phone or TV. As in the past a detailed user manual or artistic cover had been part of the complete package, the consumer had something in their hands and concluded from this to the quality of the intangible content as music, video or software. As this is missing now in many cases, people often lost the respect for the

---

[229] Scuderia Ferrari on Twitter (2019)

[230] Mercedes Benz (fetched 16.2.2019): "To drive a Silver Arrow is an honour."

product, and piracy is often perceived as a face-less crime, as nothing gets physically stolen, just additional copies elaborated. Intangible parts of a product are not limited to emotion, another important factor is quality. The potential client takes a test-drive, opens the engine to see how it works and sounds, but nevertheless you just get a non-complete picture of the car's technical quality, as you have to assume how it works in 1, 2, 5 or 10 years from now. Certain things are assumed to represent quality, as the feeling of switches and the sound of closing doors. Haptic is the science of the sense of touch. Engineers know about its importance and include it into their products. As Enzo said that his cars had to be beautiful, it is imperative that they are beautiful for at least four of the five senses: sight, hearing, smell and touch. For the taste you can visit your local Italian restaurant, even an official licensed Ferrari wine is available.

Many of the Ferrari production cars you can find inside the various lists of the world's most beautiful cars, but at the end the designs came mostly from external companies, in most of the cases from Pininfarina.

1971: Ferrari 365 GTB/4 Daytona Competition I, 4.4L, V12, 402hp @ 8300rpm, 295km/h, 1200kg, design by Pininfarina

The famous long-term business relationship started in 1951 and had been sealed in a restaurant located in the small city of Tortona, as Enzo Ferrari and Giovanni Battista Pininfarina met half-way between Modena and Turin. [231] Not untypical for the former Italian business culture that such important

---

[231] Mihalascu, Dan (2013): "Sergio Pininfarina Talks about His Collaboration with Enzo Ferrari in 2006 Interview"

business decisions had not been finalized in an office, but a restaurant. Depending on the region, it looks a bit suspicious, but in many cultures food has a high importance, and having dinner together is a sign of giving honor to the invitee. You want to learn a bit more from the potential partner, before you sign an important agreement. From a psychological point of view, it is a positive sign, as you are outside one of the participant's offices; it is a meeting on neutral space and between two parties, who meet eye-to-eye.

The result of this meeting between the two men was that Pininfarina as company received the responsibility for design, engineering, technology and construction of the Ferrari production cars. Later the relation grew even closer, as Pinin became Ferrari vice president and a partner for the Ferrari racing team. Nevertheless, both companies stayed independent, Ferrari never tried to acquire Pininfarina. This was conform to Enzo's philosophy that competency would create the best results. Even as Pininfarina had the status of a preferred supplier, other companies had the opportunity to enter. But in fact it happened just once, 1973 as Bertone created the bodywork for the 308 GT4. The situation created on the short run difficulties in-between the two men and companies, but already the order for the next chassis (the 1980 Mondial) went again to Pininfarina.

Meeting in the restaurant was a symbol of respect, which both men showed and understood accordingly. Normally Enzo preferred to hold business meetings at the factory, inside his office. Everybody who wanted something from him, should come to him.[232] This opened further the possibility to let the visitors wait, depending the grade of importance, which the Commendatore wanted the visitors to perceive. The minimalistic and functional atmosphere of Enzo's office underlined his attitudes and so supported to set a favorable business atmosphere for him.

Offering and acceptance of meals is a topic addressed by most of companies' code of conduct. A difficult situation as an invitation includes two independent dimensions: a time-frame for business discussions and

---

[232] Bentley, Logan (1979): "Behind the Ferrari Mystique Is a Lonely Man Who Lives with Fast Cars and Death"

honoring the invitee. It is not recorded whom paid, Enzo Ferrari or Battista Pininfarina. Both men met geography half-space between their companies. Eye to eye on the same level; self-confident, but also honoring the other one. We can assume that both companies worked on the topic before, but nevertheless the last step required a personal meeting of both leaders. The restaurant's location was convenient for both men and offered an additional explanation why the meeting was here instead in one of the offices. Invitations to a meal are always an instrument to foster the customer loyalty or to start the relationship. Hereby the client gets honored in two ways, by the meal itself and by the pure presence of the employee. The honor translates into influence. Ideally the employee has a slightly higher social level than the client. If it would be lower, the client could feel offended, if it is much higher, the client could feel intimidated. If the importance of the personal contact is higher than importance of food & beverage, the influence is proportional. If on the other hand, the perceived importance of good & beverage is higher than the importance of the business partner's presence, it could a non-proportional influence, or directly said a bribe. This is valid for average business relations. It is different, if the employee is a celebrity. Such people have also outside the business discussions a level of attraction, so that the personal contact itself has a value, similar to a gift. Circumstances which charity organizations use for celebrity auctions, where people bid, for example on a dinner with a celebrity.

Enzo was clearly a celebrity and lots of Ferraristi would have loved to be at that restaurant table instead of Battista, but in general it had been two men, leader of the companies. We can assume that Pininfarina perceived Ferrari not as the celebrity, but the business partner; no risk of non-proportional influence.

To share lunch or dinner is in many cultures a way to show respect for the other person, an open door to enter the circle of trust. Respect implicates a fair treatment between the individuals, as a fraud or the intend to bribe is a sign of missing appreciation. For this, if a person shows honest respect to another one, this individual will perceive a high level of trust regarding this person; often the beginning of a long-term business relation.

In the described example trust gets established between two persons, for this it is imperative that the individual's values have to be aligned with the company ones. In our case it had been a meeting between the two company founders, so it was given. But in most of the cases it is between managers or other company employees. It is a responsibility to represent the company in such meetings. For that special workshops about company, responsibility and negotiations are necessary.

Amazon CEO Jeff Bezos defined: *"Your brand is what people say about you when you are not in the room."*, Richard Branson (Founder Virgin Airways) added: *"Build brands not around products but around reputation."*[233] In fact brand is representative for reputation, further enhanced with emotion; *"The Ferrari is a dream."* (Enzo Ferrari) The personal contact between employee and potential client fosters the brand reputation, but on the other hand has the risk that the reputation got build up in relation to the employee and not so much to the company.

1983: Ferrari 126 C3, 1.5L, V6, 800hp, 552kg, design by Mauro Forghieri, Harvey Postlethwaite

For example, Rene Arnoux explained his change from the Renault-team to Ferrari in the 1983 season: *"For me, Enzo Ferrari's handshake was worth more than a signature on a contract."*[234] Of course it is positive that both men valued each other that high, so that they would not elaborate a detailed contract,

---

[233] Gattiker, Urs E. (2008): "brand versus reputation: Jeff Bezos, Richard Branson, Josef Ackermann and Pat Russo to the rescue"

[234] Ferrari.com (2014): "Rene Arnoux visits Ferrari"

but it eliminated the four-eyes-principle. In many cultures doing business between companies means first of all doing business between people. Apart from Asia, this is particularly for the Latin culture relevant. Countries with a lower level of trust, informal meetings (like in restaurant, bar or golf club) are used to build up a trustful relation.

Conducting business on a personal level bares several risk factors, including:

- The loyalty is not between two companies, but two individuals. So a decision may not be taken, because it is best for the two companies, but best for the two employees. This open ups risk like one part may subconsciously or openly (up to bribing) influences the other one.

- Through an atmosphere of euphoria & pressure and / or a manipulative counterpart, employees may get rushed into a decision.

- The four-eyes-principle gets violated. A handshake is valid for the general business, as it is legally binding. As details get not defined, it is a source for future conflicts.

5.3 A Joint-Venture

The 308 GT4 came in a time of changes for Ferrari. The company just became a part of Fiat and developed with them together the Fiat Dino, a car which none of the two companies could have developed alone. Fiat was able to produce enough units, so that the car could have been sold for an attractive price and Ferrari contributed with a new V6-engine. Both companies reached a new target-group with the car (between typical Fiat and Ferrari clients), which created additional incomes and further Ferrari needed the higher sales of the car to homologate their V6-engine for Formula 2 championship usage.

Such joint-ventures are important, as they enable the participating companies to create an additional offer to the requirements of the market. More offers lead to more competition and finally to solutions with higher quality and lower prices. For the companies they are an opportunity, as thanks to the cooperation with other companies, they can access additional markets, but on the other hand they are also a risk factor, as the corporation has no complete control over the partner and the output of its work. Quality issues, for example, can lead to problems, not just for the joint-venture itself, but also the bring down the image of the products, which are produced alone by the companies. Beside such image risks, in certain cases a company A can be legally responsible for the actions of company B.

1968: Fiat Dino Coupe, 2.4L, V6, 176hp@ 6600rpm, design by Bertone.

In the case of the Fiat Dino-project, it had effects on the Ferrari portfolio. As they needed to replace the Dino 246, they decided for the design-part against their long-time partner Pininfarina, but in favor of Bertone. This decision was based on the experience of the company, which they had collected with the Fiat Dino Coupe.[235] In opposite to Pininfarina, which preferred a more round design, Bertone was known at this time for its edgy styling, as they realized designs for Lamborghini and the iconic Lancia Stratos. Based on this, the design of the 304 GT4 became untypical for the

---

[235] Howstufworks (19.07.2014): Ferrari 308 GT4

company and Ferrari fans compared it more to the Stratos than other Ferraris. After 6 years of production the car got replaced by the Mondial, which received again a Pininfarina dress.

1973: Dino 308 GT4 2+2, 3.0L, V8, 250hp, design by Bertone (Marcello Gandini)

Apart from the Fiat Dino, there was still a second car to receive Ferrari's V6, the Lancia Stratos. Just as Ferrari, Lancia became a part of Fiat in 1969 and had been active in different kind of motorsports as Formula 1, sports car and especially successful in Rally sports. In '71 the company presented the Stratos to be the successor of the aging Fulvia. Even if the concept of the car always included the Ferrari engine, it was not easy to get it. In opposite to the Fiat, Enzo saw the radical sports car in competition to his own creations, especially to the Dino brand, and for this not wanted to supply the engines to Lancia. As part of the long negotiations, Ferrari delivered 10 testing engines in May '72 to Lancia. Project leader Cesare Fiorio (who later should join the Ferrari Formula 1 team) announced that the Stratos specifications let to 240hp and Lancia let the car already participate in November at the Tour of Corsica. At this point it was still not clear that the car really would get the engine. Then in December both sides finally agree on the deal and Ferrari started to deliver the 500 needed engines.[236]

There had been several attempts to produce a modern interpretation of the Stratos, one of them had been the "New Stratos". Ironically the project faced again problems with the Ferrari. The company made it clear in 2011

---

[236] Lanciastratos.com (fetched 30.10.2014): "History"

that it would not take the role of a supplier: "Given the situation, creation of additional vehicles seems possible only via companies that are not dependent on Ferrari." With these words president Luca di Montezemolo blocked the project, as the New Stratos was completely based on the Ferrari 430.[237]

1972: Lancia Stratos, 2.4L, V6, 240hp, 980kg, design by Bertone (Marcello Gandini)

5.4 *"My loyalty to Shell springs from my experience with automobiles."*

The relation between Ferrari and Shell already began back in 1929, when Shell became a sponsor of the racing driver Enzo Ferrari, a business connection which stayed valid and successful until today. Just some results until 2011:

- 10 Formula 1 constructor's championships
- 12 Formula 1 driver's championships
- Over 155 won Formula races[238]

---

[237] Drive.com.au (2011): "Ferrari blocks iconic sports car"

[238] Formula1blog (2011): "The Ferrari-Shell Partnership: A history"

2011: Ferrari F150° Italia, 2.4L, V8, 18000rpm, 640kg, design by Aldo Costa, Nicholas Tombazis

Such long-term relations require mutual respect, as the results cannot have the same success all the time and sometimes, one partner can get into a stronger position and some other time, the other one. To understand the benefit of a lasting business relation, the "Game theory" can be applied, which is basically a model for strategic decision making. Similar to a game of chess, every move a partner makes, provokes a counter-move by the other side. For this, the game-theory not seeks the maximization on the short run, but the long one, so after a series of moves. For example the relation between supplier and client. A client can reduce the prices of a potential supplier to a minimum, if they got into a difficult economic situation. But times can be changing. Due to a new invention, a supplier can get back to a much stronger market position and let the client then make it feel ("payback time"), for example through higher prices or simple boycotting it. Such a situation of distrust explains the "prisoner's dilemma" (explained in chapter 4.6).

Ferrari and Shell overcame the temptations of short-range profit maximization, saw the strategic value and both are now benefiting from the prosper relation. Ferrari receiving parts of their budget from Shell, including that the petrol company is developing a special fuel-combination exclusively for motorsports. On the other hand, Shell was one of the first team sponsors who had its logo on the red car, as there was still no other advertising on. Besides using the cars as communication channel, they could advertise with Ferrari at the fuel stations and even sold small die-cast models.

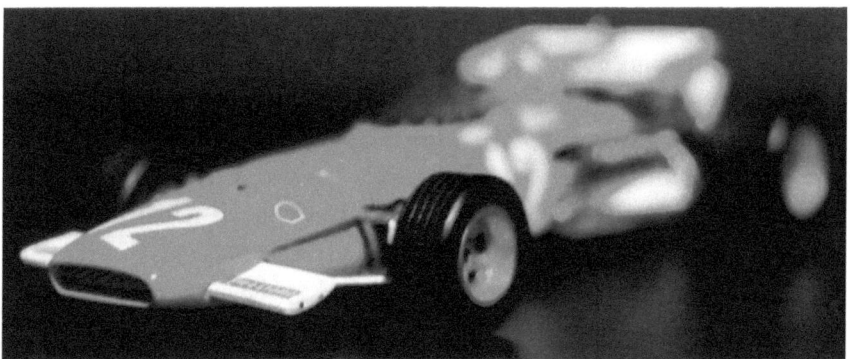

1970: Ferrari 312 B, 3.0L, V12, 450hp @ 11000rpm, 524kg, design by Mauro Forghieri

Overcoming the prisoner's dilemma is not only important for partnerships between different companies, it also applies internally in a company, between different departments and even inside the same work-teams.

Trust is an outstanding factor for successful partnerships, as positive, but also potential negative, results affects both sides on the middle and long-term. This explains why the exchange of payment streams cannot be the only base of such a relation. For Enzo Ferrari it was important that a sponsorship went further, and included an interchange of experience and technical knowledge. With this, he was child of the Italian motorsports-culture, as this philosophy was also used by others. In the beginning of the 1960s, Alfa Romeo connected again with its former employee Carlo Chiti to establish a sustainable motorsports-department. First with Auto Delta as independent partner, later embedded into the company. Carlo hat been known for his technical experience, integrity and loyalty. Auto Delta not only became responsible to develop and manage the Alfa Romeo racing team, but this experience flow back to the mother company to support the marketing and development of the street cars.

After Romeo exited Formula One after the '85-season, it will return in 2018. Again with trustful partners, the Ferrari 2018 engine and the experienced Sauber Team. Similar to Enzo Ferrari, Peter Sauber was a passionate engineer and race driver when he founded his organization in 1970. Starting with sports car, the team had its biggest success in 1989 when it won the 24 Hours of Le Mans and the World Sports Prototype Championship. This in connection with another legendary partner,

Mercedes Benz and its reborn Silver Arrow. In '91 they could secure the championship again, also thanks to drivers as Michael Schumacher.

Based in Zurich, Switzerland, the restructured Alfa Romeo Sauber F1 Team is only 280km away from Milan. This allows a required operative independence, but is still in distance to achieve the required continuous support from Italy. Team and sponsors had been presented in the Alfa Romeo Historic Museum in Arese, surrounded by the company's legendary Formula One-cars. It was on the 2nd of December, only one week after the 2017 F1 finale in Dubai.

2017: Sauber C36, 1.6L, V6, 15000rpm, 728kg, design by Joerg Zander. With friendly permission by the Alfa Romeo Sauber F1 Team.

Based on a strategic, commercial and technological cooperation, the partnership should be for multiple years and not limited to Formula One. This is comparable to the successful Auto Delta agreement, as it opens up the possibility to create special versions of Alfa's street cars, developed by Sauber. Or a cooperation in other series, for example in Touring or Endurance sports. Such ideas are based on Alfa's experience in the first and Sauber's in the second.

5.5 *"I don't smoke and neither do my cars."*

In opposite to the Shell offer, later in the 60s Enzo was not convinced, as a tobacco company wanted to sponsor the Ferrari team, as for him it was important that the sponsoring on the car was sharing the same values as he did. Quite untypical for time and country, Enzo was non-smoker so declined the tempting offer with his famous quote: *"I don't smoke and neither do my cars."* For the proud Italian this sentence had a slight double-meaning, as he declined the offer for the reason that he as an individual was not smoking, but also as he saw car racing as non-compatible with tobacco sponsoring, as smoking cars usually are a bad sign, announcing a technical problem and in most of the cases a retirement from the race. Especially for him as engineer, who always emphasized the importance of a functional car, an unpleasant vision.

1965: Ferrari 250 LM Berlinetta Speciale, 3.3L, V12, 310hp @ 7500rpm, design by Pininfarina

Later in the 90s, after Enzo's death, Ferrari yes accepted the offer by the Philipp Morris company, and Marlboro became the main sponsor of the Formula 1-team, including that they firmed now as "Scuderia Ferrari Marlboro". Even as the business relation continued, in 2011 they returned to their classical name "Scuderia Ferrari".

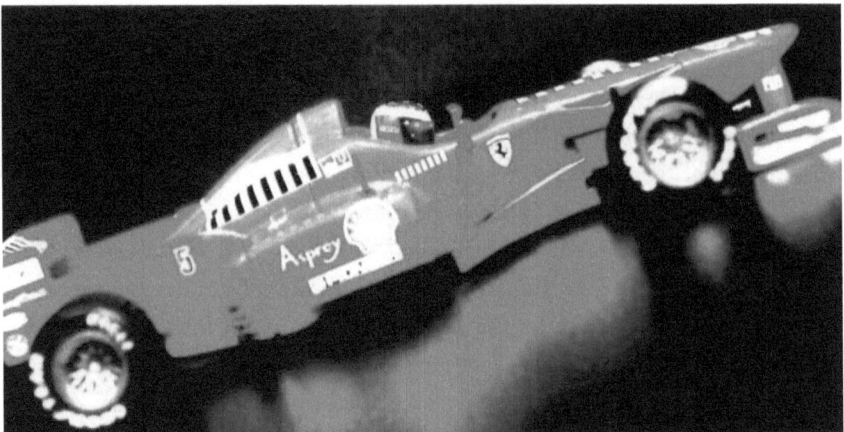

1997: Ferrari F310 (Launch Version), 4.7L, V10, 705hp @ 15500rpm, 595kg, design by John Barnard.

In early 2018 Philip Morris made a drastic business decision and published a manifesto where the company announced to concentrate on the development of smoke-free products, which in future should completely replace cigarettes.[239] To communicate this disruption, the organization started the same year its initiative "Mission Winnow".[240] This with a new internet platform to promote science, knowledge and leadership, embedded into a social media-strategy including all relevant channels. Nevertheless they stayed true to their classic communication partners and consequently "Mission Winnow" replaced Marlboro as one of the Scuderia's main sponsors. In addition, one year later the sponsorship extended to include Ducati Corse. As valid for all good partnerships, both sides profited from it. For the Scuderia it was not only a way to finance its activities, furthermore it supported to establish the team inside the internet and made it relevant for younger generations, which may turn into future clients. Not all buyers for the cars, but at least for the merchandising and other licensed products.

---

[239] Philip Morris International (fetched 16.2.2019): "Our Manifesto – Designing a Smoke-Free Future)"

[240] Mission Winnow (fetched 16.2.2019)

5.6 "A man has no need of entertainment. Entertainment only distracts from his duty."

This philosophy applied Enzo Ferrari for himself, his employees, but also externals. In opposite to many other companies, the Ferrari Corporation never got involved into a mayor corruption scandal. As described before, lunch and dinners got used for business talks and discussions, but as it was part of the Italian culture, all parties interpreted it accordingly. Furthermore, Enzo had no special preference for luxury, he invited to good traditional restaurants, but nothing out of the ordinary. As, for example, the "Restaurante Il Cavallino" in Maranello, where he often ate, as it was just across the factory. High quality local food, with a focus on family and business dining, no extravagant place. In fact, the this restaurant is property of the Ferrari Corporation. The idea was to have a place to meet and enjoy the traditional food of the Emilia Romana. A place for all kind of employees, from mechanics to drivers, including family and business partners, furthermore friends, neighbors and tourists. It was established in 1985 near the company, but outside its gates.

Enzo had no particular preferences, nevertheless it is reported that he enjoyed "Tagliatelle alle Bolognesa" (a meat-based pasta), and especially "Gnocco Fritto", a typical local dish, which combines few and simple ingredients. It started in the mid-1900s as a popular street food, especially at festivals.[241] Enzo liked his Gnocco Fritto together with salami, but nevertheless it is combinable with all kind of cold cuts and cheeses. As Enzo understood, the dish is ideally combined with a good bottle of Lambrusco. Similar to today's startup companies, working times at Ferrari, especially the racing team, could had been long, often up to late at night. His personal chauffeur Dino Tagliazucchi remembered that Enzo had been well aware what he requested from this employees, so often when his team had to work the night, he ordered bread, salami and Lambrusco from a nearby restaurant for his mechanics.[242]

---

[241] San Pellegrino (2018): San Pellegrino Fruit Beverages

[242] Art City Emilia Romagna (fetched 30.03.2018): "Enzo Ferrari"

As food plays an important part in the Italian culture, the restaurant had high importance for Enzo. He himself appointed in 1984 Giuseppe Neri to become the restaurant manager.[243] Mario Neri S.pA. was founded in 1933 as an building construction company. Their projects included the Paddock Building of the Mugello race-track (property of Ferrari) and the enlargement of the Ferrari museum.[244] Later they extended their portfolio and included catering and the management of restaurants. Their successful business relation with Ferrari grow over the time, for example they had been responsible for the catering of Enzo's 90th birthday.

Traditional Italian food, like the Mediterranean diet in general, is perceived as healthy. Extra-virgin oil or nuts reduce the risk of cardiovascular events.[245] In addition, children get socialized to spend adequate time for eating, not so much in the morning, but for supper and dinner. Eating slower is not only more healthy for the human body, but it is interlinked with culture, as taking time for the food means paying tribute to it. This interprets into that Italian consumers not only use more time for eating, but also for sourcing the ingredients and preparing the dishes. Fresh local meat and vegetables are preferred. The healthy habits get completed by up to 32 paid days off a year, and an efficient public healthcare system. So it is no surprise that Italy is one of the countries with the highest life expectancy.[246]

A healthy condition fosters cognitive performance, such as attention, decision-making and reasoning.[247] The wellness initiatives of many companies and organizations not only help to reduce sick leave, but actively prevent accidents and corruption cases. Especially low level corruption and facilitation payments aim to make the victim tired and give in to do the illegal payment. To resist this requires a certain standing and willingness to engage in a longer discussion. Enzo Ferrari's lifestyle and eating habits had

---

[243] Ristorante Cavallino (fetched 23.09.2014): "History"

[244] Mario Neri S.p.A. (fetched 29.03.2018): "Building Work"

[245] Miller, Lee J. / Lu, Wei (2019): "These Are the World's Healthiest Nations"

[246] World Health Organization (fetched 28.2.2019): "Italy"

[247] Martin, Jennifer L. (fetched 29.4.2017): "Travel & Jet Lag"

been rooted in the local culture, learnt by his parents. Surely, it supported him to stay active and involved into all business activities until high age.

Ristorante "Il Cavallino". With friendly permission by the Ristorante "Il Cavallino"

Ristorante "Il Cavallino". With friendly permission by the Ristorante "Il Cavallino"

As it is known from Eskimo cultures, the best place to store one's surplus is in another one's stomach.[248] Meaning, for an integrant of a hunting culture it is a more successful strategy to share the results of his hunting luck with the group than to store the surplus and come back later to continue eating. This is explainable as hunting luck is changeable. A hunter can be days or weeks without capture or if you want to capture a bigger or faster animal, one hunter is not enough and the task has to be executed by a group. Even if the person had been lucky today, tomorrow he can be dependent on others. To ensure that his colleagues think of him, when they had been lucky, he shares today his surplus. As all human cultures developed from a society of hunters and collectors a long time ago, it is psychologically inside us that we want to have balanced relationship accounts with others. If we perceived that we received more gifts from someone than we gave back, we feel an inner pressure to get this relation in balance again. This can be conscious as giving something back or even sub-conscious that we start a preference for this person in relation to other ones. The last situation is even more dangerous as procurement employees have to find the best supplier for a company and besides the pure numbers, also experience plays an important factor. This experience or "feeling" can subconsciously get manipulated by a non-balanced relation. As entertainment is perceived as a gift, they can bring the relationship account into a non-balance. We try to return to the former status and this distracts us from your duties, right as Enzo analyzed.

This is not only relevant for gifts & hospitality, but also internal relations. Independent if employees are intrinsically ("enjoying the flow") or externally ("pressured") motivated, if they perceive that over a certain period they invert more into the job position as they receive back from the employer, they understand the relationship as un-balanced. This is a risk, as employers often try to motivate the employees "to go the extra mile". If they do so, but on the other hand individuals not see that their company does the same, they perceive that they saved on their relationship account and expect an interest rate. Translated to behavior this means that if several times they went beyond the expected, the employee perceives to gain the right to, on the other hand, do something wrong, as for example, violate an

---

[248] Wright, Robert (2001): "Nonzero - The Logic of Human Destiny"

internal guideline or even external law. This psychological bias is known as "moral licensing", as doing good things would give us the license to do bad things later.[249] Such an effect gets fostered, if the employee perceives that based on the equity theory (chapter 2.11), other employees have a more balanced account than he or she. This is why managers not always have to motivate their employees to do more, but also stop them from regular overtimes and ensure that they take their annual vacation days. To protect the employees, even against their-selves, many countries have this defined in their local labor laws.

5.7 Donations & Gifts

The Ferrari factory saw a lot of politicians and celebrities, but the June 4th of 1998 should became a special day, as Pope John Paul II came to visit, bless the installations and celebrate a Holy Mass on the company's Fiorano race track. Formula 1 Team Manager Marco Piccinini organized the event, as he had the necessary connections with the Vatican. In 2010 81.2% of the Italian population had been Roman Catholic.[250] With this, it is by far the strongest religion in country and explains why nearly all Ferrari employees had been there that Saturday. Enzo had been the one big exception, as due to a sickness he had to stay at home in bed. At least he spoke with the Pope, as he took Enzo's call while he was in the Ferrari headquarters.

Of course the visit was not complete without one lap on the Fiorano track, greeting the attending employees. Against the normal procedure, he used not his bullet-proofed Papamobil, but an open Ferrari Mondial 8, driven by Enzo's son Piero.[251] Being the processor of the 308 GT4, the Mondial was the most humble car in production that time.

---

[249] Yam, Kai Chi (Sam) / Klotz, Anthony C. / He, Wei / Reynolds, Scott (2016): "Pushing Employees to Go the Extra Mile Can Be Counterproductive"

[250] Pew Research (2013): "The Global Catholic Population"

[251] Pisarzewski, Bernardo (fetched 09.09.2014): "The Visit of the Pope"

1983: Ferrari Mondial Cabrio, 3.0L, V8, 214hp, 1420kg, design by Pininfarina

Beside the appreciation for the employees, the Pope's visit was also perfect external communication for Ferrari, as the visit had been topic for tv-news, magazines and newspapers around the world. The visit showed again the unique position of the Ferrari company. Giving the message that the company does not only produce ordinary sports cars, but is a part of the Italian culture, strongly connected to the Catholic church. It could be also understood as drawing a line under the Saturn comparison which had been written decades ago by the Vatican's own newspaper.

A Ferrari sports car as gift or donation normally makes management and compliance officers nervous, especially if it would be the last of the produced Enzos with a value of 1 Million US-Dollar and more. Donating it to a religious organization would deviate the policies of most of the global companies. But nevertheless, the Ferrari Corporation donated in 2004 the 400th and last produced Enzo to the Vatican. Of course the company had been very well aware that it was not an adequate automobile for the Pope to use. For this it became no surprise that John Paull II felt honored, but respectfully declined the acceptance. Instead he requested to give it to an auction and donate the money for the victims of the same year's Tsunami. He should not get these proceeds, as months later he died due to his long-term illness. Ferrari gave the achieved money to his successor, Pope Benedict XVI. Ten years later, this special Enzo were sold again at a Sotheby's auction, this time in Monterey, California and its proceeds had

BUSINESS PHILOSOPHY ACCORDING TO ENZO FERRARI

been 6,050,000 US-Dollar.[252]

2002: Ferrari Enzo, 6.0L, V12, 651hp @ 7800rpm, 335km/h, 1365kg, design by Pininfarina; photo with friendly permission from David Lee

This example presents a best-practice how to politely decline a non-appropriate gift, without displeasing the giver. To avoid the situation, a company can proactively inform clients, suppliers and other external stakeholders that employees are not permitted to receive presents. Of course, this can be combined with charity; as such information can include the company's preferred charity organization to which donate instead. Now the external party has the possibility to donate instead of sending a gift. Nevertheless the knowledge of a donation can trigger the same psychology effects as directly receiving the contribution.

---

[252] Blackwell, Rusty (2015): "Monterey Auctions Day 1: Top 10 Includes Pope John Paul II's Enzo"

Gifts and donations can easily produce an image of not being adequate. If they are too cheap they can offend and become contra-productive, if they are too expensive they can be perceived as attempt to "buy" the receiver. This can be successful and the gift or donation worked as a bribe or it can be rejected, and again the receiver feels offended and the process gets contra-productive.

A special red flag would be, if the potential receiver actively requests a gift or donation. An act of giving should be voluntary and made without the idea to receive something back. If yes, it looks like a bribe or as Enzo Ferrari defined it, it could distract someone from his or her duty.

Was the Enzo car an adequate donation? A topic to discuss, some questions, which can help us here:

- Who was the receiver? – In this case it was not a single person, but the Vatican itself. As the donation was publically communicated, no none could use the car for his or her personal benefit. No risk that, for example, a procurement employee could have taken the donation and decided in favor of Ferrari or Fiat in deviation to the Vatican's internal policies.

- Was the donation before the closing of a potential business opportunity? – This we do not know, but we can assume that the Vatican is a potential client for the Fiat corporation. However, traditionally the Vatican never limited itself to one supplier, but used different providers. A fact which got reflected by the Papamobils, which came from various manufacturers, including Fiat and Lancia, but also Mercedes Benz or Land Rover.

- As donation, Ferrari could deduce it from its annual tax declaration? – We do not know if it was a donation to a charity organization or the head of country. But at the end for transparency reasons it is not important, as it was tax relevant, but not de- or increased a potential corruption risk.

- Was it altruistic? – Ferrari had known that the Vatican would not keep the car, as a luxury good it was not compatible with the core values of the Catholic church. If the company wanted to support the church for pure charity reasons, it would had been much easier just to transfer 1 Million US-Dollar. Today exist thousands of charity organizations and even more good reasons to support a cause. For this, a company has to decide what it wants to support, mostly it will be a cause that has a more or less direct relation to the company's business or core values. A company which uses strongly this strategy is Benetton. Founded in 1963, since the beginning they followed the idea to offer colorful clothes and accessories, what they called "united colors". With this, they had the easy connection to diversity. Around this topic they started in 1991 a visible marketing campaign, including civil, social and political issues.[253] It got controversial discussed, but ensured that Benetton and its values were widely known in the market and by the target-group. Besides, the diversity topic was compatible to the company's sports marketing, in the early eighties the company became main sponsor for Tyrell and later the Alfa Romeo team.

---

[253] Benetton.com (fetched 10.09.2014): "Advertising"

1984: Alfa Romeo 184T, 1.5L, V8, 550kg, design by Mario Tolentino, Luigi Marmiroli

In this time as sponsor, positive race results had been rare. The highlight was in 1984 with Riccardo Patrese's third position at the Italian Grand Prix on an Alfa Romeo 184T. An historic result, as this became Alfa Romeo's last podium position in Formula One. Already in '51 Enzo said after his first victory: *"It's just like I've killed my mother."* In fact he did not killed her, it was a single victory based on special circumstances. Alfa Romeo still dominated these years. Ferrari had been more similar to a rebel teenager. Only later the team dominated the sports. After the '85 season, Alfa Romeo left Formula One. Mainly as the former governmental company became part of Fiat. As it did not make sense to have two companies competing in the same tournament, it was decided that this should be Ferrari, while Alfa Romeo successfully concentrated on other tournaments, as touring cars. As adult, the Scuderia Ferrari took now officially the responsibility from "her mother". Only later in 2017 the company decided to return and became technological partner of the Swiss Sauber F1-Team. Now the roles changed, as Alfa became Ferrari's junior team.

Benetton decided in '85 to focus strongly on Formula One and bought the Toleman-team, what became the base for the new Benetton F1-team. Later Ferrari driver Michael Schumacher won his first two world championships with this team and even had the role of a taxi driver, as Jean Alesi at his first Formula 1 victory ran out of gas and had to stop his car shortly after the finishing line. Thanks to Michael he nevertheless got the opportunity of greet the tifosi in an celebration lap around the Canadian track.

1995: Benetton Renault B195, 3.0L, V10, designed by Ross Brawn and Rory Byrne

With the donating of the Enzo to the Vatican, Ferrari made a statement that the company is connected to the catholic faith and with this, a strong part of the Italian culture. An important step to keep Ferrari away from being a normal car manufacturer, but keep company and products in the general mindset being an Italian culture good, fostering the company's iconic status.

Even if not directly related to the Vatican, a nice example for this is a tradition, which started in 1951, as the Father of a Local church in Modena began to ring the church bells after the first victory of the independent Ferrari team. A tradition, which can be heard after each Ferrari victory in Formula 1 until now.[254]

A decade later, Ferrari resurrected the company tradition and will produce one car more than the planned 499 of the actual super sports car LaFerrari to donate the revenue for the victims of the Italian 2016 earthquake.[255] This time there was no detour of giving the car first as a gift, but it got sold directly at an auction. The hybrid car had a reported price of approximate 1,4 Million USD, but as the last car of the series had an unique history and some differences in details to distinguish it from the 499 others, it got auctioned at a Ferrari weekend at the Daytona racetrack for 7 Million US-Dollar. So far the highest price achieved at an auction for a 21st Century automobile.[256] Ferrari announced the donation in summer 2016.

For a clear example of a gift we have to travel further back in time. In the beginning of the 1950's, Lancia was the leading team in motorsports. An important part of this success-story was written by Enzo Ferrari's long term fellow Vittorio Jano, who left the Scuderia to work for its competitor. Here he created in '53 the racing car D24.

---

[254] F1 Al Dia (2011): "Silverstone 1951: Que hiciste, Pepe!"

[255] Ferrari.com (2016): "The 500th La Ferrari to be built to benefit the people affected by the earthquake"

[256] Adams, Laurence (2016): "LaFerrari Auctioned for Charity Raises $7 Million for Earthquake Relief"

1953: Lancia D24, 3.3L, V6, 265hp, 260km/h, design by Pininfarina

The car proved its capability in the world's most difficult races, including it was able to win the '53 Carrera Panamericana and the '54 Mille Miglia and Giro di Sicilia. Further Pininfarina gave with this car an outlook on the design of the later '58 Ferrari Testa Rossa.

1958: Ferrari 250 Testa Rossa, 3.8L, V12, 360hp @ 7200rpm, design by Pininfarina

After these two successful years, Lancia officially left sports car racing to concentrate on Formula One and the new D50, also designed by Jano. Nevertheless the D24 was still in '55 a very competitive car and an excellent choice for rich and famous gentlemen driver. One of the few cars became a gift from the Lancia company, in person of Gianni Lancia, to the Argentinian president Juan Perón.

For a company it is a problematic question if their employees are allowed or not to receive gifts, especially around Christmas-time. One the one hand, gifts are always meant to positively influence the relation between two organizations and persons, but on the other hand it is also a sign of respect and to forbid receiving gifts may lower the employee's motivation level. Due to this, most companies allow their employees to receive adequate gifts. "Adequate" is a grey area and often explained that the employee should ask him or herself: *"You feel comfortable to read about it in tomorrow's newspaper?"* Perón answered this question for himself with a big "yes", in fact he was so proud of the car that he got it painted in the Argentinian national colors celeste & white and in the following time raced it personally in different local races.

As discussed earlier, values and attitudes are learnt in early age. It may look strange that a politician, who also officially defended worker rights and left-wing ideas, felt no shame to accept such luxury toys. More, he enjoyed to be seen with the car. Similar cases can be found until today, especially in cultures, which are based on families and friendships; in other words circles of trust. Inside these circles the different members support and care for each other. But with people outside these circles exist much less emotional connections, this explains why high governmental offices or politicians often do not feel ashamed to show their luxury lifestyle or even their received gifts.

Today we still may face a similar culture, but nevertheless, in opposite to 1955, such a gift would be forbidden, as it would be defined as bribery in many local laws and further, in the US Foreign Corrupt Practices Act and the UK Bribery Act. The last two laws are important, as the US and the UK also apply their laws for acts of corruption outside their borders, at least if the individual or the company has connection to the two countries. In today's connected world this is nearly always the case, as these are important markets or at least interesting places to have a bank account.

In 1980 the D24 returned from Argentina to Italy, being today one of only two existing models.²⁵⁷ For giver and receiver it not brought much luck. Perón had been overthrown September 21, '55 and Lancia had to sell its racing department in '56 after Alberto Ascari's tragic accident and financial problems.

5.8 Middlemen

Before Ferrari worked nearly exclusively with Pininfarina, their cars received designs by several Italian coachbuilders. Some of the most original ones came from Vignale. The contact between its director Arturo Vignale and Enzo Ferrari not started directly, but with the help of a middleman. Franco Cornacchia had a Ferrari and Maserati dealership in Milano and besides that was a gentleman driver for the Ferrari team.²⁵⁸ Later he should build up the Scuderia Guastalla, utilizing different kind of Ferrari sports cars. As he liked Ferrari cars, but also Vignale designs, he introduced Enzo to Arturo in 1950.²⁵⁹ We can assume that neither of the two had paid him a success fee for this new business, but nevertheless Cornacchia received his personal benefit out from the deal, as he later drove Ferrari cars with Vignale bodywork in several races, including at the famous Monza.²⁶⁰

---

[257] Conceptcarz.com (fetched 27.12.2015): 1954 Lancia D24 Sport Spyder

[258] Autosport.com (fetched 11.09.2014): "Who was Franco Cornacchia"

[259] Lehbrink, Hartmut, Schlegelmilch, Rainer (1995): "Ferrari"

[260] Barchetta.cc (fetched 11.09.2014): "Inter 212"

1955: Ferrari 225 Export Vignale Spyder,

Middlemen or Agents can play an important role for a company, as due to their experience and connections, new markets or clients could be exploited. But on the other hand it is also a critical topic, as this kind of third parties include not legal, but also reputational and business risks.

From a legal point, a company can be held responsible for its agents, especially if they are not properly controlled. This is a significant risk factor as most of the global corruption cases included the usage of an agent. But it must said clear here that in most of these situations the company was not the victim of the agents, but that corporation or at least single employees actively involved the agent to bypass internal policies and external laws. There is guidance available, how to control such third parties: "Good Practice Guidelines on Conducting Third-Party Due Diligence"[261], published for free by the World Economic Forum's Partnering Against Corruption Initiative.

In many cases a middleman gets included to utilize his or her good connections, as on the first view using this third party is cheaper than building up this knowledge and / or infrastructure internally. As the agent first of all behaves based on its own ideas and strategy, there is no insurance, that the company or physical person stays faithful until the end or maybe someday prefers working for the competitor. Other questions are what happens with our business, if the agent wants to retire or if we want to

---

[261] World Economic Forum (2013): "Good Practice Guidelines on Conducting Third-Party Due Diligence"

replace the agent finally with internal resource, he or she would understand our decision or in future would work against us. Important from legal side, a company can be held responsible for the action of its middleman, meaning if a sales agent bribed, the company behind is in the center of an investigation and could receive delicate fines.

The Carozzeria Vignale got forgotten with the time, acquired first by De Tomaso and later by Ford. But the US company has plans to resurrect the name and use it in future as additional brand for the most luxurious versions of its cars.

5.9) *"La Ferrarina"*

First of all, Enzo Ferrari saw his company as an engine manufacturer, for this he understood the motor has the key factor and competitive advantage in relation to other car companies. Already the first Ferrari car, the 125, had a 12-cylinder engine. This became for the company more than just a motor, but a philosophy. Originally constructed by Giocchino Colombo, every year the engine got further developed and is still the base for the actual Ferrari 12-cylinders.

As it was time to decide how the company would expand, Enzo decided against further in-sourcing, as for example to build up an internal design department, but consequently concentrated on additional engine types. As the technical state-of-the-art, the V12 cylinder should stay the engine of choice for the Ferrari cars, but the company identified a market below and wanted to commercialize its V6 engine, which was before only found in their racing cars.

1966: Dino 206 S, 2.0L, V6, 218hp @ 9000rpm, 580kg

The smaller and less powerful engine opened a new possibility for the company, to change the position of the motor also for street cars from the front to the middle. A solution which Enzo declined before, as he was afraid that this solution together with the powerful V12 would overexert the unexperienced drivers. To not to harm Ferrari's premium image, a new company was founded. On the one hand separated to avoid damage to the Ferrari philosophy, but on the other hand connected to ensure an image transfer from the original to the new company. The strongest sign of their connection was the name, as the new company got named Dino to honor Enzo's son. But at the same time it should be clear that a Dino is not a Ferrari and what would be a clearer statement than that cars were not sold in the traditional red. Involved customers found other details of connection as both company logos used the same yellow background and maybe more important, both companies used Pininfarina to design their cars.

1967: Dino 206 Competizione Prototipo, V6, 175hp @ 6500rpm, design by Pininfarina (Paolo Martin)

Based on the '66 Dino sports car, designer Paolo Martin created the Competizioni Prototipo. His favorite creation, as it represented the pure joy of driving.[262] His colleague Leonardo Fioravanti used this inspiration and created later the Dino 206 GT with softer lines, but still similar to the prototype. One year later, in '68, the company introduced the 246 GT.

---

[262] Martin, Paolo (2017): "Martin's Cars - Pensieri in tre dimensioni"

1969: Dino 246 GT, 2.4L, V6, 196hp @ 7600 rpm, 238 km/h, 1080kg, design by Pininfarina (Leonardo Fioravanti)

The cars received soon a positive image based on their design and handling. Thanks to this, the cars found to be worthy to get the Ferrari name. In '76 the Dino company closed and the cars received the original Ferrari badge.

Dino was the second attempt to establish a separate company to manufacture cars with smaller engines. Already at the end of the 1950s Ferrari tested a prototype with a small 850cc 4 cylinder engine. The goal was to offer a proper car for the fast growing middle class, not just in Italy and Europe, but also in the US. Ferrari used the same strategy, as later for Dino, have an external designer, in this case Carrozzeria Bertone and sell the car under a separate company. The prototype was presented at Turin Auto Show 1961, but not to find clients for the car, but for the whole concept. The de Nora family became interested, as they not only had been the owners of an electromechanical factory, but also long term Ferrari clients. Their plan had been to produce the car in one of their existing plants under the brand AVA (Autocostruzione Società per Azioni). Niccolò de Nora, ASA's director elaborated an agreement with Enzo Ferrari, which was excluding the usage of the famous brand, but they could win the participation of the former Ferrari engineer Giotto Bizzarrini, who had been involved in the original development of the small car. Thanks to his modifications, the engine reached 97HP, 5 more than the 1.6L Alfa Romeo engine.[263] Enzo's friend and partner Luigi Chinetti involved himself to sell

---

[263] Cavaliere, David (2016): "The History of Italian Automobiles Part 6" Autocostruzioni Societa per Azioni (ASA) and the Ferrarini

the ASA cars via his official Ferrari dealership in the US.

Even if Ferrari officially not had been involved anymore in the project, the public called their first car, the 1000 GT, immediately *"Ferrarina"*, Italian for "Little Ferrari".

But all this should not help, as the relative high prices (In the US the car costed slightly more than the Jaguar E-Type) prevented the cars to become a success. In '67 ASA had to close its doors and the 4 cylinder concept was buried.[264] The same year as Pininfarina presented the prototype for the later Dino.

5.10 *"Racing amuses me"*

Enzo Ferrari himself brought it to the point what his main motivator was: *"Racing amuses me."* To ensure the financing of a competitive racing department, we started selling sports cars. Until today these street cars include the DNS of the company's race cars. This requires to have a target group who values this relation, independent if they race themselves or just follow motor sports as spectators. Traditionally the motor sports virus was given from father to son, starting from Sunday visit at a local racing event.

The times changed and the Ferrari company found solutions to ensure customer loyalties via a strong portfolio of merchandising and communication measures. Even the youngest are included with a line of Ferrari strollers, children seats and teddy bears. These early contacts lead to an early embossing of the child and to sympathy for the brand. A first step, the second is to excite the girl or boy for motor sports, especially Formula One.

Activision published in 1983 one of the first video games for the Atari console. Due to the limited technical possibilities, in-game graphics still could not be used to show a specific car, but the green game cartridge had the iconic Lancia Stratos on the cover. Even with the technical limitations

---

[264] International ASA Register (fetched 14.04.2015): "A bit of history"

the programmer Larry Miller reached to simulate the typical situation of a rally, including day, night, streets, fog and snow.

Already five years later, modern home computers, as the Commodore Amiga, offered an adequate base to simulate a complete Formula One Championship. Electronic Arts presented "Ferrari Formula One Racing Simulation. The software house understood that the combination of software with famous brands made a commercial success more predictable. As producer Richard Hilleman's grand-father raced stock cars, he spent many week-ends on race tracks and practically grew up in the pits. So he had a different approach, not creating another arcade game, but a simulation. Similar to earlier EA titles as Earl Weaver and John Madden, the software should present real cars and real race tracks. In the middle of the 1980s, Ferrari was successful with the Testrarossa or the F40, but the Formula One team was not competitive. Nevertheless, Electrical Arts decided to create the simulation around the Scuderia, this as it was by far the most famous Formula One team, especially on the important US market.

EA contacted the Ferrari company and made them an initial offer for the brand license. EA represent Richard Hilleman flew to Maranello for negotiation and to close the deal. Ferrari was open to the idea, even if their marketing focus was on winning clients for the F40.

Later, game designer Rick Koenig programmed the software in nine months. He himself never visited the Ferrari plant or had the a direct contact with the F1-86, the car that he simulated.

The F1-86 was one of the technological most advanced cars of the 1986 Formula One season, including modern materials as carbon fiber and Kevlar. The car had been sharped in Ferrari's one wind tunnel and the engine was one of the strongest in the field. Nevertheless the hoped results never came. Because of missing test kilometers before the start of the season, the engineers never achieved reliability.

1986: Ferrari F1-86, 1.5L, Straight 4, 850hp @ 11500rpm, 330km/h, 548kg, design by Harvey Postlethwaite

Rick based his creation on Rich Hilleman's descriptions, a book by former Ferrari driver Niki Lauda: "The new Formula One: A turbo age"[265] and calibrated the simulation that way, that the virtual car reached similar lap times as the real Ferrari in that season. Even if he never had a direct contact with the car or the company, Rick Koenig created the first real 3D Formula One simulation with race, qualification, set up, including the Ferrari team and the Fiorano track. This ten years before "Formula One" came for the Playstation and other platforms. An interesting side note is that the game programming started in 1987, the simulation had been published in '88, but nevertheless it is presenting the '86 season, including car and drivers. As Rick Hilleman had the motorsports virus, he produced later the further titles "Indianapolis 500" and "Andretti Racing". In that time he presented "Ferrari Formula One" to the former Ferrari driver Mario Andretti, but as Mario had problems with the Mouse, he wasn't able to keep the car on the track and due to this, could not give further feedback. Richard stayed in contact with motorsports. Even if after "Indianapolis 500" he never produced any racing title, he built high performance go-karts and raced different kind of cars.

Nearly 20 years later, in 2016 it is not required anymore to create an own racing game. Established titles as "Gran Turismo" offer an ideal opportunity to promote a brand. Mercedes Benz designed a prototype exclusive for Gran Turismo 6, the AMG Vision Gran Turismo. Only later the company presented a 1:1 model in the real world. The internet connections make temporary events possible, as a Ferrari Challenge, where

---

[265] Lauda, Niki (1984): " A new Formula One: A turbo age"

players can participate for the certain period of a month.

Computers and video game consoles can present a technical accurate copy of a real car, but it is difficult to simulate here the physical exposure of the drivers. Due to this, Ferrari went one step further. Not everybody has the opportunity to drive once a real Formula One car. For this the company opened in its Milan store the Ferrari Simulation Center. Here the everyday visitor can get a realistic experience, how it is to drive a modern F1 car. What looks on TV as an easy job, is in reality an extreme sport, as even on a long straight it is difficult to keep the car under control, as all the time you have to slightly counteract and keep the steering wheel in a firm grip. As it is only a simulation, it not includes real g-forces, but nevertheless the hobby driver exists the simulator with a different opinion about the sports. The amateur gets a good impression of the physical requirements to drive the whole race distance on the limit. Especially in the last laps fatigue may lead to the loose of concentration and regarding accidents.

2016: Ferrari Simulation Center, Milan, Italy

If you prefer physical racing, kart tracks offer an adrenaline filled experience. These small, but agile vehicles are the natural first step to become one day a famous race driver. Because of their direct handling, even later, drivers always like to go back to their karts. Three times Formula One champion Ayrton Senna described it once: *"I started racing go-karts. And I love karts. It's the most breath taking sport in the world. More than F1, indeed, I used to like it most."* It is only consequent that Ferrari's theme park "Ferrari World Abu Dabi" in Dubai has its own Karting Academy, featuring modern electric karts. Who live it even faster can ride on "Formula Rossa", one of the world's fastest roller scooter, which accelerates from 0 to 240km/h in only 4.9 seconds.[266]

Ferrari World Abu Dabi, photo with friendly permission from Ferrari World Abu Dabi

---

[266] Ferrari World Abu Dabi (fetched 21.9.2016): "Formula Rossa"

Formula Rossa, photo with friendly permission from Ferrari World Abu Dabi

Former Ferrari driver Mario Andretti opened two indoor kart centers in the Atlanta region. Here the visitor can chose between electric and the more powerful gasoline karts, which can reach up to 65km/h.

This for ones, who dream about being or becoming a famous driver, but Ferrari also always stood for engineering skills. Due to this, a cooperation with Lego was logical. Here the future engineers can construct models of different difficulty levels. Independent if you prefer to drive or engineer, the Ferrari company sets the foundation stone for future "Ferraristi".

5.11 Project Sigma

Even if we have today a romantic view on 60's motorsports, in reality it was also much more dangerous as on present day, with regular fatal accidents and drivers dying in each season. A reality that also affected the Ferrari team, not only in Formula One, but also in the different sports car-events. On the other hand, the end of the '60s was a time, where people had a positive attitude towards technology and believed that most of the world's problems could be solved by new developments.

In 1969, the Swiss car magazine Automobile Revue suggested Pininfarina a project to develop a potential grand prix car to test and include different safety devices. Paolo Martin was Pininfarina's rising star and received the task to create the Sigma Gran Prix. An interesting choice has he stated once that he is dreaming in three dimensions and his models had been an impression of his original ideas. The Scuderia Ferrari supported the project with a bearing structure of a 312 F1-car, including its 12-cylinder engine. At that time neither Paolo or Pininfarina as company had further experience with Formula One.[267] It was an unique situation of disruption, as fresh sources thought about a given situation. This especially as the designer received a maximum of freedom to develop his own ideas. Later Steve Jobs said: *"It doesn't make sense to hire smart people and tell them what to do; we hire smart people so they can tell us what to do."*

"Disruption" is in fashion today, to stop the current and give opportunity to the new. Disruption does not automatically mean that something will be implemented, but that a break can be used to think about the status quo and potential alternatives. A new decision making process will choose between continuing on the known path or change to a new one.[268]

For the Sigma, Paolo came up with new ideas, such as buffer zones, enforced fuel tanks and even the concept to lock the driver's helmet to the car to prevent damages to the most vulnerable part: the human head.[269]

---

[267] Martin, Paolo (2017): "Martin's Cars - Pensieri in tre dimensioni"

[268] Henz, Patrick (2017): "Tomorrow's Business Ethics: Game On"

[269] Martin, Paolo (2017): "Martin's Cars - Pensieri in tre dimensioni"

1969: Pininfarina Sigma Gran Prix, 3.0L, V12, 436hp, 590kg, design by Pininfarina (Paolo Martin). Photo with friendly permission from Paolo Martin.

1969: Ferrari 312, 3.0L, V12, 534kg, design by Mauro Forghieri.

Probably the most common difference between the Sigma and the '69 Formula One cars had been that the wheels had not been free, but the car's body was constructed around them. This should prevent a typical monoposto-risk that cars touch each other's wheels and lift off. Especially the idea that the front-wing is no separate part, but instead integrated into the car's body had been later in 1971 taken on by the Tyrell-Ford team, the car (Tyrell 002) that helped Jackie Stewart to win the championship. Nevertheless the integrated front-wing not stayed inside Formula One as even it offered higher safety levels, it limited the team's flexibility. Not only as you could not change the wing inside the race, if there was a slight accident, furthermore teams developed the aerodynamics over the season, so hardly the car ran in the final race the same wings than it did at the season's start. Beside safety, cost reduction would be a positive side-effect, if the FIA would change the regulations for F1-design.

The Sigma was a statistic model, meaning it was based on the Ferrari F1 312 and included its engine, but it was not drivable. It was never meant to be, as it was first of all, an exercise to understand how new safety features could be integrated into a Formula One car. As a technical documentation, Paolo created two 1:4 scale models. Today, one is exhibited at the Pininfarina-, and the other one at the Ferrari-museum. Ferrari itself presented in 2017 the "Formula 1 Concept".[270] As sign of the times, there is no physical model existing, only a virtual one. Ironically, this gave the F1 Concept the theoretical advantage that it could be driven, at least inside virtual reality. The design itself presented similarities to the car, which was done nearly 50 years before, as also the F1 Concept included wings integrated into the body. Other parallels were the top-wing and the driver's helmet fixed to the car.

Today disruption allows fresh ideas to enter the company. A vividly example is the autonomous cargo vehicle "Gita", developed by Piaggio Fast Forward, a daughter company of the original Vespa company[271] (where Paolo worked in the 1980s and created the '88 Cosa).

They used the traditional concept of urban individual transportation and interpreted it completely new. Instead of personal transport as the Vespa, they came up with Gita. The robot can work autonomously or follow an individual. Doing so, it can transport laptops, food or other cargo. Even if the basic design reminds to the Star Wars-droid BB-8, Piaggio's designers did a perfect job to include retro-touches, including colors, to keep the spirit of the Vespa alive. With this, the design supported the image-transfer from Vespa to Gita and kept Piaggio's claim up to be a leader in individual transportation.

---

[270] Ferrari (2017): "Formula 1 Concept"

[271] Piaggio Fast Forward (2017): "Gita"

2017: Piaggio Fast Forward Gita, press photo. With friendly permission from Element Public Relations.

6 THE CHEQUERED FLAG

6.1) *"Whom am I in this world."*
6.2) *"I think fundamentally I belong to another time."*
6.3) Enzo for Startups
6.4) Puccini, Ferrari & The Return of the Artists
6.5) Ferrari today
6.6) The Day that Enzo Ferrari predicted Industry 4.0
6.7) Enzo 4.0
6.8) The Legacy

BUSINESS PHILOSOPHY ACCORDING TO ENZO FERRARI

6.1 *"Whom am I in this world."*

Enzo Ferrari was a complex person, as besides his preference for epic histories with himself as the tragic hero, he was humble. Ironically in opposite to a part of his clients, he never was a someone who liked to show off with his financial possibilities and never drove his own cars with the idea to be seen. If he drove one of his own creations, it was full of respect for the machine and the wish to make the good even better. For pure transportation he used less expensive and sophisticated automobiles. Luxury was not important for him, but his life's work.

Further he was a strong believer of competition (chapter 4.6) and its positive impact on the final product. Conversely, the absence of competition would lead to stagnation, as often seen in a monopoly market, independent if with a private or public company. Even worse, such a situation can get dangerous for the company, as the absence of competition could let to missing experience how to defend against competitors, until unawareness that such may arise through the appearance of new companies.

You are leading the race and because of the huge gap to second, you already perceive the race as won. As in competition it is most important to know where the competitor is, it is no surprise that the rear mirror was originally invented for the motorsports and then later introduced in two steps for streetcars. In the 1970s and early 80s, most car manufacturers thought it is enough to have a mirror on the driver's side, for this the mirror on the co-driver's side was often only available against additional charge. In motorsports, since the beginning the rear mirrors had been on both sides, as the driver had to see if the competitor is directly behind or still far-away. Maybe the other car tries to overtake on the left or right. Only if you know where your competitor is, you are able to execute counter-measures as, for example, leave the ideal line and block the car behind you.

For the case of a monopoly, the ideal line means the company will set up a relative high price for its product, so that based on its cost structure it will reach the highest profit. As results many potential clients are not able or not want to buy the product. If the market is not protected and it is possible to produce a similar product, such a constellation will attract competitors.

There are many examples that a market leader lost this position until leaving the race

- Sony: With the rise of Japanese technology companies in the 1980s, Sony reached a leadership position, which is comparable to Apple thirty years later. Their claim "It's not a trick, it's a Sony" brought it perfectly on the point. The 80's iPod was Sony's "Walkman", the first device for masses to take their music everywhere with them. Walkman was the synonym for portable cassette-players and everybody wanted the original and not the competitor's product, because of quality, but also its image. With the raise of CDs, Sony weakened the trademark, as they called their portable CD-Players "Discman". In the beginning the product was still successful in the market, but slowly the downfall began. Today the "Walkman" still exists as MP3-Player, but has no standing against the Apple products, also as today's consumers do not see any special Walkman image anymore.

- Lego: The company had been founded in 1949 and became famous for its brick construction toys. But then in the 80s and 90s, children began to prefer playing with the new home computers and video consoles. At the end of century, Lego was near bankruptcy. Coming from McKinsey, the young Jørgen Vig Knudstorp became the company's CEO. He changed the organization of the former family company, including outsourcing of the theme parks and signing of expensive, but attractive licenses. With this Lego was able to offer brick sets with Superheroes, Disney Princesses, Harry Potter, Star Wars and, yes, Ferrari. Especially with the last, Lego was not limited anymore to the young target group, but had been able to keep them and today also have products for the young-at-heart clients, including that a special set of Legos only had been available at the fuel stations of Ferrari's sponsor Shell. But the company went further, it created a bridge to its former competitors and designed Lego sets, which you can construct in the real world and connect to the virtual one, so that these constructions can be used inside computer games.

The other car gets bigger and bigger in rear mirror. As result, before the curves you will leave the idea line and look for another brake-point. To translate this into business language, it means that the company has to leave its comfort-zone and to lower the price and / or make the product more attractive.

As there is still an advantage, the company can afford to ask for a higher price than the competitor, even if the products are identical. This thanks to the fact, that for the buyer the positive experience with the product in the past also has a value. It can be that the buyer is adapted to the usage of the product or simple that from the positive experience in the past the buyer assumes to the actual quality. This is especially valid for goods, where the actual quality cannot be examined in the buying situation. This is, for example true for the purchase of a car. With a test drive you are able to understand how the car is today, but not how well it will be in 5 years.

The race is on for a while and now it would be time for a pit stop to get fresh tires or perform some updates on the car's setup. In the 1996's DTM (German Touring Car) series, it was even possible to change the complete car's engine in less than 15 minutes. A long time for a sprint race, but if you in an endurance competition, it may lead to victory. For the company, the tires symbolize a short-term change and the exchange of engine, for the deeper change of strategy.

The 90's Alfa Romeo DTM team

If the other car is faster, based on technical superiority, better tire conditions or surprisingly weather conditions; in one moment both cars will be par. In business life we have now the perfect competition. If products are exchangeable; the prices must be identical. Profits in the market are minimal, and the race is not attractive for new competitors to enter.

Similar as in sports, there is a psychological advantage for the company, which closed the gap, as the potential buyers and trade press recognize the positive development, while the other one shows a negative tendency. This is not only important in the competition for clients, but also in the one to get the best employees.

The described scenario for a car without rear mirrors is fatal. The driver has no information where the competitor's car is, still far-away or right behind. Maybe it is already trying to overtake on the left or on the right? Especially if the driver has the wrong impression that he or she thinks that the competitor is still far away, but in reality is not, this leads to a wrong strategy. In a comfortable lead you do not drive at the limit as you want to save on fuel and gasoline. To achieve this you use the track's ideal line. If you are unaware of a near and faster opponent, this one has no difficulty to overtake you in the next opportunity.

Perception is subjective to the viewer, for this not only the existing and seize of rear-mirrors is important, but further who is looking into them. A success-seeker tends to overestimate the distance to the following opponent and a failure-avoider will perceive the other car closer than it is really is. A realistic view on the competitors is needed!

Enzo Ferrari was well aware of his own capabilities. Thanks to his friendship with Tazio Nuvolari, he early recognized that he self was a good driver, but could not compete with the best. Also as engineer he could understand the technology, but was not able to build the perfect engine or race-car, for this he had people as Vittorio Jano. Enzo's biggest talent had been in the management of the company and racing team. As a humble person, he had the required respect regarding his competitors and a good view on the complete picture, including where he has persons stands in the world and the specific situation. *"Whom am I in this world"*, he analyzed for himself. This capability was essential to for the company's success until today.

Thanks to his emotional intelligence and self-education, he was able to handle difficult situations and different kind of characters. With his strong will and the capability to combine product and company with his person, he was surprisingly near to another famous manager and leader, who was born nearly 60 years later on another continent, Steve Jobs. We have modern theories and vocabulary, but if you analyze the person, Enzo's skills and methods still would make him today a modern and successful leader. Independent that he lived in another century and culture.

Integrity based leadership is not just comfortable for the employees, but it is an important success-factor for the company. Due to the brand evaluation consultancy "Brand Finance" Ferrari is the world's most powerful brand today. With an overall ranking of AAA+, it received top scores in the categories desirability, loyalty and consumer sentiment to visual identify, online presence and employee satisfaction; just as Enzo described it as "elite works".[272] Being leader in these categories allow the company to sell their cars with attractive margins and use the prancing horse further for other merchandising as clothes, watches and even strollers.

In 2014 Ferrari is 90% owned by Fiat Chrysler Automobiles and the other 10% belong to Piero Ferrari. Less than 3000 employees[273] produced 7,318 cars in 2012.[274] With this they reached 2013 a revenue of 2.3 billion Euro.[275]

On the track, the Scuderia won 16 Formula 1 Constructors' Championships and 15 driver ones, more than any other team. Beside Formula 1, the team won most of the prestigious races as Le Mans, Daytona, Sebring and the road courses Targa Florio, Mille Miglia and the Carrera Panamericana.

Ferrari is not the exception, but the rule that integrity leads to profitable and sustainable business. According to research by Simon Webley and Elise More, companies with an explicit commitment to conduct business ethically presented from 1997 to 2001 and 18% higher profit/turnover ratios than

---

[272] Brand-Finance (2014): "Ferrari – The World's Most Powerful Brand"

[273] Fiat (2012): Annual Report 2011

[274] Fiat (2013): Annual Report 2012

[275] Fiat (2014): Annual Report 2013

the ones without such a commitment.[276] In the same direction is Ethisphere going, as their comparison of the "World's Most Ethical Companies" against the Standard & Poor's 500 showed in 2007 around 7% better development of the regarding stocks and in 2011 even over 30%. The better performance is notable in times of recession, but also a positive economic environment.[277]

The mentioned "elite work" is not just a sign of respect from the employees to the employer. Furthermore it is a sign of respect of the whole company towards its clients. By this means are the same trust concepts valid as between two persons. If the client does not understand the offered product, not esteems it or, even worse in the business-two-business-relation, asks for in-proper discounts, the supplier loses the respect for the potential client. When negotiations are only about the money, elite work cannot get maintained. Not only because the invested time does not pay, but because dedication gets not appreciated. Positive recognition is an important motivational factor. Employees need it from the management, but also to receive it from the customer. This is another reason why it is imperative to have an internal control and compliance system, because if parts of the company, as sales or procurement would start doing business in a non-proper matter, for example with giving or receiving bribes, on the long run this behavior would spread out in the whole company and even affect the production unit. As they would see that their products do no not receive any more the wanted appreciation, as the client's procurement department chooses them based on personal benefits (bribe), it is impossible for these engineers and factory workers to motivate themselves and produce elite work.

Building up respect between supplier and client was the Italian way of doing business, which was also practiced by Enzo. He gave this respect to others, but also demanded it from employees and customers. If he perceived that this was not the case, he stayed consistent and separated the employees from the company or boycotted the client. On the short run, he risked sales figures and race results, but on the long run this business philosophy

---

[276] Webley, Simon / More, Elise (fetched 09.10.2014): "Does Business Ethics Pay?"

[277] Ethisphere (fetched 09.10.2014): "2011 World's Most Ethical Companies"

fostered the Ferrari myth and made corporation and race department successful. Further, respect cannot only be showed and perceived between different people, integrity based behavior leads to respect four yourself. As individuals need a positive self-perception, such self-respect is a priceless reward.

Because of their differences, Enzo refused to speak anymore with Ferruccio Lamborghini, but nevertheless the stop of communication, they never lost the respect for each other and the competition stayed clean between the two company. Ferruccio remembered Enzo in a later interview: *"He was a great man, I admit, but it was so very easy to upset him."* [278]

1953: Ferrari 340 MM Vignale Spider, 4.1L, V12, 300hp @ 6600rpm, design by Carrozzeria Vignale

6.2 *"I think fundamentally I belong to another time."*

Interesting that Enzo said this with the idea that he belonged to the past. His several alignments to Machiavelli or the history of the Roman Empire underlined this attitude. But analyzing his business decisions, makes it clear that he fitted perfectly into the Italy of the 20th century. Especially because of his knowledge and sensibility he could built up the company to the one, we know today.

---

[278] Thoroughbred & Classic Cars (1991): "Interview with Ferruccio Lamborghini"

Further if we understand his philosophy and actions, we can see that most of this has not lost any meaning and Enzo is still an inspiration for today's managers and leaders; for the sustainability of the company and the benefit of most employees. For all employees? Definitely not, as history showed that he was indeed a leader with edges. But this is not different from two other celebrated leaders as Steve Jobs[279] or Richard Branson.[280] Enzo was aware of his weaknesses, but could say that he always stayed faithful to his own philosophy.

Enzo Ferrari
"Equally valuable lessons are learnt in defeat and victory"

Bill Gates[281]
"Success is a lousy teacher. It seduces smart people into thinking they can't lose."

Richard Branson[282]
"Do not be embarrassed by your failures, learn from them and start again."

Enzo Ferrari
"The client is not always right"

Steve Jobs
"A lot of times, people don't know what they want until you show it to them."

Enzo Ferrari answering to the question, which is his favorite model
"That which is yet to be built"

Steve Jobs[283]
"I think if you do something and it turned out pretty good, ... Just figure out what's next"

---

[279] Tate, Ryan (2011): "What Everybody is Too Polite to Say About Steve Jobs"

[280] Chakrabortty, Aditya (2013): "Don't be fooled by Richard Branson's defense of Virgin trains"

[281] Brainy Quotes (fetched 28.04.2015): "Bill Gates Quotes"

[282] Brainy Quotes (fetched 28.04.2015): "Richard Branson Quotes"

[283] Levy, Karyne / Love, Dylan (2014): " Steve Jobs' 14 Most Inspiring Quotes"

Enzo Ferrari
"What we do here is elite work."

Steve Jobs
"Quality is more important than quantity"

6.3 Enzo for Startups

If you ask the experts which was the first Ferrari car, you will get different answers. Some will mention the 1935 Alfa Romeo Bimotore. The concept of having two engines, one in the front and one in back perfectly aligns with Enzo's philosophy that *"aerodynamics are for people who can't build engines."* At that time, the in the year '32 presented Alfa P3 was technically inferior against the new competitors from Mercedes Benz and Auto Union. This not only in relation of power, but further the German companies included the latest knowledge about aerodynamics in the creation of their race cars. Also because of a limited budget, Enzo wanted to counter this development with the double of engine power. This solution was less technical complex and expensive, as it was mainly based on the idea to include a second identical engine into the car.

The Bimotore is an ideal example that motivated employees can achieve their liberty inside a company, it is not always necessary to leave a big organization and found an own company, especially as this means risk and limitation of leisure time. Depending on the personal character, responsibility and freedom to decide can motivate or demotivate an employee. To keep its key-employees, a company creates the required environment. If this is not possible or responsibilities get limited, the employee loses its motivation and may decide to change the company or create its own.

After ten years successful as Alfa Romeo employee, Enzo Ferrari had more and more disagreements with the company's new technical director, and his direct manager, Spaniard Wilfred Ricart. As his responsibilities got cut down, Enzo saw no other possibility than to leave Alfa in 1939. As key-employee he had signed a non-competing agreement and due to this, he could not use the "Scuderia Ferrari" name for the next four years. To nevertheless start his own business, he founded already in '39 "Auto Avio Construzioni".

The company created the 815, another often-heard answer to the question which was the first Ferrari car. It is known about Enzo that is favorite engine construction was the twelve cylinder, since he saw a Packard 299 race car. This US race car featured a 4.9 V12 engine and had been brought to Italy to participate there in different events from 1920 to 22. The Packard was owned and driven by Baroness Maria Antonietta Avanzo. Enzo recalled her later as *"the first courageous woman driver of the postwar era"*. In 1932 she started with an Alfa Romeo 6C 1750 GS Spider as official part of the Scuderia Ferrari. The Packard brought her not too much luck, once the car had been on fire at a race in Denmark, so that she had to drive the car into the sea to stop it. Later she sold the car to Alberto Ascari and remembered it with the words that the Packard *"went from owner to owner, and no-one managed to get any good results from it except Enzo Ferrari, who said that it had given him the inspiration for his future 12-cylinder cars."*[284] Due to Maria Antonietta, Enzo's fascinating for the twelve cylinder engine started with seeing her drive that Packard 299. A car which he had known before only from photos, as it participated at Indianapolis 500.

Nevertheless for his own company's first car he resisted to create a twelve cylinder, but instead used a more conventional eight cylinder engine. As most of the car's components, AAC not manufactured them their selves, but bought them from the Fiat company. Thanks to this realistic project approach and have as much parts as possible bought and not made, the young company could achieve to finish its crucial first project, not only present the 815, but also employ it in such prestigious races as the 1940 Mille Miglia.

Of course Enzo's vision was to build a successful twelve cylinder race car, what he realized seven years later, now not only with his own company, but also under his own name: Ferrari S.p.A. To develop this motor, Enzo could motivate Gioacchino Colombo, whom he still knew from his time at Alfa Romeo, to join the new Ferrari company. Colombo just had been laid off

---

[284] Ludvigsen, Karl (2010): "Genesis 1.5:12"

and so was free to take on new tasks. Both men had the same philosophy and been passionate about the twelve cylinder solution. The result, the famous "Colombo Engine" became an important step to establish the company in the market and fostered Ferrari's myth. The 1946 version became base for many motors and could be found, for example, later in the '48 125 F1, '58 Testa Rossa until the '89 412.

6.4 Puccini, Ferrari & The Return of the Artists

Giacomo Puccini's opera "Madame Butterfly" premiered 1904 at Milan's La Scala. But in opposite to his earlier works, the reaction from the audience and critics had not been favorable. They claimed that music and story had been too similar to his earlier creations.

2016: Milan's La Scala

As a sensible artist, Puccini withdrew the opera and rewrote it, so that it had its second premiere only three months later in Brescia. Now it received a more positive reaction. In the following years Madame Butterfly travelled all over the world, including performances at the famous opera houses of Buenos Aires, Paris and the US. Puccini accompanied the opera to most of these places to arrange the performances and see how the local audience reacts to it. Based on this, Puccini still made sever changes to the opera and in 1907 finished the fifth and final version.

As he was an artist it was important to him to create a perfect work. A similar attitude, what had also his fellow countryman Enzo Ferrari: *"I should like to put something new into my cars every morning."* As child, before getting the idea to become a race driver, he wanted to be an opera singer. Still later he comprehended manufacturing as the art to build hand-made cars. Until the 1960's hardly one of his cars had been identical to an earlier one. This as the company tailored them after the individual client, but also Ferrari always included new ideas to build better cars. For this it is understandable that Enzo never became a friend of the automated factory production. He understood that it was the necessary next step for the company, but as it was not inside his nature, he searched for a partner and found it in 1969 with Fiat.

A good example of his artisan way to build cars is the 330 TRI ("Testa Rossa Independente"). After the first of the legendary Testa Rossa debuted in '56, six years later the company built with the 330 TRI the last of them. With this car the era of the front-engine prototypes should find its final chapter, as the 330 TRI became the last car with a front-engine to win the traditional 24 Hours of Le Mans. But the car itself was not an end, as the race car development was a continuous flow. Its design included elements from other Ferraris, like the shark from 156 F1 or the back from 250 GTO, and inspired later cars.

1962: Ferrari 330 TRI, 4.0L, V12, 390hp @ 7500rpm, 820kg

The sound of its traditional twelve cylinder engine is like an orchestra and the combination of acceleration and deceleration composes its own opera. No surprise that 2015 Puccini and Ferrari officially came together, while the operas had been performed at Bologna's Enzo Ferrari Auditorium.[285]

Enzo never became a friend of industrial production. Ironically is that today's and tomorrow's production seems to give his approach a comeback:

- Content is liberated from physical storage mediums as CD, DVD, books and newspaper. This means that content does not have to be static, but can be in a flow to be adapted when necessary. Articles at news portal can be rewritten as soon as new information is available. With this tablets have an advantage against printed daily newspapers. Even if here the effect is most obvious, it affects also other media: books can printed on demand and musicians do not have to create a whole album, but can release continuously their songs.

- New production possibilities, including 3D-printers, give small scale production a possibility to compete with the mass producers. A good example is today the electric car manufacturer Tesla, but can go much further than that. Further it is a new possible re-manufacture spare parts for classic automobiles and so give them a longer productive life. The physical production of an idea gets easier for the young entrepreneur. Even more today than in the last century, Enzo Ferrari's quote: *"If they are good ideas, then they work"* is valid. But still it should not be underestimated that the development of a business idea, stays a challenge.

- Needs and wishes from today's and tomorrow's generations create new solutions to old topics. Often these ideas come from companies outside the traditional market. Apple revolutionized the music sector, Uber takes on the established Taxi business and online sales is slowly replacing the established department-stores.

---

[285] Bologna 2000 (2015): "Giovedì 17 dicembre all'Auditorium Enzo Ferrari la rassegna "Recitar Cantando": musiche di Mascagni e Puccini"

Some established companies are not able to change and adapt, but for the consumer it is a change to see again more diversity. This offers new perspectives for artists, startups and craftsmen to challenge the big global players.

6.5 Ferrari Today

In 2017 Ferrari celebrated its 70th company anniversary. It is nearly 30 years ago when Il Commentadore died. Since then, as before, the Ferrari Corporation continued its success story by following its founder's vision & values and adapt them to the actual environment. This could be reached by officially incorporate these values and not only proudly present them on the company website and use them as base for its Code of Conduct[286], but live them. As discussed earlier, integrity is defined as value-based behavior, so it is no surprise that the Ferrari Code of Conduct starts with the chapter "Road to Integrity". On the website the company did something interesting, it paired their values:

- Individual & Team
- Emotion & Integrity
- Tradition & Innovation
- Passion & Excellence[287]

The reader of the book remembers that these combinations are not the invitation of a corporate communication department, but directly can be linked to Enzo himself:

- Individual talent is needed and has to be integrated into the complete team.
- Positive emotion requires a value-based lifestyle.

---

[286] Ferrari (fetched 11.6.2017): "Ferrari Code of Conduct"

[287] Ferrari (fetched 11.6.2017): "Values"

- Tradition does is not limited itself to the achievements of the past, but includes the respect of the original vision to develop the fastest car of all.
- Excellence cannot reached alone by hard work, but requires a high level of motivation: passion.

For the Ferrari excellence is defined with *"working your heart"* and stay open-minded about the world.

Liberty Media bought in 2016 the Formula One organization and implemented Chase Carey as its new director. The new owner changed the championship's strategy and brought the series a bit more back to roots and with this, nearer to the fans. As part of this, drivers and teams gained more possibilities to interact with their fans, including on social media platforms.

The 2017 Barcelona grand prix saw an entertaining race, where Mercedes driver Luis Hamilton won with less than 4 seconds advantage before Ferrari's Sebastian Vettel. Noticeable had been also the start where in the first curve Valterri Bottas, Kimi Raikkkonen und Max Verstappen had to experience that there was only place for two cars. The result: Bottas could continue, but Räikkönen and Verstappen had been out of the race. On the main tribune, a small Kimi fan broke out in tears, what cameras effectively showed for the millions of TV viewers in the whole world. The Ferrari team saw it too, and decided to act. Their press team tracked down the boy and his family and invited them to the motor-home, where he not only could see the cars, but met Kimi, who gave him his Ferrari cap.[288] Little Thomas not stayed only with the Scuderia, but met also other drivers as Haas' Romain Grosjean and started his reporter career with interviewing the Renault team. Without doubt, the misery turned into his happiest day so far.

---

[288] Negative Camber (2017): "Carey: Crying Kimi fan wouldn't have smiled in old F1"

As Chase Carey stated later, such an action had not been possible last year with the anterior processes and guidelines. Now with less rules, the teams have more freedom to act based on their own decisions and so on their values and attitudes. Ferrari's corporate values include excellence, connected with passion. As they appreciate their fans (which automatically are potential clients for the merchandising), they acted accordingly. They stopped their actual tasks to show heart, what was not only in benefit for the young fan, but also for their own employees, directly inside the race-team, in the factory and sales-rooms. A message that they can be proud of their employer. An achievement of a positive corporate culture, honoring the founder's vision and values, which later became the official company values.

Skilled and motivated employees is the key factor for successful and sustainable business. On Wall Street the Ferrari share (with the fitting acronym RACE) presented from Q4 2015 to Q4 2016 a 111% increase.[289] With this they outperformed most of the other car manufacturers. Acting

---

[289] Parker, John (2017): "Ferrari Reported Solid Q416 Results"

on values is a form of respect, for internal and external stake holders. Respect does not avoid hard negotiations, but if both play by rules, it comes to a positive result and both parties not only keep the respect for each other, but if you are able to keep the self-respect inside the negotiations, your respect for other side will even raise.

Being respected means responsibility, as people put their trust in you. A positive reputation is a sales advantage. Acting based on values, and not only guidelines, supports this advantage. To achieve this position, the rules must leave enough space for the heart. This is no contradiction, as guidelines could be designed to include this freedom. Furthermore clear rules can protect the employees, as they can act based on their values inside the defined space.[290]

Kimi Raikkonen showed value-based behavior already earlier that year. The Friday's training session for the 2017 Bahrain Formula One Grand Prix went not as planned for the Ferrari driver. After a problem with the engine, he had to abandon his car beside the race track and walk back to the pits. The temperatures showed 37C, but he started his journey in full race suit and helmet on. Even if he was being collected later by a Scooter, an impressive behavior. Due to the Ferrari corporate values, a true example of commitment *"to the utmost professional, respectful and exemplary behavior."*[291]

Most companies have the core values defined, but it cannot stop there. The corporate culture has to ensure that the values get combined with actions. Based on our believes, we develop our attitudes towards ideas and philosophies. If we identify a situation, the attitude works as motivational spark to start the action. Integrity means that our behavior is based on values & attitudes.

Imperative for the concept is experience and knowledge. Even if the values are right, a misinterpreted situation would lead to inadequate behavior. A company shall require its employees to comply with the values, but it is also obliged to train the personnel, so that attitudes will lead to the desired

---

[290] Henz, Patrick (2017): "Compliance is a Race Car."

[291] Ferrari (fetched 11.6.2017): "Values"

behavior.

As Kimi had to experience, values are a clear message, but it should not be mixed up with making it easy for the personnel. Employees will face difficult situation and all kind of temptations. The values guide the individual, but often it means that the employee will choose the hard way instead of taking the shortcut.

Integrity does not automatically lead to continuous success, as Kimi reached only the fifth position in the Sunday training, but on the long run integrity leads to sustainability. Thanks to this, Ferrari can celebrate this year its 70th company anniversary and Kimi already 16 years in the world's highest and most competitive race series, including crowning his career with the driver title in 2007.

Corporate values are a positive message and organizations shall communicate them adequately, internally, but also to the external shareholders.

Ferrari combined passion and excellence. Enzo said once *"racing amuses me."* A common observation, humans like and want to compete. For this cognitive learning needs a reward as motivation. This can be a title or other benefit. After a while the psychological effect changes. Individuals start to appreciate not only the reward, but the whole process. This can mean that they even execute it, if there will be no related reward at all. As Gilles Villeneuve stated: *"As long as my car goes, I drive it. I like racing to the limit, first and last."*[292] Later Michael Schumacher added: *"The more precisely I can drive, the more I enjoy myself."* Individuals appreciate if they are able to apply their knowledge and experience. It is up to company to provide them an adequate environment. Meaning, on the one hand guidelines and processes have to protect the employees, but also that these processes have to support the human and should be reduced to the required minimum.

---

[292] Musée Gilles Villeneuve (2012): "30 ans Gilles Villeneuve – Jamais Oublie!"

6.6 The Day that Enzo Ferrari predicted Industry 4.0

The Philosophy of Industry 4.0 is to perfectly connect the employees with optimized IT-infrastructure, but also efficient processes. Indeed, bricks and machines lose their importance in comparison to the human factor.

In 2018, Ferrari achieved the third position at Forbes' "The World's Best Regarded Companies". This index includes the opinions of 15,000 surveyed individuals about trustworthiness, social conduct, performance of the company's product or services, and the company as employer.[293]

Due to another study from the same year, Ferrari achieves an average profit of 69,000 USD/car.[294] This makes it clear that clients not only pay for the physical product itself, but also the image, including the myth. Based on history and experience, the consumer trusts the product to deliver similar or better performance now and in the future than it did in the perceived past. Paying for the non-physical part of the product is rational and even compatible with the concept of the homo-economicus. As conclusion, if clients pay a premium for the product (physical good plus the emotional charged image), the company cannot rely only on its physical production-lines, but has to focus on its employees' knowledge, integrity and creativity. Enzo perfectly understood this: *"Factories are made of people, machines and bricks. Ferrari is made mostly of people."*

With this understanding he anticipated Industry 4.0. Even if this is no revolution, it is nevertheless an important step inside the continuous industrial evolution. In opposite to earlier, now computer & machines are designed to adapt to the human employee and not the other way around. Of course jobs get automated, but the remaining employees get fostered, as human characteristics as curiosity, passion, integrity, creativity and critical thinking become imperative for the sustainable success of the corporation.

---

[293] Murphy, Andrea (2018): "Global 2000: The World's Best Regarded Companies 2018"

[294] WirtschaftsWoche (2018): "Ferrari macht 69.000 Euro Gewinn pro Auto"

Furthermore, new developments as 3D-printing, the cloud and crowd-sourcing decrease still existing economics of scale. Depending the industry and solution, it is not mandatory anymore to invest into production-lines and machinery. New business models are on the market, so that companies do not directly have to invest into fixed inventory, but shift this investment to the supplier. As result, the company only pays for the produced good. In future, extended production lines may get obsolete, as thanks to 3D-printing even small companies can craft required parts out of different materials, including steel and titanium.

6.7 Enzo 4.0

Actual technologies make it possible to create an electronic version of a human actor. This not only gets used to create alien characters, but also to bring back passed away actors to the silver-screen. Of course, this is always connected with discussions about ethics, as the dead cannot read the script or deny a role. Less problematic is to create a younger version of the actor, if the story requires such. The last was done, for example, for the movie "Terminator Genisys", as a younger version of Arnold Schwarzenegger's character was in need.

What about simulating not only the individual's outer appearance and movements, but his or her mind? Empathic and knowledgeable advisors are important for employees to take the right decision, but it is not always possible to have such around.

Artificial Intelligence can make this possible. Based on information like biographies and documentations, software designers can create a chat-bot with the required character and knowledge, including its strengths and weaknesses. This is the starting point, as the software will learn thru the continuous interactions with its human students. Based on the programmed character, the chat-bot perceives information and processes it. In this process the software connects today's topics with the simulated attitudes and believes. As result, leaders from the past can give relevant advise for today's challenges. The sophisticated software is based on a cloud-server and with apps connects to the user. With this, the counselor is independent from locations, as thanks to smart phones and watches, the user can activate it. Furthermore, the AI is capable of multitasking and attends several users at the same time.

New inventions come with new legal challenges. The AI learns through additional information and the conversations with the users. If the software does not keep the different user accounts separated, it can learn much faster, as it learns from a big number of users instead of just one. On the other hand, experiments showed that humans build up a relation of trust with a robot or even other kind of machine. Due to this, they may discuss confidential information with the AI. If the user accounts are not strictly separated, the software uses the confidential information to learn, and counsel other users. Even if it not directly forwards the information, it will become the base of guidance.

Companies can take this idea and create such an app for internal use, where they recreate their founders. An interesting idea, as for many of these figures starting their own company was not only a way to earn money, but they had a vision that their products and solutions could change the market or even whole societies. As conclusion, they had been aware that taking on short-term risks could jeopardize the future of the company, sustainability had a high importance for them. The interaction with the founder's digital twin may create a disruptive moment, what is required that the employee can re-think his or her decision; this to avoid getting rushed to into a wrong agreement.

The technology can go further. Already today exist applications which analyze the user's behavior to conclude on his or her mood, including state of mind. This up to understand when the human individual is in a depressive state and may think about suicide. The app is not passive to answer the user's questions, but gets effective when a special behavior triggers it. The reaction can be the start of a discussion, but also that the software automatically contacts the organization's Human Resources-department. Again, a relevant usage, but requires robust data privacy processes.

First Virtual Counselors may come from a non-expected side. The video game industry licenses sports leagues and events directly from the official organizers. This way they are able to simulate the original teams including the real players. The actual "FIFA Soccer" titles not only feature the outer appearance of the original stars, but also their individual strengths and weaknesses. Such a digital twin can include also values as honesty, as the simulation may include a tendency to foul or not. Less obviously, the video game not only simulates the soccer players, but also the coaches, as every team plays with different strategies.

We already have the technical possibility to simulate real humans, as it is possible instead of creating the individual style of playing, picture the individual's philosophy of life and business. We can imagine that in a near future a Playstation game as "Ferrari Racing Legends" not only includes detailed digital twins of the original race cars from up to 70 years ago, but also Enzo Ferrari himself, who not only interacts with us, but learns from these dialogues.

The impression gets more impressive, if not only the outer appearance is near to the original, but also the voice. Startups, but also established companies, are working on AI algorithms, which can analyze speech samples and offers an application the possibility to speak with the same tone.[295] This gives the user the ability to include additional words into the recorded voice or create complete new speeches. Similar to today, where we can manipulate reality on photos and video, it will be tomorrow also possible to do this with voice recordings.[296] This opens up ethical concerns, as it will become easier to create "fake news", but also as human individuals may tend to humanize computer applications.

That way the digital counselor is similar to a digital twin, only that the AI is not created based on an existing individual, but an idealized, and so partly fictive, character. Also the purpose is different, the classic digital twin wants

---

[295] Vincent, James (2017): "Lyrebird claims it can recreate any voice using just one minute of sample audio"

[296] Statt, Nick (2016): "Adobe is working on an audio app that lets you add words someone never said"

to simulate reality and the AI counselor to influence and advice human individuals.

In many ways Industry 4.0 lowers the economics of scale and with this the advantage of big organizations. Additional to this, Artificial Intelligence is in the process to replace human workers, including white collar employees. The more standardized the position, the higher the risk to get replaced. The best protection for the human is to have a creative job-position. As even though AIs will be capable to create art, human customers appreciate the human expression. Doing business may get similar to the first half of 20th Century again, where car manufacturers developed the vehicle it-selves, but external coach companies designed and build the car's body individually to the specific needs and the customer's wishes. That way some of Ferrari's most famous and beautiful cars arose. It is no surprise that Enzo himself not liked industrial mass production, but understood himself and the company as creative craftsmen. Based on his decisions, the workshop's employees crafted the individual cars. Art on the highest quality level.

Intelligent software can take on administrative tasks and combined with 3D-printing, employees can create individual pieces for relative low costs. Thanks to this, a more individual car production gets possible again. Similar to today's craft beer market, smaller automobile manufacturers get the opportunity to compete against big organizations. Or at least work together with them to take the mass product and include individual changes, like a different body. This is an opportunity, but no automatic development, as artists are rare. If such a talent is not available, the solutions from the craftsmen would not be more creative as the industrial mass product.

The possibilities of the new technology open up great opportunities. Some of them existed before and will come back. A discussion with Enzo Ferrari's Digital Twin would be a great support to understand its opportunities and challenges from a complete different angle. Disruption!

6.8 The Legacy

"Death will destroy my body, but my creatures will keep on living ever after, in the years to come." The late Enzo Ferrari was aware of his mortality, this at a time, where his creations already entered the Olympus. What is true for the cars it-selves has to be ensured day-by-day for the company, independent if we talk about the racing team or the production facility. A task for all employees and other stake-holders. Management has the responsibility (and tools) to create the adequate environment, what includes effective processes, guidelines and tools, but also non-tangible assets as a positive & creative work-atmosphere. All parts are required to keep the legend alive. Imperative to attract talent and clients. The message gets understood, as Sebastian Vettel confirmed: *"People talk about a legend, to me it appears that this legend is still alive because of the people who work for it, day in, day out."*

PATRICK HENZ

"COMPLIANCE IS A RACE CAR."

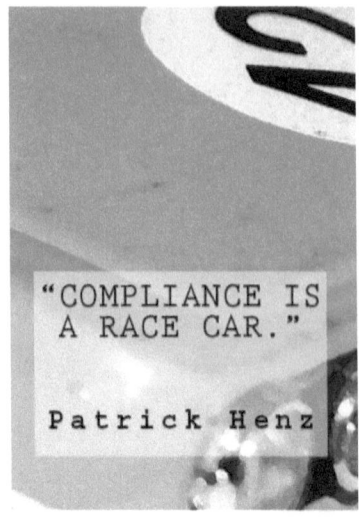

"Compliance is a Race Car.", Patrick Henz, 2017, 2.edition, 168 pages

ISBN-10: 1545157634, ISBN-13: 978-1545157633

The idea of this book is to go further than being a manual for Compliance, as it should work on different levels. Newcomers and experts can learn about the different parts of an effective Ethics & Compliance program. The toolbox questions support the reader to understand if the own program is adequate or requires optimization. Furthermore, the book demonstrates that all parts of the program interact with each other, and the whole is more than the pure addition of the single items.

The book invites the reader to a time travel, as it goes to the past to analyze what Compliance can learn from the structures of a traditional Mafia organization (always keeping in mind that Compliance and Mafia stand on opposite sides). Then it brings us back to the creation of a successful race car, to blast off and take a look into the near future to present the new challenges based on robotics and Artificial Intelligence.

The different trips not only underline that "travelling educates" and due to this, Compliance is not a function to stay behind a desk, but furthermore Ethics & Compliance is a task, which can be interpreted based on the own character and offers the required space and flexibility to climb up Maslow's Pyramids.

PEPE, THE RED RACE CAR

"Pepe, the Red Race Car", Patrick Henz, 2014, 1.edition, 30 pages

ISBN-10: 1503358739, **ISBN-13:** 978-1503358737

Pepe was the fastest race car in the early 1950's and on the best way to win the World Championship. But then his opponent John started to use unfair measures and the deserved success seemed to be out of reach.

Pepe decided not to give up and to fight for his dream and against the corruption! A fast and entertaining book for children of 6 years and older. As ethical or corrupt behavior is learnt already in young years, the story is a good base to discuss this topic with parents or teachers.

BIBLIOGRAPHY

- Acerbi, Leonardo (2015): "Ferrari – all the cars"
- Adams, John Stacy (1965): "Inequity in social exchange"
- Adams, Laurence (2016): "LaFerrari Auctioned for Charity Raises $7 Million for Earthquake Relief": http://gtspirit.com/2016/12/04/laferrari-auctioned-for-charity-raises-7-million-for-earthquake-relief/?utm_source=feedburner&utm_medium=feed&utm_campaign=Feed%3A+GTspirit+%28GTspirit%29
- Argentina Autoblog (2009): "La Ferrari ex Menem reapareció en La Plata": http://autoblog.com.ar/2009/03/la-ferrari-ex-menem-reaparecio-en-la-plata/
- Arshad, Sameer (2014): "How money is Generated in Formula 1 and then Distributed?":
- Art City Emilia Romagna (fetched 30.03.2018): "Enzo Ferrari": http://www.artcityemiliaromagna.com/characters/modena/enzo-ferrari
- Asch, Solomon (1940): "Studies in the principles of judgments and attitudes: II. Determination of judgments by group and by ego-standards."
- Asch, Solomon (1951): "Effects of group pressure on the modification and distortion of judgments"
- Attracion360 (2015): "10 frases de Enzo Ferrari para personas exitosas", http://m.atraccion360.com/enzo-ferrari-frases-para-personas-exitosas
- Auto Italiana (1961): "Perche' si sono dimessi gli otto dirigenti della S.E.F.A.C.-Ferrari"
- Autoblog.com (2016): "This electric Ferrari 308 GTE would do Magnum PI proud": http://www.autoblog.com/2016/05/04/electric-ferrari-308-gts/?utm_source=twitterfeed&utm_medium=twitter
- Autocar (2016): "Autocar confidential: Aston Martin, Honda NSX, Renault, Nissan Nismo": http://www.autocar.co.uk/car-news/confidential/autocar-confidential-aston-martin-honda-nsx-renault-nissan-nismo
- Automobile catalog (fetched 22.11.2015): "1954 Ferrari 375 MM Berlinetta Speciale Pininfarina Ingrid Bergman": http://www.automobile-catalog.com/car/1954/2066480/ferrari_375_mm_berlinetta_speciale_pininfarina_ingrid_bergman.html
- Autosport.com (fetched 11.09.2014): "Who was Franco Cornacchia": http://forums.autosport.com/topic/82621-who-was-franco-cornacchia/
- Bandura, Albert (1993): "Perceived Self-Efficacy in Cognitive Development and Functioning"
- Banovsky, Michael (2014): "Audi Quartz by Pininfarina": http://www.banovsky.com/archive/audi-quartz-by-pininfarinaBanovsky, Michael (2015): "More than Luck: the Story of Alfa Romeo's Quadrifoglio Badge: http://petrolicious.com/more-than-luck-the-story-of-alfa-romeo-s-quadrifoglio-badge
- Barchetta.cc (fetched 11.09.2014): "Inter 212": http://www.barchetta.cc/english/all.ferraris/detail/0237eu.212inter.htm
- Barnes, Hannah (2013): Lauda, Hunt and Rush: How deadly was 1970s Formula 1?, http://www.bbc.com/news/magazine-24172885
- Benson, Andrew (2017): "Toto Wolff: Mercedes boss says this year's battle with Ferrari has revived his love for F1": http://www.bbc.com/sport/formula1/40000702

- BBC (2015): "Green cards: Italy's Serie B to reward positive player behaviour": http://www.bbc.com/sport/football/34162999
- Before it's news (2015): "the Ferrari 375mm owned and raced by Briggs Cunningham in the 1954 Le Mans, the two huge air intakes on its hood cooled the heat exchanged for the water cooled brakes": http://beforeitsnews.com/motor-junkies/2015/02/the-ferrari-375mm-owned-and-raced-by-briggs-cunningham-in-the-1954-le-mans-the-two-huge-air-intakes-on-its-hood-cooled-the-heat-exchanged-for-the-water-cooled-brakes-2510644.html
- Benetton.com (fetched 10.09.2014): "Advertising": http://www.benettongroup.com/group/communication/advertising
- Benetton, Lorenzo (2014): "Enzo Ferrari and Gilles Villeneuve": https://www.linkedin.com/pulse/enzo-ferrari-gilles-villeneuve-lorenzo
- Bennis, Warren G. / Nanus, Burt (1985): "Leaders: The Strategies for Taking Charge"
- Bentley, Logan (1979): "Behind the Ferrari Mystique Is a Lonely Man Who Lives with Fast Cars and Death": http://www.people.com/people/archive/article/0,,20073075,00.html
- Berger, Peter L. / Luckmann, Thomas (1966): „The Social Construction of Reality"
- Bevis, Daniel (2013): "Eight Driving Innovations which came from F1": http://www.gocompare.com/covered/2013/03/eight-driving-innovations-which-came-from-f1/
- Blackwell, Rusty (2015): "Monterrey Auctions Day 1: Top 10 Includes Pope John Paul II's Enzo", http://blog.caranddriver.com/monterey-auctions-day-1-top-10-includes-pope-john-paul-iis-enzo/
- Blake, R.; Mouton, J. (1964). The Managerial Grid: The Key to Leadership Excellence
- Bologna 2000 (2015): "Giovedì 17 dicembre all'Auditorium Enzo Ferrari la rassegna "Recitar Cantando": musiche di Mascagni e Puccini": http://www.bologna2000.com/2015/12/16/giovedi-17-dicembre-allauditorium-enzo-ferrari-la-rassegna-recitar-cantando-musiche-di-mascagni-e-puccini/
- Botsford, Keith (1977): "The pride and passion of Enzo Ferrari": http://www.carmagazine.co.uk/Community/Car-Magazines-Blogs/Guest-Blogs/The-pride-and-passion-of-Enzo-Ferrari/
- Brainy Quotes (fetched 28.04.2015): "Bill Gates Quotes": http://www.brainyquote.com/search_results.html?q=bill+gates
- BrainyQuote (fetched 24.04.2014): "Enzo Ferrari Quotes": http://www.brainyquote.com/quotes/authors/e/enzo_ferrari.html
- Brainy Quotes (fetched 28.04.2015): "Richard Branson Quotes": http://www.brainyquote.com/quotes/authors/r/richard_branson.html
- Brand-Finance (2014): "Ferrari – The World's Most Powerful Brand": http://www.brandfinance.com/news/press_releases/ferrari--the-worlds-most-powerful-brand
- **Bridgestone (fetched 29.05.2015): "Think before you drive": http://www.bridgestone.com/responsibilities/corporate_citizenship/safety/tbyd/**
- Brundtland, Gro Harlem (1987): " Our common future", part of the Brundtlandreport
- Buchhorn, Eva (2014): " Beliebteste Arbeitgeber – BMW schlägt Google" (in Spiegel): http://www.spiegel.de/karriere/berufsstart/beliebte-arbeitgeber-absolventen-fahren-auf-autokonzerne-ab-a-965486.html
- Business Anti-Corruption Portal Italy (fetched 07.07.2014): http://www.business-anti-corruption.com/country-profiles/europe-central-asia/italy/snapshot.aspx
- Cardiff University: Edgar Schein's Career Anchors (Fetched 13.08.2014):

- http://www.cardiff.ac.uk/learn/assets/PDF/CPD/CPD-membership/person/Edgar%20Scheins%20Career%20Anchors.pdf
- Carlei, Carlo (2003): "Enzo Ferrari"
- Carscoop (2011): "1980 Ferrari Pinin Four-Door Sedan Concept up for Grabs": http://www.carscoops.com/2011/10/1980-ferrari-pinin-four-door-sedan.html
- Cavaliere, David (2016): "The History of Italian Automobiles Part 6" Autocostruzioni Societa per Azioni (ASA) and the Ferrarini", http://www.italiantribune.com/part-6-autocostruzioni-societa-per-azioni-asa-and-the-ferrarini/
- Chakrabortty, Aditya (2013): "Don't be fooled by Richard Branson's defense of Virgin trains", http://www.theguardian.com/commentisfree/2013/jun/24/richard-branson-defence-virgin-trains
- Cherry, Kendra (fetched 23.06.2014): "What is Emotional Intelligence?": http://psychology.about.com/od/personalitydevelopment/a/emotionalintell.htm
- Chierici, Sergio (2007): "Speciale Virtual Car: A.L.F.A. 40/60 HP Aerodinamico (carr. Castagna), 1914"
- Chizzola, Gianni (2004): "AUTODELTA and surroundings"
- Ciotti, Gregory (2014): "Why Steve Jobs Didn't Listen to His Customers" in Help Scout: https://www.helpscout.net/blog/why-steve-jobs-never-listened-to-his-customers/
- Coachbuild.com (fetched 24.10.2015): "Touring Ferrari 166MM Barchetta #0024M", http://www.coachbuild.com/index.php?option=com_gallery2&Itemid=50&g2_itemId=24046
- Collins, Peter / McDonough, Ed (2006): "Tipo 33"
- Colosseum.net (fetched 25.08.2015): "Who were the Gladiators?": http://www.colosseum.net/listingview.php?listingID=18
- Conceptcarz.com (fetched 27.12.2015): "1954 Lancia D24 Sport Spyder": http://www.conceptcarz.com/vehicle/z12481/Lancia-D24-Sport-Spyder.aspx
- Corruption Perception Index 2015: http://cpi.transparency.org/cpi2015/results/
- Cowgil, Charles (1997): "Carl Jung": http://www.muskingum.edu/~psych/psycweb/history/jung.htm
- Crash.net (fetched 29.05.2015): "F1: Ferrari duo back 'think before you drive' campaign: http://www.crash.net/f1/news/52089/1/schumi-and-barrichello-think-before-they-drive.html
- Crassey, David (1973): "Other People's Money: A Study in the Social Psycology of Embesslement"
- Curtis, Sean: "Jaguar E-Type"
- Da Vinci, Leonardo / Richter, Irma A. (1999): "The Notebooks of Leonardo da Vinci"
- Dal Monte, Luca (2018): "Enzo Ferrari"
- Danziger, Nira (2008): "The construct validity of Schein's career anchors orientation inventory"

- De Graaf, Mia (2013): "Mussolini's magic motor sells for £6million: Legendary Alfa Romeo which was built to beat Hitler can still do top speed of 165mph", http://www.dailymail.co.uk/sciencetech/article-2421111/Grand-Prix-car-Mussolini-race-Nazi-Germany-sells-6million-record-breaking-auction-deal.html

- Deaton, Jamie Page (Fetched 10.08.2014): Top 10 Everyday Car Technologies That Came From Racing: http://auto.howstuffworks.com/under-the-hood/trends-innovations/top-10-car-tech-from-racing.htm#page=0

- DeMeza, Todd (2010): "Michael Schumacher's Bugatti EB110 Super Sport For Sale": http://www.motorauthority.com/news/1045391_michael-schumachers-bugatti-eb-110-ss-for-sale

- Di Montezemolo, Luca (2019): "Beyond the Grid": https://www.youtube.com/watch?v=8GunkhliNgk

- Diseno-Art.com (fetched 17.9.2016): "Alfa Romeo Proteo": http://www.diseno-art.com/encyclopedia/concept_cars/alfa_romeo_proteo.html

- Drive.com.au (2011): "Ferrari blocks iconic sports car": http://www.drive.com.au/motor-news/ferrari-blocks-iconic-sports-car-20110714-1hes7.html

- Drucker, Peter Ferdinand (1967): "The Effective Executive"

- DTM.com (fetched 06.01.2015): "Die DTM-Saison 1993", http://www.dtm.com/statistik-jahr.php?jahr=1993

- Dutton, Fred (2012): "F1 driver uses videogame for practice", http://www.eurogamer.net/articles/2010-10-12-f1-driver-uses-videogame-for-practice

- Dye, Noug (2002): "How Evita helped Fangio to the top", http://www.telegraph.co.uk/motoring/4757528/How-Evita-helped-Fangio-to-the-top.html

- Dymock, Eric (1981): "Postwar Sports Cars"

- Ellis, Matteson (2014): "Don't Bribe for Me, Argentina": Corruption risks on the Rio de la Plata: http://fcpamericas.com/english/anti-corruption-compliance/dont-bribe-me-argentina-corruption-risks-rio-de-la-plata/

- ESPN (2015): "'When it looks good it should be a pretty good car' – Kimi",http://en.espnf1.com/ferrari/motorsport/story/189867.html?CMP=OTC-RSS;utm_content=f1+formula1+noticias+espa%C3%B1a;utm_medium=twitter;utm_source=twitterfeed;utm_term=f1+formula1+noticias+espa%C3%B1a

- Ethisphere (fetched 09.10.2014): "2011 World's Most Ethical Companies": http://m1.ethisphere.com/wme2013/index.html

- Ewing, Steven J. (2014): "Ferrari to launch new model every year, keep production limited": http://www.autoblog.com/2014/05/06/ferrari-new-model-every-year/#aol-comments

- F1 Al Dia (2011): "Silverstone 1951: Que hiciste, Pepe!": http://www.f1aldia.com/12494/silverstone-1951-que-hiciste-pepe/

- Fast Lane Daily (2014): "James Glickenhaus Garage": https://www.youtube.com/watch?v=O6qpq7hyQlY

- Fearnley, Paul (2016): "Lauda's comeback": http://www.motorsportmagazine.com/opinion/f1/laudas-comeback

- Finch Stoner, James Arthur (1959): "A comparison of individual and group decisions

involving risk"
- Fischer, Lorenz / Wiswede, Guenter (1997): Grundlagen der Sozialpsychologie
- Felipe, Juan (2013): "Ferrari Sales 2012 Full Year Analysis": http://fiatgroupworld.com/2013/06/01/ferrari-sales-2012-full-year-analysis/
- Ferrari.com (2016): "70 Style Icons": http://auto.ferrari.com/en_US/70-anniversary/
- Ferrari.com (2015): "Italian Grand Prix – Best second place ever": http://formula1.ferrari.com/en/italian-grand-prix-best-second-place-ever/
- Ferrari.com (fetched 09.09.2014): "Discover the first car ever featuring Apple CarPlay": http://auto.ferrari.com/en_EN/news-events/news/ferrari-ff-first-car-world-feature-apple-carplay/
- Ferrari.com (fetched 28.04.2014): "Enzo Ferrari – an example for the future": http://auto.ferrari.com/en_EN/news-events/news/enzo-ferrari-an-example-for-the-future/
- Ferrari.com (2015): "New stylistic notes for Ferrari: The SP12 EC is born. EC like Eric Clapton", http://auto.ferrari.com/en_EN/news-events/news/new-stylistic-notes-for-ferrari-the-sp12-ec-is-born-ec-like-eric-clapton/
- Ferrari.com (2014): "Rene Arnoux visits Ferrari": http://auto.ferrari.com/en_EN/news-events/news/rene-arnoux-visits-ferrari/
- Ferrari.com (2016): "The 500th La Ferrari to be built to benefit the people affected by the earthquake": http://auto.ferrari.com/en_EN/news-events/news/the-500th-laferrari-to-be-built-to-benefit-the-people-affected-by-the-earthquake/
- Ferrari.com (fetched 10.01.2015): "The evolution of singleseaters", http://formula1.ferrari.com/cars
- Ferrari.com (2015): "Enzo Ferrari in your own words": http://auto.ferrari.com/es_ES/noticias-y-eventos/news/enzo-ferrari-in-your-own-words/
- Ferrari (2017): "Formula 1 Concept": http://f1concept.ferrari.com/
- Ferrari (fetched 11.6.2017): "Ferrari Code of Conduct": http://corporate.ferrari.com/sites/ferrari15ipo/files/codice_condotta_ferrari_eng_def.pdf
- Ferrari (fetched 11.6.2017): "Values": http://corporate.ferrari.com/en/career/values
- Ferrari World Abu Dabi (fetched 21.9.2016): "Formula Rossa": https://ferrariworldabudhabi.com/attraction/formula-rossa/

- Festinger, Leon (1957): „A Theory of Cognitive Dissonance"

- Fiat (2012): "Annual Report 2011": http://www.fiatspa.com/en-US/investor_relations/financial_reports/FiatDocuments/Bilanci/2011/Fiat_AnnualReport_2011_ENG.pdf
- Fiat (2013): Annual Report 2012
- Fiat (2014): Annual Report 2013
- Formica, Piero (fetched July 29, 2014) : Enzo Ferrari – The Making of the Motor Racing and Sport Cars Knowledge Cluster – Case study of an inspired leader
- Formula1.com (2015): "Do you remember… Mario Andretti's superb Monza comeback", https://www.formula1.com/content/fom-website/en/latest/features/2015/8/do-you-remember_-mario-andrettis-superb-monza-comeback.html
- Formula1.com (2015): "Gene Haas Q&A: We're no Ferrari junior team": https://www.formula1.com/content/fom-website/en/latest/interviews/2015/11/gene-haas-q-a-no-junior-f1-ferrari-team.html
- Formula1blog (2011): "The Ferrari-Shell Partnership: A history": http://www.formula1blog.com/top-story/the-shell-ferrari-partnership-a-history/

- Noticias-F1.com (2016): "Todt: Ayrton queria venir a Ferrari y lo queríamos": http://www.noticias-f1.com/2016/03/08/21311-todt-ayrton-queria-venir-a-ferrari-y-lo-queriamos.html
- **Franks, Norma (2000): "Aces of World War 1"**
- **Franz, Annette (2013): " 31 Henry Ford Quotes about Leadership and Customer Experience" in CX Journey: http://www.cx-journey.com/2013/08/31-henry-ford-quotes-about-leadership.html**
- **Gallagher, Jake (2013): "Gianni Agnelli's 10 Top Best Style Moves":** http://www.esquire.com/style/advice/g1553/gianni-agnelli-best-style-0813/
- Gattiker, Urs E. (2008): "brand versus reputation: Jeff Bezos, Richard Branson, Josef Ackermann and Pat Russo to the rescue": http://commetrics.com/articles/branding-versus-reputation-jeff-bezos-richard-branson-josef-ackermann-and-pat-russo-to-the-rescue/
- Geographic.org / Weather Data (fetched 06.03.2019): "Palermo": https://geographic.org/global_weather/weather_data.php?month=11&year=1919&id=ITE00105250&path=weather_stations/in020000000_iz999999999/ITE00105250.dly&name=Palermo&country=Italy
- Gillespie, Jorden (2013): "Enzo Ferrari": http://prezi.com/gev5bd2hqd1q/enzo-ferrari/
- **good reads (fetched 20.09.2015): "Quotes / Warren Buffet":** http://www.goodreads.com/quotes/76790-somebody-once-said-that-in-looking-for-people-to-hire
- **GP Update (2009): "Second is the first loser – Vettel": http://www.gpupdate.net/en/f1-news/222138/second-is-the-first-loser-vettel/**
- **Grandprix.com (2019): "Clemente Biondetti": http://www.grandprix.com/gpe/drv-biocle.html**
- **Grandprix.com (fetched 02.09.2014): "People: Luigi Bazzi":** http://www.grandprix.com/gpe/cref-bazlui.html
- Grand Prix History (fetched 09.07.2014): "Vittorio Jano": http://www.grandprixhistory.org/jano_bio.htm
- Gran Prix History (fetched 24.10.2014): "Alfa Romeo Bimotore": http://www.grandprixhistory.org/alfabimotore.htm
- Grand Prix History (fetched 31.05.2015): "Horribly Beautiful – Ferrari 166/212 Ouvo at the Mille Miglia": http://grandprixhistory.org/ferrari-uovo.htm
- **Gulett, Mike (2013): "Giotto Bizzarrini – A Body Designer? – Oh Yes":** http://mycarquest.com/2013/07/giotto-bizzarrini-a-body-designer-oh-yes.html
- Gute Zitate (fetched 09.09.2014): "Gerhard Berger": http://gutezitate.com/autor/gerhard-berger
- Gutenberg, Erich (1979): "Grundlagen der Betriebswirtschaftslehre, Band 1: Die Produktion

- H-G, Rachel (2010): "Anna Maria Peduzzi":
  http://speedqueens.blogspot.com/2010/01/anna-maria-peduzzi.html

- Hall-Geisler (fetched 28.08.2014): "The Italian Stallion: A History of Ferrari":
  http://exoticcars.about.com/od/overviewsofmaker1/p/FerrariHistory.htm

- Handelsblatt (2015): "Vettel fährt den Pavarotti-Ferrari":
  http://www.handelsblatt.com/motorsport-formel-1-vettel-faehrt-den-pavarotti-ferrari/11394978.html

- Hawk, Steve (2016): "Authenticity's Paradox: If You Flaunt It, You Lose It":
  http://www.gsb.stanford.edu/insights/authenticitys-paradox-if-you-flaunt-it-you-lose-it?utm_source=Stanford+Business&utm_campaign=15e5243bd1-Stanford-Business-Impact-Issue-96-9-18-2016&utm_medium=email&utm_term=0_0b5214e34b-15e5243bd1-74013277&ct=t(Stanford-Business-Impact-Issue-96-9-18-2016)

- Henz, Patrick (2017): "Compliance is a Race Car."

- Henz, Patrick (2017): "Access Granted Vol. 2 - Tomorrow's Business Ethics"

- Herzberg, Frederick (1964): "The Motivation-Hygiene Concept and Problems of Manpower"

- History.com (fetched 26.09.2014): „October 5, 1919: Enzo Ferrari makes his debut as a race car driver":http://www.history.com/this-day-in-history/enzo-ferrari-makes-his-debut-as-a-race-car-driver

- Hoffmann, Maren (2015): "Gut, dann fahre ich eben woanders" – Niki Laudas sieben Verhandlungs-Regeln: http://www.manager-magazin.de/lifestyle/leute/niki-lauda-die-7-verhandlungsregeln-des-formel-1-weltmeisters-a-1062403.html

- Hofstede, G. (1980): Cultures consequences: National differences in work-related values.

- Hogan, K. / Stubbs, R. (2003): Can't get Through 8 Barriers to Communication

- Holiday (fetched 07.09.2014): "Erfindungen in der F1": http://forum.motorsport-total.com/cgi-bin/bbs/ultimatebb.cgi?ubb=get_topic;f=6;t=000799;p=0

- Howard, Bill (2013): "Ferrari's new 'mild hybrid' LaFerrari supercar produced 963 hp":
  http://www.extremetech.com/extreme/150495-ferraris-new-mild-hybrid-laferrari-supercar-produces-963-hp

- Howstufworks (fetched 19.07.2014): "Ferrari 308 GT4":
  http://auto.howstuffworks.com/ferrari-308-gt4.htm

- Hyde, Justin (2014): „February 18: Enzo Ferrari was born on this date in 1898":
  https://ca.autos.yahoo.com/blogs/motoramic/february-18--enzo-ferrari-was-born-on-this-date-in-1898-134251434.html

- International ASA Register (fetched 14.04.2015): "A bit of history":

http://www.asaregister.com/lang1/history.html

- International Chamber of Commerce, Transparency International, United Nations Global Compact, World Economic Forum (2011): RESIST – Resisting Extortion and Solicitation in International Transactions"

- Investiopedia (fetched 16.03.2015): "White Elephant": http://www.investopedia.com/terms/w/whiteelephant.asp

- Italiancar (fetched 07.06.2016): "Autodelta – a history": http://www.italiancar.net/pilot/ms054.htm

- Jaber-Lopez, Tarek / Garcia-Gallego, Aurora / Perakakis, Pandelis / Georgantzis, Nikolaos (2014): "Physiological and behavioral patterns of corruption": http://journal.frontiersin.org/article/10.3389/fnbeh.2014.00434/full
- Jones, Jonathan (2002): "And the winner is…": https://www.theguardian.com/culture/2002/oct/22/artsfeatures.highereducation
- Kiisel, Ty (2012): "3 Reasons Why the Customer Isn't Always Right" (in Forbes): http://www.forbes.com/sites/tykiisel/2012/09/25/3-reasons-why-the-customer-isnt-always-right/
- Kirby, Gordon (1999): "Bobby Rahal: The Graceful Champion"
- Kleophas, Klaus / Dziedzic, Andreas / Hörner, Wolfgang / Kistler, Henry T. (1997): Ferrari – Alle Serienmodelle von 1947 bis heute
- Koobs de Hartog, Jack (2011): "Bizzarrini P528 Anniversario"
- Kubrik, Stanley / Clarke, Arthur C. (1968): "2001: A Space Odyssey"
- Lauda, Niki (1984): " A new Formula One: A turbo age"
- Lauda, Niki / Voelker Herbert (1986): „To hell and back"
- Lazzarini Design (fetched 30.12.2017): http://www.lazzarinidesignstudio.com/
- Lehbrink, Harmut / Schlegelmilch, Rainer (1995): Ferrari

- Levy, Karyne / Love, Dylan (2014): " Steve Jobs' 14 Most Inspiring Quotes": http://www.businessinsider.com/14-inspiring-steve-jobs-quotes-2014-10

- Ludvigsen, Karl (2010): "Genesis 1.5:12": http://www.forza-mag.com/issues/100/articles/genesis-1-5-12#.VytvUIQrLIU

- Mario Neri S.p.A. (fetched 29.03.2018): "Building Work": https://www.marioneri.it/building-work/?lang=en

- Marjoram, Stefan (2014): The Beast of Turin trailer, http://vimeo.com/113158655

- Markides, Constantinos / Geroski, Paul A. (2004): "Fast Second: How Smart Companies Bypass Radical Innovation to Enter and Dominate New Markets"

- Martin, Jennifer L. (fetched 29.4.2017): "Travel & Jet Lag"

- Martin, Paolo (2017): "Martin's Cars - Pensieri in tre dimensioni"

- Maslow, Abraham (1943): "A Theory of Human Motivation", published in Psychological Review

- Mc Cafferty, Hugo (2013): "Enzo Ferrari: A driving passion": http://www.swide.com/sport-man/formula-1/enzo-ferrari-biography-of-a-driving-passion-in-the-25th-anniversary-of-his-death/2013/08/14
- McCluggage, Denise (2014): "Ferrari in America at 60: Luigi Chinetti, first Ferrari dealer in US, also a Le Mans Champion": http://autoweek.com/article/sports-cars/ferrari-america-60-first-ferrari-dealer-us-luigi-chinetti-was-also-racer
- McCoy, Carbon (2002): "Ferrari Road Car Models and Production Numbers": http://www.ferrarichat.com/forum/ferrari-discussion-not-model-specific-sponsored-algar-ferrari/196388-ferrari-road-car-models-production-numbers.html
- McGuire, W.J. (1969): The nature of attitudes and attitude change, in Lindzey, G. & Aronson E.: The handbook of social psychology, Vol.3
- Melissen, Wouter (2005): "Ferrari 712 Can-Am": http://www.ultimatecarpage.com/car/625/Ferrari-712-Can-Am.html
- Melissen, Wouter (2013): "Alfa Romeo 8C 35": http://www.ultimatecarpage.com/car/2889/Alfa-Romeo-8C-35.html
- Mercedes Benz (fetched 16.2.2019): "To drive a Silver Arrow is an honour.": https://www.mercedes-benz.com/en/mercedes-benz/classic/history/mercedes-benz-silver-arrows/
- Mihalascu, Dan (2013): "Sergio Pininfarina Talks about His Collaboration with Enzo Ferrari in 2006 Interview": http://www.carscoops.com/2013/03/sergio-pininfarina-talks-about-his.html
- Mihalascu, Dan (2013): "Michael Schumacher's Unique Black Ferrari FXX Could be Yours for EURO 2.03 Million": http://www.carscoops.com/2013/06/michael-schumachers-unique-black.html
- Miller, Aaron / Gushue Ted (2014): "20 things you did not know about Enzo Ferrari": http://www.supercompressor.com/rides/20-enzo-ferrari-facts-that-you-might-not-know
- Miller, Lee J. / Lu, Wei (2019): "These Are the World's Healthiest Nations": https://www.bloomberg.com/news/articles/2019-02-24/spain-tops-italy-as-world-s-healthiest-nation-while-u-s-slips
- Mission Winnow (fetched 16.2.2019): https://www.missionwinnow.com/
- Modern Issues: Psychology (2013): The Halo Effect of Beautiful People, https://psychologybits.wordpress.com/2013/01/29/the-halo-effect/
- Monticello, Mike (2010, in Road & Track 61): "2011 Ferrari 599 GTO"
- Moss Kanter, Rosabeth (2011): How Great Companies Think Differently in Harvard Business Review November 2011: http://hbr.org/2011/11/how-great-companies-think-differently
- MotorSport (1982): "Thin Wall Special 1952": http://www.motorsportmagazine.com/archive/article/september-1982/100/thin-wall-special
- MotorSport (2006): "Great racing cars: 1971-73 Ferrari 312PB": http://www.motorsportmagazine.com/race/sports-cars/great-racing-cars-1971-73-ferrari-312pb/

- Motor Trend (2007): " Ferrari FXX Evoluzione: Maranello's track toy gets even faster": http://www.motortrend.com/auto_news/112_news290710_ferrari_fxx_evoluzione/

- Motor Trend (2007): "The Secret History of Ferrari: Outtakes:" http://www.motortrend.com/features/112_0709_secret_history_of_ferrari_outtakes/viewall.html

- Murphy, Andrea (2018): "Global 2000: The World's Best Regarded Companies 2018": https://www.forbes.com/sites/andreamurphy/2018/09/12/global-2000-the-worlds-best-regarded-companies-2018/#7a78287e7b2f

- Murray, Alan (fetched 26.07.2014): "Leadership Styles", in The Wall Street Journal": http://guides.wsj.com/management/developing-a-leadership-style/how-to-develop-a-leadership-style/

- Musée Gilles Villeneuve (2012): "30 ans Gilles Villeneuve – Jamais Oublie!"

- Myers, David (2008): "Exploring Psychology"

- Nedelea, Andrei (2014): "Did You Know that Enzo Ferrari's Personal Cars Until the Early 70s Were Peugeots?": http://www.carscoops.com/2014/03/did-you-know-that-enzo-ferrari-personal.html

- Negative Camber (2017): "Carey: Crying Kimi fan wouldn't have smiled in old F1": https://www.formula1blog.com/f1-news/carey-crying-kimi-fan-wouldnt-have-smiled-in-old-f1/

- Nero Horse (2013): "Legendary quotes from "Il Commendatore" Enzo Ferrari": http://www.thescuderia.net/forums/showthread.php/31826-Legendary-quotes-from-quot-Il-Commendatore-quot-Enzo-Ferrari

- Nick D (2016): "1967 Ferrari 350 Can-Am": http://www.supercars.net/blog/1967-ferrari-350-can/

- Nye, Doug (1993): "The Autocourse History of the Grand Prix Car 1945-65"

- Lanciastratos.com (fetched 30.10.2014): "History": http://www.lanciastratos.com/en/history

- Lazzari, Michael John (2014): "A.T.S. - The Italian Team that challenged Ferrari"

- Levin, Doron (1988, in The New York Times): "Enzo Ferrari, Builder of Racing Cars, Is Dead at 90": http://www.nytimes.com/1988/08/16/obituaries/enzo-ferrari-builder-of-racing-cars-is-dead-at-90.html

- Life in Italy (fetched 12.12.2015: "Life in Italy 1970s to 1980s": http://www.lifeinitaly.com/content/life-italy-1970s-1980s

- Lorio, Joe (2012): "Collectible Classic: 1971-1979 Fiat 128": http://www.automobilemag.com/features/collectible_classic/1208_collectible_classic_1971_1979_fiat_128/#ixzz2GeEPgVrk

- OECD: Society at a Glance 2011: OECD Social Indicators: Trust: http://www.oecd-ilibrary.org/social-issues-migration-health/society-at-a-glance-2011/trust_soc_glance-2011-26-en

- Oreovicz, John (2013): "When Ferrari Almost Came to Indy": http://www.indianapolismotorspeedway.com/default/news/show/52020-when-ferrari-almost-came-to-indy/

- Orosz, Peter (2009); "Steve McQueen's $2.3 Ferrari 250 GT Lusso: What Can Brown Do For You?": http://jalopnik.com/5252193/steve-mcqueens-23m-ferrari-250-gt-lusso-what-can-brown-do-for-you

- Orosz, Peter (2010): "Brabham BT46B Fan Car: Making Lemonade from Lemons":

- http://jalopnik.com/5442597/brabham-bt46b-fan-car-making-lemonade-from-lemons
- Owen, Richard (fetched 17.11.2015) : «1954 Ferrari 375 MM Coupe Scaglietti »: http://www.supercars.net/cars/3783.html
- Owen, Richard (fetched 25.09.2014): "1988 Ferrari F90": http://www.supercars.net/cars/4206.html
- Palazzo, Guido / Krings, Franciska / Hoffrage, Ulrich (2012): "Ethical Blindness": http://www.huoj.hr/files/File/Sud_Casti/PalazzoKringsHoffrage_EthicalBlindness_JBusEthics2012.pdf
- Pander, Juergen (2016): "Alfa Romeo Alfasud Caimano: Gib Gas!": http://www.spiegel.de/auto/fahrkultur/alfa-romeo-alfasud-caimano-utopie-auf-bestseller-basis-a-1078135.html
- Papadopoulos, Dimitris (2014): "Senna & Ferrari: Wie es beinahe zur Traumehe gekommen waere": http://www.motorsport-total.com/f1/news/2014/05/senna-ferrari-wie-es-beinahe-zur-traumehe-gekommen-waere-14050108.html
- Parker, John (2017): "Ferrari Reported Solid Q416 Results": http://marketrealist.com/2017/02/investors-cheer-ferraris-4q16-results/
- Perfil.com (2009): "Reapareció la famosa Ferrari que perteneció a Menem": http://www.perfil.com/politica/Reaparecio-la-famosa-Ferrari-que-pertenecio-a-Menem-20090326-0021.html
- Perkins, Chris (2016): "Porsche Left a Cheeky Message on the 911 GT3 Acura Bought to Develop the NSX": http://www.roadandtrack.com/new-cars/news/a30121/porsche-911-gt3-acura-nsx/

- Persol History (fetched 21.4.2019): http//www.persol.com/usa/history

- Petrolicious Productions (2013): "Ferrari 250 GTE on Special Assignment": http://www.petrolicious.com/ferrari-250-gte-on-special-assignment

- Pew Research (2013): "The Global Catholic Population": http://www.pewforum.org/2013/02/13/the-global-catholic-population/
- Philip Morris International (fetched 16.2.2019): "Our Manifesto – Designing a Smoke-Free Future": https://www.pmi.com/who-we-are/designing-a-smoke-free-future
- Phillips, Tom (2015): "Flavio Manzoni designs Ferrari UFO": http://cardesignnews.com/media/imported/197939/197939.html
- Piaggio Fast Forward (2017): "Gita": http://www.piaggiofastforward.com/gita
- Pisarzewski, Bernardo (fetched 09.09.2014): "The Visit of the Pope": http://www.vea.qc.ca/vea/articles/pape1.htm
- PM Magazin (fetched 06.01.2014): "Telemetrie: Der 'gläserne Rennfahrer' verstrickt in 3.700 Meter Kabel", http://www.pm-magazin.de/a/telemetrie-der-gl%C3%A4serne-rennfahrer-verstrickt-3700-meter-kabel

- Racing.Reference.info (fetched 8.7.2016): "1957 Grand of Argentina": http://racing-reference.info/race/1957_Grand_Prix_of_Argentina/F
- Rampton, John (2016): „Here's How to Know for Sure if You're Emotionally Intelligent",https://www.shopify.com/content/114369734-heres-why-emotional-intelligence-is-more-important-than-you-think
- Ristorante Cavallino (fetched 23.09.2014): "History": http://www.ristoranteilcavallino.it/inglese/main_ita.html
- Road Show (fetched 8.8.2016): "Inside Ferrari's program to turn mere mortals into Formula One racers": https://www.cnet.com/roadshow/news/yes-you-can-drive-a-ferrari-formula-

- one-car/?utm_content=bufferf5d7e&utm_medium=social&utm_source=twitter.com&utm_campaign=buffer
- Roebuck, Nigel (2013): "Lauda's falling out with Ferrari": http://www.motorsportmagazine.com/ask_nigel/laudas-falling-out-with-ferrari/
- Rosenthal, R. / Jacobsen, L. (1968): "Pygmalion in the classroom: teacher expectation and pupils' intellectual development."
- Rossbach, Rainer (2011): "Ferrari 212 E Montagna: Ueberflieger": http://www.prova.de/archiv/2011/00-artikel/0003-ferrari-212e/index.shtml
- Rotter, Julian (1954): "Social learning and clinical psychology"
- Russel / C.P. (1921): "How to Write a Sales-Making Letter"
- San Pellegrino (2018): San Pellegrino Fruit Beverages: https://www.sanpellegrinofruitbeverages.com/intl/en/gnocco-fritto-1695
- Saward, Joe (1999): "Stranger than fiction: Strange Formula One team owners.": http://www.grandprix.com/ft/ft00343.html
- Schleuning, Sarah / Gross, Ken (2014): "Dream Cars"
- Schwab, Klaus (World Economic Forum, 2014): "The Global Competitiveness Report 2013-2014"

- Science Daily (2015): "Anticipating temptation may reduce unethical behavior, research finds": http://www.sciencedaily.com/releases/2015/05/150522083509.htm

- Seligman, Martin / Maier, Steve (1967): "Failure to escape traumatic shock"

- Shippingnet (2016): "JUNE 1 in history, Lampredi the myth of Ferrari, died: http://www.shippingnet.eu/june-1-in-history-lampredi-the-myth-of-ferrari/

- Siano, Joseph (1994): "Luigi Chinetti Sr. 93, Automobile Importer and Champion Driver": http://www.nytimes.com/1994/08/20/obituaries/luigi-chinetti-sr-93-automobile-importer-and-champion-racer.html

- Sidepodcast (fetched 29.08.2014): "F1 People – Enzo Ferrari": https://sidepodcast.com/static/transcript/people3.pdf
- Spears, John (2011): "Why Chrysler boss Sergio Marchionne always wears black": https://www.thestar.com/business/2011/11/22/why_chrysler_boss_sergio_marchionne_always_wears_black.html
- Sportscars.tv (fetched 24.11.2015): "For Negotiations to Buy Ferrari": http://www.sportscars.tv/Newfiles/66fordbuyferrari.html
- StarTalk Radio (2017): "The Science of Creativity, with David Byrne": https://soundcloud.com/startalk/the-science-of-creativity-with-david-byrne?utm_source=soundcloud&utm_campaign=wtshare&utm_medium=Twitter&utm_content=https%3A//soundcloud.com/startalk/the-science-of-creativity-with-david-byrne
- St. Antoine, Arthur (2015): "Luca di Montezemolo is the Other Enzo Ferrari", http://www.automobilemag.com/features/columns/1503-luca-di-montezemolo-is-the-other-enzo-ferrari/?utm_medium=referral&utm_source=t.co
- Stefan_ (fetched 10.01.2015): "Built but unraced Formula 1 cars", http://www.f1technical.net/forum/viewtopic.php?f=12&t=15297
- Sports Car Market (2000): "1951 Ferrari 212 Inter Ghia Coupe", http://www.sportscarmarket.com/columns/profiles/ferrari/1504-1951-ferrari-212-inter-ghia-coupe

- Supercars.net (fetched 5.12.2015): "1959 Ferrari 250 SWB California Spyder Competizione" : http://www.supercars.net/cars/4232.html
- Supercars.net (fetched 17.03.2015): "1966 Ferrari 365 P2 Spyder", http://www.supercars.net/cars/535.html
- Tajfel, Henri (1974): Social Identity and Intergroup Behavior
- Tartakovsky, Margarita (fetched 03.09.2014): "4 Things Introverts Do that Makes Them Effective Leaders": http://psychcentral.com/blog/archives/2013/09/28/4-things-introverts-do-that-makes-them-effective-leaders/
- Tate, Ryan (2011): "What Everybody is Too Polite to Say About Steve Jobs", http://gawker.com/5847344/what-everyone-is-too-polite-to-say-about-steve-jobs
- The Best Artists (2011): "Why Michelangelo Disliked Leonardo da Vinci": https://100swallows.wordpress.com/2011/05/01/why-michelangelo-disliked-leonardo-da-vinci/
- The Maserati Enthusiasts' Page (fetched 24.10.2015): "From Giorgio in Italy"; http://www.maserati-alfieri.co.uk/alfieri06xx.htm
- Thompson, Cadie (2016): "Here's the stunning electric car Porsche is making to take on Tesla": http://www.techinsider.io/porsche-reveals-mission-e-all-electric-concept-car-2016-7/#with-two-motors-the-all-wheel-drive-mission-e-packs-the-equivalent-of-600-horsepower-1
- Thoroughbred & Classic Cars (1991): "Interview with Ferruccio Lamborghini": http://web.archive.org/web/20030409114059/http://www.geocities.com/lamboguy/Intervu1.html
- Tracy, David (2016): "Ferrari's 70th Anniversary Cars Pay Homage to Great Race Drivers And Also Steve McQueen": http://jalopnik.com/ferraris-70th-anniversary-cars-pay-homage-to-great-race-1787219147
- Transparency International Corruption Perception Index 2016 (2017) : https://www.transparency.org/news/feature/corruption_perceptions_index_2016

- Tuck, Michael (2010): "Gestalt Principles Applied in design": http://sixrevisions.com/web_design/gestalt-principles-applied-in-design/
- Tucker, Albert William (1950): "A Two-Person Dilemma – The Prisoner's Dilemma"

- UDLAP (2015): "Índice Global De Impunidad (IGI) 2015": http://www.udlap.mx/cesij/resultadosigi2015.aspx

- United Press International (1985): "Niki Lauda Closes In on Formula One Mark", http://articles.latimes.com/1985-03-24/sports/sp-30269_1_niki-lauda

- Unknown: Enzo Ferrari Biography: http://lgc.150m.com/ENZOFERR.htm
- Unknown: Enzo Ferrari Quotes: http://www.evancarmichael.com/Famous-Entrepreneurs/7173/Enzo-Ferrari-Quotes.html
- Unknown: The Alfa Romeo Logo History (fetched 22.08.2014): http://www.homdrum.net/alfa/alfahistory_logo.html
- Vack, Pete (2013): "Carlo Chiti: An Appreciation in English and Italian"

- Van Osten, Phillip (2019): "Humble Irvine: 'Not many out there better than me - except Schumacher' ":http://f1i.com/news/328507-humble-irvine-not-many-out-there-better-than-me-except-schumacher.html

- Vaughan, Daniel (2007): "Ferrari 166/250 MM Abarth": http://www.conceptcarz.com/vehicle/z8715/Ferrari-166/250-MM-Abarth.aspx

- Walthert, Matthew (2014): „Ferrari, Italy and Formula 1: Where Have the Italian Drivers Gone, and Why?": http://bleacherreport.com/articles/1923944-ferrari-italy-and-formula-1-where-have-the-italian-drivers-gone-and-why

- Wan, Mark (2009): "De Tomaso": http://www.autozine.org/Manufacturer/Italy/DeTomaso.html
- Webley, Simon / More, Elise (fetched 09.10.2014): "Does Business Ethics Pay?": http://www.ibe.org.uk/userfiles/doesbusethicpaysumm.pdf
- Wikipedia: http://en.wikipedia.org
- Williams, Richard (2004): "Mistress of the maestro of Maranello": http://www.theguardian.com/sport/2004/jan/23/formulaone.comment

- WirtschaftsWoche (2018): "Ferrari macht 69.000 Euro Gewinn pro Auto": https://www.wiwo.de/unternehmen/auto/studie-ferrari-macht-69-000-euro-gewinn-pro-auto/22889008.html

- World Health Organization (fetched 28.2.2019): "Italy": https://www.who.int/gho/countries/ita/en/

- Wright, Robert (2001): "Nonzero - The Logic of Human Destiny"

- World Economic Forum (2013): "Good Practice Guidelines on Conducting Third-Party Due Diligence": http://www.weforum.org/reports/good-practice-guidelines-conducting-third-party-due-dilig

- Yam, Kai Chi (Sam) / Klotz, Anthony C. / He, Wei / Reynolds, Scott (2016): "Pushing Employees to Go the Extra Mile Can Be Counterproductive": https://hbr.org/2016/09/pushing-employees-to-go-the-extra-mile-can-be-counterproductive

- YellowBirdRS on FerrariChat (2007): "Strange Question - Enzo Ferrari's Glasses": https://www.ferrarichat.com/forum/threads/strange-question-enzo-ferraris-glasses.146444/

- Yoon, Eddie (2016): "The Benefits of Hiring Your Best Customers": https://hbr.org/2016/12/the-benefits-of-hiring-your-best-customers?utm_campaign=harvardbiz&utm_source=twitter&utm_medium=social

- Zorfas, Alan / Leemon, Daniel (2016): "An Emotional Connection Matters More than Customer Satisfaction": https://hbr.org/2016/08/an-emotional-connection-matters-more-than-customer-satisfaction?utm_source=twitter&utm_medium=social&utm_campaign=harvardbiz

ABOUT THE AUTHOR

Patrick Henz started his career in Corporate Information and Compliance at the end of 2007, when he was responsible for the implementation of an Anti-Corruption program in Mexico and several Central American and Caribbean countries. Together with these tasks, he gained valuable insights into global Compliance programs, with a focus on Latin America. Since 2009 in his role as Compliance Officer he is responsible for an effective Compliance program; based on identification, protection, detection, response & recovery and combined with integrity, respect, passion & sustainability. With these means, he defines Compliance as pro-active function, being perceived as guardian, expert and facilitator. The focus is on information to ensure adequate behavior, not only of the human employee, but Artificial Intelligence included.

This includes the regular planning and execution of Compliance Risk Assessments and further global reviews. According an effective sustainability strategy, where Compliance plays a key role, he actively promotes this idea at university workshops and conferences (including the ACI Compliance Boot-Camp 2013, '15 and '17 in Houston). In so doing he became two times President of Honor of Marcus Evans' Latin-American Corporate Compliance Conference 2011 and '12 in Mexico City, panelist at The Economist's Mexico Summit 2015 and co-founder of the Ethics & Compliance Forum Mexico, including editor and co-author of the Ethics & Compliance Manual, published in April 2014.

Since 2013 he lives and works in Atlanta, USA.

www.ingramcontent.com/pod-product-compliance
Lightning Source LLC
Chambersburg PA
CBHW021809170526
45157CB00007B/2518

50 THINGS TO KNOW BOOK SERIES REVIEWS FROM READERS

I recently downloaded a couple of books from this series to read over the weekend thinking I would read just one or two. However, I so loved the books that I read all the six books I had downloaded in one go and ended up downloading a few more today. Written by different authors, the books offer practical advice on how you can perform or achieve certain goals in life, which in this case is how to have a better life.

The information is simple to digest and learn from, and is incredibly useful. There are also resources listed at the end of the book that you can use to get more information.

50 Things To Know To Have A Better Life: Self-Improvement Made Easy!

Author Dannii Cohen

This book is very helpful and provides simple tips on how to improve your everyday life. I found it to be useful in improving my overall attitude.

50 Things to Know For Your Mindfulness & Meditation Journey
Author Nina Edmondso

Quick read with 50 short and easy tips for what to think about before starting to homeschool.

50 Things to Know About Getting Started with Homeschool by Author Amanda Walton

I really enjoyed the voice of the narrator, she speaks in a soothing tone. The book is a really great reminder of things we might have known we could do during stressful times, but forgot over the years.

Author Harmony Hawaii

---

50 Things to Know to Manage Your Stress: Relieve The Pressure and Return The Joy To Your Life

Author Diane Whitbeck

There is so much waste in our society today. Everyone should be forced to read this book. I know I am passing it on to my family.

50 Things to Know to Downsize Your Life: How To Downsize, Organize, And Get Back to Basics

Author Lisa Rusczyk Ed. D.

Great book to get you motivated and understand why you may be losing motivation. Great for that person who wants to start getting healthy, or just for you when you need motivation while having an established workout routine.

50 Things To Know To Stick With A Workout: Motivational Tips To Start The New You Today

Author Sarah Hughes